LIVE
FROM
AMERICA

LIVE FROM AMERICA

HOW LATINO TV CONQUERED THE U.S.

JAVIER MARÍN

Original title: *En vivo desde América: Cómo la televisión latina conquistó Estados Unidos*

Translation: © Ezra Fitz
Cover design: © Genoveva Saavedra / aciditadiseño
Cover illustration: © iStock / spxChrome
Author photo: © Carolina Olavarría M.
Interior design: © Juan Carlos González

Under the imprint PLANETABOOKS
Avenida Presidente Masarik 111, Piso 2, Polanco V Sección,
Miguel Hidalgo, Ciudad de México, MEX 11560
www.planetadelibros.us

First edition in this format: November 2025
ISBN: 978-607-39-3162-5

Printed by Lightning Source, LLC.
1246 Heil Quaker Blvd., LaVergne, TN 37086, USA.
Impreso en EE.UU. - *Printed in the United States of America*

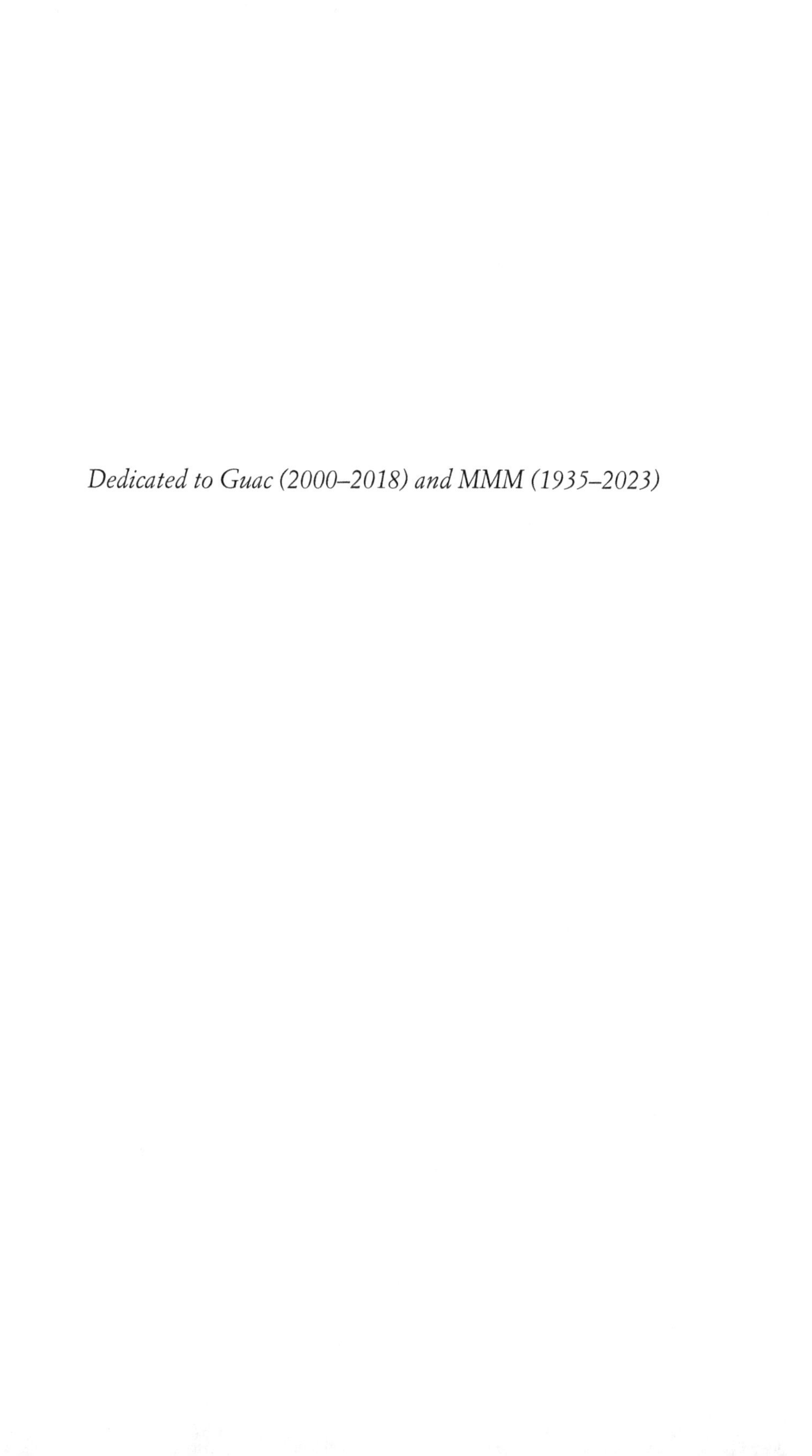

Dedicated to Guac (2000–2018) and MMM (1935–2023)

CONTENTS

PREFACE

International Waters, April 1997

El Tigre, having lost all hope, was ready to die. He asked for one of his brand-new white Oxford shirts. From that moment forward, only his English butler, who knew exactly what needed to be done, would accompany him, while the crew, under the captain's command, would handle the route and the mysterious itinerary. The *ECO*, his yacht, set sail for an unknown destination. The formally registered documents listed Saint-Tropez, in the South of France, though El Tigre's final destination lay elsewhere.

During the last months of his life, El Tigre chose as his lair a marina in the Atlantic waters near Miami. One April afternoon in 1997, he decided to leave the United States in order to evade any laws that might complicate his wish for an assisted death. He had decided to meet his end onboard the *ECO*, having been defeated by pancreatic cancer that started as melanoma. His black hair with its striking white streak had already gone, and his imposing height had yielded to the all-consuming cancer, leaving his torso so hunched that it pained anyone who looked at him.

Between 1960 and 1990, there was one figure who dominated Mexico's economic skyline. Emilio "El Tigre" Azcárraga Milmo was one of the first Hispanic business magnates to emerge as one of the richest men on the planet. More than nine million Mexicans were already making a living north of the Rio Grande during those tumultuous years of interrupted presidencies in the United States. In 1963, John F. Kennedy was assassinated in Dallas, marking a time of great shock and upheaval in the country. A decade later, in 1974, Richard M. Nixon became the only president in U.S. history to resign, doing so in the wake of the Watergate scandal.

The story of El Tigre sailing through international waters on his floating deathbed wasn't unique. Before the legalization of assisted death, some millionaires chose to be euthanized in open waters, sparking controversy based on the existence of the Montego Bay Treaty. This international legal framework established that a country's territorial waters extend up to twelve nautical miles from shore and that its exclusive economic zone extends up to two hundred miles from it, but beyond that lie waters with neither territoriality nor jurisdiction. So what would happen, then, if no nation's flag were flown for a few hours out in the open ocean? In this legal gray area, some experts suggest that an individual may choose to undergo euthanasia in international waters—a practice that has continually raised ethical and legal debates.

Emilio Azcárraga Milmo was known as El Tigre, a nickname approved by his father, Emilio Azcárraga Vidaurreta, who was himself known as El León.

El Tigre was born in San Antonio, Texas, but at the age of eighteen and without his father's approval, he decided to renounce his U.S. citizenship. It's been said among El Tigre's friends that he vociferously declared, both mockingly and celebratorily, that he was no longer a "gringo."

El León always rebuked his son for his decision, and El Tigre always resented his father for having sent him to an American military academy for high school. In 1946, El León decided to enroll his son at Culver Military Academy in Indiana, with the goal of completing high school and perfecting his English. Sending their children to Culver remains a symbol of social status among upper-class Mexican families. Affluent parents have a number of reasons for choosing the United States as the destination for their teenage children. They send them to elite boarding schools in Massachusetts to foster connections with other young intellectuals and facilitate access to the world's most prestigious universities. When they want a more lenient environment, they opt for Seattle, where their children not only learn English but also experience a degree of boredom that ensures their eventual return to Mexico. Attending Culver, however, serves a different purpose: it's where parents hope to foster strong social and disciplinary characteristics in their children, teaching them that part of personal growth often requires knowing how to navigate tough social environments without having everything they need within their immediate reach.

Looking back on those times, El Tigre's friends recount his negative experience at Culver Military Academy, where he "became more anti-gringo than Pancho Villa. They made him clean bathrooms and make the beds of his superiors while being subjected to strict military discipline." Whenever he had the chance to criticize the most challenging times from his youth, El Tigre would recall how Americans ("damn gringos") at Culver discriminated against him for his darker skin tone, Indigenous features, and accent. It was there that El Tigre learned to master the English language, though he could never hide his strong Mexican accent. In 1948, he returned to Mexico a few months before the end of his final semester without having graduated. After that, he never studied again.

El León was a strategist, and he knew that the north was a necessary stop along the road to achieving his dreams. He spent time as a child in Austin, Texas, where he learned to speak English, married a wealthy Mexican American woman born in San Antonio, and learned to understand Anglo-American ways.

Emilio Azcárraga Vidaurreta, quietly and without the knowledge of his business partner Rómulo O'Farrill, was laying the groundwork for a bold venture. From the privacy of his office, El León cleverly designed the plans for what could be considered an extension of Telesistema Mexicano (the Mexican television network founded by O'Farrill and El León) into the United States. It's the same company that today is known as Televisa.

When the secret of what he intended finally came to light, Rómulo O'Farrill reacted not only with surprise but also disbelief and ridicule. He openly mocked El León, suggesting that it was madness to think a Mexican could achieve something even close to that level of business success in the competitive U.S. market. Despite his partner's doubts and mockery, Azcárraga Vidaurreta was undeterred and decided to move forward with his plan, convinced that his vision was both viable and revolutionary.

O'Farrill was right, though not for the reasons he thought. Despite Azcárraga Vidaurreta's audacity and determination, neither he nor O'Farrill would live long enough to see the outcome of that ambition. El León would never see his project become the leading Spanish-language television network in the United States. For his part, O'Farrill's son would bear witness to this, even becoming something of a supporter of El Tigre, his friend in social and corporate circles, in continuing this vast undertaking.

This is a story marked by perseverance and attrition. The rise of Univision, far from being a tale of uninterrupted success, is a chronicle of anguish and resistance in a hostile environment where discrimination, resignations, betrayals, and the constant cycle of collapse and resurgence paint a portrait of unending struggle. This book reveals how a non-English-language start-up was able to survive in the U.S. market. For those who think Univision's story was one of seamless organic growth, this book offers a raw, moving, and often thrilling account of what really happened during the building of a Spanish-language media giant in the most powerful country on the planet.

After the Treaty of Guadalupe Hidalgo ended the Mexican-American War in 1848, Mexicans who chose to remain in the territory ceded to the United States were promised citizenship and "the right to their property, language, and culture."

In a context where prejudices and stereotypes toward people of Mexican origin prevailed, however, many began to feel marginalized and excluded from Texan society. During the twentieth century, Mexicans in the United States faced severe forms of discrimination. In Texas, for example, numerous racially motivated lynchings were recorded, and in the workplace, Mexicans were often relegated to low-paying jobs with poor conditions and a lack of opportunities to advance and grow compared with their non-Mexican colleagues.

Another prominent example was school segregation, in which children of Mexican origin were often bussed to separate, lower-quality schools. During World War II, the Zoot Suit Riots reflected these racial tensions as Mexican youth were targeted for attack based on their appearance and cultural heritage.

In the 1980s, the search for a better quality of life and economic opportunities for their families drove many Mexicans to leave their home country and venture north in pursuit of the so-called American dream. They were followed by Guatemalans, Salvadorans, Nicaraguans, and Hondurans, with each group being motivated by similar circumstances. Later, Panamanians also began undertaking this journey, as did Cubans, Puerto Ricans, and Dominicans from the Caribbean. Furthermore, political crises, dictatorial regimes, and guerrilla warfare in countries such as Chile, Peru, Argentina, and Colombia triggered significant exoduses of their citizens, all seeking refuge and new opportunities.

It was during this time that the term "Hispanic" began being recognized as an identity in the United States. Families from Cuba arrived in Florida; Puerto Ricans, Dominicans, and Colombians arrived in New York; and Central Americans joined Mexicans in crossing the borders of California, Arizona, and Texas. However, the term had already been formally registered by Richard Nixon in 1973, just before his abrupt departure from the White House after the Watergate scandal. His administration recognized the importance of grouping U.S. citizens of Latin American descent under a single designation. After six months of committee deliberation on a name that would represent this group, "Hispanic" was selected.

In 1981, Ronald Reagan became president, marking a significant change. This new Reagan-Bush administration recognized the value of the Hispanic community as an influential bloc, both in political and socioeconomic terms.

The evolution of Univision is a journey of ambition, manipulation, conflict, extravagance, social control, politics, activism, patriarchy, collaboration, and business acumen: one in which each protagonist in the story left their own unique mark.

After its early days were shaped by Mexican visionaries, Univision's leadership passed through various hands: Chileans, Cubans, and Venezuelans assumed key roles, though always under an Anglo-American supremacy that maintained a firm grip on ownership. This power struggle between Anglos and Hispanics, with its tug-of-war dynamics, is one of the central narratives of this book, which could itself easily be the inspiration behind an epic telenovela with all the victims, villains, and innocent actors caught in the middle of it all. And in this case, the innocent protagonist is the audience itself: the massive Hispanic immigrant community here in the United States whose population continued to grow rapidly during this time.

Unlike a population that has directly experienced the ravages of war, Hispanic media audiences were largely unaware of the conflicts and tensions between Univision's proprietors. As such, the primary focus of this book is to narrate this bellicose conflict between the owners who, by ingenuity or luck, managed to keep their audience isolated from these internal conflicts.

While researching and collecting testimonies for this book, I encountered a significant split in opinions regarding how to portray the history of the Latino community in the United States. On the one hand, some of my friends and interviewees urged me to avoid portraying Latinos exclusively as victims of oppression and discrimination. They argued that, despite the obstacles, the Latino community has made remarkable strides, not only occupying but thriving in political and socioeconomic spaces that once seemed unattainable. These voices highlighted achievements and resilience, emphasizing progress over victimization.

On the other hand, more liberal historians urged me to thoroughly detail the ongoing struggle Latinos face against injustice and discrimination, pointing out that recognizing these challenges is essential to understanding the overall dynamics of their experience in the United States. These scholars insist that omitting or minimizing these struggles would perpetuate an incomplete and unbalanced narrative that fails to do justice to this community's true tenacity.

I wrote reality as I saw it, heard it, and believed it based on the sources I spoke with and the people I studied. My intent is not to sway the reader toward one particular perspective or another on the actions or decisions of the characters in this saga; rather it is to offer a balanced account that encompasses both the achievements and defeats as well as the challenges faced by the trailblazers who conceived and built Univision.

In the 1970s and 1980s, a mere three national television networks held all the power in the United States: ABC, NBC, and CBS. But El León and El Tigre laid the groundwork for a fourth one that snuck in right under the noses of Ted Turner and Rupert Murdoch. Their story must reach U.S. leaders: businesspeople, politicians, and dreamers hoping to delve deeper into the origins of a media empire, the interracial psychological battles between leadership positions under a single umbrella, and the evolution of audience behavior in an age of streaming, artificial intelligence, and digital platforms. Beyond that, it's an opportunity to understand how the Spanish language not only reached the United States but also took root, becoming forever ingrained in the country's cultural fabric.

The true purpose of this work is to not only present the milestones and highlights that appeared along the way but also to decipher the mysteries of the human spirit that forged Univision. Each character, episode, triumph, and setback is a piece of a larger puzzle that allows us to better understand the consolidation and significant presence of the Hispanic community—as well as the Spanish language—in the United States.

CHAPTER 1

The Transition: El León, René Anselmo, and El Tigre

In the summer of 1972, Emilio Azcárraga Vidaurreta, El León, traveled to Houston to visit the MD Anderson Cancer Center, one of the world's leading cancer treatment clinics, for a review of his already advanced pancreatic cancer. There was nothing to be done, and the businessman knew this, so he'd asked his two daughters, Laura and Carmela, ages forty-six and forty-four respectively, to be by his side. On September 9, doctors notified the sisters that their father had been admitted to the Houston Methodist Hospital, which is affiliated with the cancer center, for surgery. It was on that date that El León's son, El Tigre, decided to fly from Mexico City to Houston to be with his father during the delicate procedure.

While El Tigre asked his sisters to wait for him to arrive before allowing the surgery, the doctors advised against any further delays. El León was taken into the operating room and never woke up. On September 23, 1972, he stopped breathing. He was seventy-seven years old, and his son, Emilio, was forty-two. The founder and owner of what had already become a powerful Mexican television empire (known at the time as Telesistema Mexicano) had passed away. He also left behind a separate project in

El Tigre (left) and El León (right). (Photo: Museo de la Radio y la Televisión, Jalisco, Mexico.)

the process of being launched in the United States. El Tigre was never able to say goodbye to his father.

Porfiriato (1876–1911)

During the robust yet violent period known as Porfiriato, when Mexico was ruled by the military leader Porfirio Díaz, El León's father, a native of Tampico with a Basque heritage who was named Mariano Azcárraga López de Rivera, sent his sons to Texas to finish their final years of middle school and high school in San Antonio and Austin, respectively. El León was one of the fortunate ones who took full advantage of that opportunity.

Like many businessmen of his time, Azcárraga López lived under the constant shadow of political instability. In an environment ripe for dictatorial regimes, a common fear among entrepreneurs is the inherent transience of such governments; in other words, the knowledge that no dictatorship lasts forever. This uncertainty is exacerbated when changes in government are frequently marked by revolutions or other abrupt transitions that can bring to power new leaders with radically different ideologies. Such changes often pose significant risks for businesspeople who may be viewed with suspicion or even hostility by the new ruling class. Revolutionaries often look to dismantle existing power structures and, in the process, businesspeople pay a heavy cost because they're perceived as collaborators or beneficiaries of the previous regime, regardless of whether they had an actual relationship with it or not.

Before becoming known as El León, Azcárraga Vidaurreta began his career as a successful salesman, distinguishing himself through his business acumen and skill. His marriage to Laura Milmo Hickman, who was eleven years his junior and the daughter of a wealthy family, was not only an act of love but also a reflection of the common marital aspirations of the time. Back then, marrying someone from a wealthy family was seen as both a significant and strategic achievement, especially for ambitious men seeking to consolidate their economic and social standing. Born in San Antonio, Texas, Laura brought youth and family connections to their union, but she also represented an opportunity to strengthen Azcárraga's social status. She became his lifelong wife.

In an ironic twist to the story, during the Porfiriato era, many affluent Mexican families chose San Antonio as the ideal place to give birth to their children. This choice was due in part to their search for somewhere with the stability and security that Mexico's volatile political environment at the time couldn't offer. San Antonio, with its cultural and geographic proximity to Mexico, offered these families a safe and accessible refuge. And Laura Milmo Hickman, born there in 1906, was a prime example.

Following this Porfiriato tradition and looking to ensure the benefits of U.S. citizenship for his descendants, El León also chose that city for the birth of his son. Months before she gave birth, he sent Laura to San Antonio, where Emilio Azcárraga Milmo was born in September 1930 at Santa Rosa Hospital, located just a few blocks from the historic site of the Battle of the Alamo, a landmark in the conflicts between Texas and Mexico. This act not only symbolized the continuation of a practice established by Mexico's elites but also marked the intersection of personal and national history in a place charged with meaning for both countries. El Tigre was born there as if fate knew his life would be marked by the conflicts and complicated history between Mexico and the United States.

1950: First Entrepreneurial Steps

El León began his entrepreneurial career selling shoes imported from Boston, capitalizing on the boom created as the United States more aggressively entered the Mexican market. At that time, English proficiency in Mexico was a rare and highly valued skill, particularly in the business world. El León stood out not only for his shrewd commercial sense but also for his fluency in English, which gave him an edge when it came to negotiating and helped him forge strong relationships with American suppliers.

At the same time, his ability to communicate effectively in Spanish while living in the United States was equally beneficial. Unlike many other Mexican businessmen of the time who were attempting to conduct business in the United States without a strong command of English or a deep understanding of Anglo-American culture, El León used his bilingualism and cultural knowledge to successfully navigate between and adapt to both markets.

After a number of business ventures, some more successful than others, he decided to invest in, register, and acquire a radio station in Mexico. This industry gave him a great sense of satisfaction along with plenty of connections in music and broadcasting. Taking full advantage of these relationships, he joined forces with businessmen Guillermo González Camarena, Rómulo O'Farrill, Ernesto Barrientos Reyes, and Miguel Alemán Valdés to secure the first license to open a private television channel, which they named Telesistema Mexicano. This was in 1951, and at the age of fifty-six, he and his partners began building a Mexican media empire that, by 1969, owned nearly one hundred TV stations stretching all across Mexico. At that point, Telesistema Mexicano was already the largest TV network in the country, but they still lacked a solid, centralized national broadcasting system. They didn't yet have the technology to consolidate and transmit a unified message nationwide. In other words, each station operated its own independent broadcast.

After consolidating his presence in the broadcasting industry and participating in the founding of Telesistema Mexicano, El León began to envision even broader horizons. And while his alliance with Rómulo O'Farrill was essential to his success in Mexico, he began to independently plot his next big move.

Recognizing the growing demand for Spanish-language content in the United States, especially when it came to films and shows produced in Mexico, he devised a bold plan that he didn't initially share with his partners in Mexico. His vision was to expand his media empire beyond his nation's northern border and tap into the growing Mexican diaspora in the United States: a community looking to stay connected with their culture and roots through media in their native language. And so El León began to quietly explore opportunities in the U.S. market. His first foray was selling Mexican films to a movie theater owner in Los Angeles, California, by the name of Frank Fouce Sr.

The First Hispanic TV Station in the United States

The pioneers of Hispanic radio and television in the United States were Emilio Nicolás Sr. and his father-in-law, Raoul Cortez, both based in San Antonio. In 1955, Nicolás Sr. decided to devote himself entirely to radio and television stations KCOR-AM and KCOR-TV, which were the first stations to offer continuous Spanish-language broadcasts in the United States: a project founded and led by Cortez. KCOR-TV changed its call sign to KWEC, and it was then that Cortez and Nicolás Sr. created the Spanish International Network, abbreviated SIN. Nicolás Sr. oversaw the news department during the day and produced a variety of live programs at night. He also presented his own editorials on current events, such as immigration and education. In his search for Mexican content, Cortez met Frank Fouce Sr., who connected him with El León, his own main supplier of Mexican films.

Despite its popularity among Mexican residents and other Spanish speakers in San Antonio, SIN struggled to survive. Its early years were extremely challenging because advertisers underestimated the commercial value of the Hispanic audience and rarely targeted the channel for promotions.

El León had begun selling Mexican films to SIN and pitched the idea to Nicolás Sr. and Cortez that they allow him to invest in the network. He even convinced Fouce Sr. to partner with him to propose a partial acquisition of SIN. The two businessmen made numerous unsuccessful attempts at investment by offering content in exchange for shares in the company.

In 1961, El León put his political acumen on full display by convincing Mario Moreno, the actor known worldwide as Cantinflas, to accompany him to San Antonio and support the election campaign of Henry Barbosa González, a Mexican American Texan running to represent his district in the U.S. Congress. Much to the surprise of the local Hispanic community, Lyndon Johnson, who was vice president at the time, was also in attendance, and El León convinced Emilio Nicolás Sr. to have SIN cover the historic visit by the Johnson–Cantinflas–Barbosa González trio. Johnson had been a U.S. senator from Texas before John F. Kennedy invited him to be his running mate in the 1960 presidential campaign. With Johnson's implicit endorsement—he was the state's preferred political son, after all—González emerged victorious and became the first Hispanic member in the history of the United States House of Representatives, and coverage of the campaign helped the Hispanic community understand, more than ever, the power and importance of the ballot. González would go on to be undefeated in reelection campaigns and remained the representative of Texas's 25th district, which includes the city of San Antonio, until 1998, when he retired two years before his death. SIN played a significant role throughout Congressman González's career.

Cantinflas was always grateful to the Azcárragas for facilitating his friendship with Johnson who, just two years after that first meeting, suddenly became president of the United States following the assassination of JFK in Dallas on Friday, November 22, 1963.

El León bore witness to the power television wielded when it came to politics, having seen how Cantinflas's presence influenced González's victory. The dots were easy to connect: his films, broadcast on SIN, were hugely successful, especially *Pepe*, in which Cantinflas starred alongside such Hollywood legends as Tony Curtis, Kim Novak, Judy Garland, Bing Crosby, Carlos Montalbán, César Romero, and Sammy Davis Jr., among others.

The First Investment in SIN

Due to SIN's ongoing financial struggles, and after witnessing El León's political influence, Emilio Nicolás Sr. convinced his father-in-law to sell a portion of SIN in exchange for content and cash.

In 1961, El León and Frank Fouce Sr. formalized their investment in the Spanish International Network, which broadcast through KWEX, the call sign identifying its signal, which was authorized by the Federal Communications Commission (FCC), the U.S. telecommunications regulatory agency.

The creation of a Spanish-language television network in the United States was not only a logical extension of El León's newly formed empire in Mexico. It was also a way to address the nascent Hispanic market north of the border. At the time, Spanish-language broadcasts were limited and fragmented, and as such, this Mexican entrepreneur saw a golden opportunity to provide high-quality Spanish-language content to an underserved nationwide audience. El León was often heard proudly stating that "los mexicanos invadidos" (referring to the U.S. invasion of Mexico during the nineteenth century) never wanted to "agringarse": to assimilate themselves, to become "gringified."

By the late 1960s, El León had undertaken his bold move: acquiring several television channels in the United States. But his plan ran up against U.S. federal law, which presented numerous obstacles to achieving his goals. No broadcast TV channel in the United States could have more than 20 percent of its ownership in foreign hands. This "20 percent rule" was an unwavering mandate that required stakeholders to be U.S. citizens in order to hold a larger share. This federal law remained on the books until February 2017.

El Tigre's impulsive decision to renounce his U.S. citizenship at the age of eighteen stripped El León of his protective shield, leaving him exposed to the rapacious 20 percent rule. Perhaps, at that age, El Tigre, wealthy, handsome, and somewhat spoiled, lacked the business insight to see the bigger picture. Awash in youthful arrogance, he might have felt alienated from his father's American dream, choosing instead to forge his own path forward. Through some legal acrobatics, El León was able to weave a shareholder web around his U.S. television stations in order to evade the 20 percent rule.

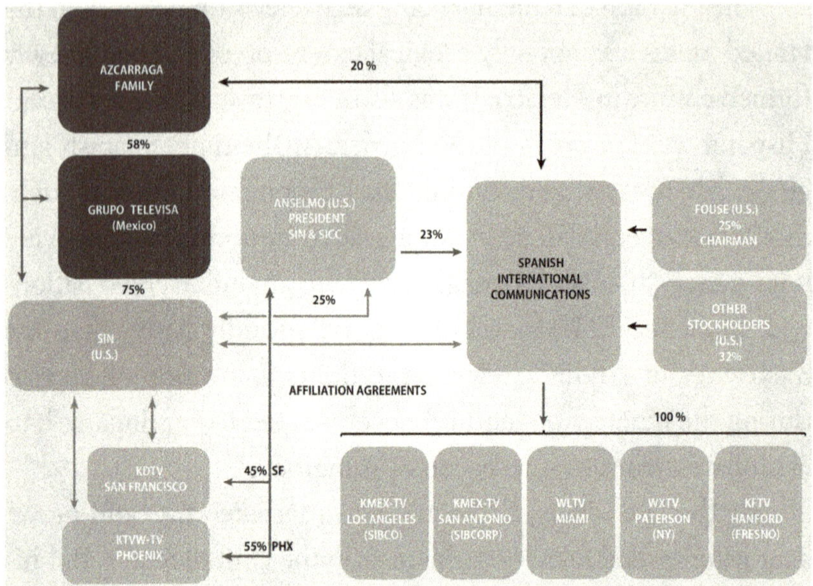

Chart: Norm Leventhal, attorney for Emilio Azcárraga Vidaurreta and Emilio Azcárraga Milmo

El León never truly respected the maximum percentage he was allowed to hold. Legally, yes, but de facto, no. He always used his connections to assign controlling interests to front men, allies, friends, and even his wife, Laura, who did have U.S. citizenship.

El León's increased focus on expanding his television network in the United States began to generate tensions with his partners at Telesistema Mexicano. While he saw potential in the American market, his partners, Rómulo O'Farrill in particular, were skeptical and concerned about the risks this expansion entailed. O'Farrill and others felt this obsession with developing this new market diverted attention and resources from their operations in Mexico, where they still faced significant challenges. This divergence in business vision not only revealed a strategic rift between El León and his Mexican partners but also threatened to destabilize the internal cohesion of their original company.

El León knew he needed allies who shared his vision and who were well versed in the complicated American legal and business environment. This need led him to forge new partnerships with individuals who understood the value of an expanding Spanish-language market and were willing to invest time and money in consolidating a network that would eventually become a touchstone for the Hispanic community in the United States. This strategy not only allowed El León to further his dream but also to form the foundation for what would become a revolution in Hispanic television in the United Sates.

To bolster his operations north of the border, El León decided to retain the SIN brand name while also making the strategic decision to relocate one of his most valued and competent colleagues from Mexico, Reynold Vincent "René" Anselmo, to San Antonio to work at SIN. Anselmo, born in 1926 in Bedford, Massachusetts, possessed a blend of qualities that made him ideal for the mission. A World War II veteran of Italian descent, Anselmo was not only fluent in both English and Spanish but he was also a U.S. citizen, which significantly streamlined operations and navigation around the 20 percent rule. This move demonstrated El León's commitment to making his vision a reality, and the trust he placed in Anselmo underscored the importance of having one of his own at the head of this important venture.

At that time, the relationship between El León and his son, El Tigre, wasn't the best. The father was constantly downplaying the son's presence. The young man's attitude as a coveted wealthy bachelor always bothered his father, who reproached his son for his behavior, especially when it came to his treatment of women.

Nor did he accept his son's public romantic relationships with young ladies who didn't belong to Mexico's elite and upper classes. El León also made no effort to acknowledge his son's work and professional development. This cold shoulder treatment made El Tigre only that much more rebellious.

Meanwhile, El Tigre turned a blind eye, instead seeking visibility within the network by openly talking about the family business and suggesting he was the future heir to El León's throne. He took it upon himself to recruit talent, including writers and actors, for shows produced by Telesistema Mexicano, his father's empire. Of course, El Tigre was quite taken with his role as the son of a media mogul, and being the tall, handsome, and well-educated young man that he was, he began to savor and wield power with greater ease and affinity than his own father. El León, an entrepreneurial and family-oriented man, was never suspected of ever having had an extramarital relationship. In fact, after the death of his wife, Laura, in the late 1960s, he never remarried. Meanwhile, El Tigre was becoming increasingly known for his legendary parties where he could often be seen whispering in English with Reynold Anselmo, exchanging contact info of future girlfriends, many of whom were actresses hoping to achieve stardom in Mexican theater, film, and television.

Anselmo was known to everyone simply as René, a name he adopted following an amusing anecdote with El Tigre. Early in Anselmo's career, while still trying to find his footing in the Telesistema Mexicano environment, El Tigre gave Reynold a playful warning: some would likely try to nickname him Rey, the Spanish word for "king," but there was already an undisputed ruler of this organization: his father, the patriarch. Besides, the line of succession was clear: the future king would be El Tigre himself.

From that moment forward, Reynold stopped going by his original name and everyone, both in Mexico and the United States, recognized him and referred to him as René.

"From now on, you're René. I'm the only 'rey' around here, cabrón!" El Tigre is said to have told Reynold Vincent Anselmo.

The First Program Lineup

SIN's programming consisted primarily of content from Mexico. Among many others, some of Cantinflas's films that were in constant rotation were *El bolero de Raquel* (1957), one of his most memorable films in which he plays a shoeshine boy who cares for a young orphan; *Sube y baja* (1959), in which Cantinflas plays a store clerk who gets involved in various comical situations and, due to plenty of mistakes, is demoted to the position of elevator operator; *El padrecito* (1964), in which Cantinflas plays a young priest who arrives in a small town only to face various social and cultural challenges; and *Un Quijote sin mancha* (1969), with Cantinflas playing a lawyer dedicated to helping the needy, in a modern adaptation of the classic *Don Quixote*. Another film broadcast on SIN was *Simón del desierto* (1965), directed by Luis Buñuel and starring Silvia Pinal and Claudio Brook. This film is known for its surrealist style and religious themes.

Other notable movies that became big ratings hits for SIN were *Los cuervos están de luto* (1965), directed by Francisco del Villar and starring Silvia Pinal, Kitty de Hoyos, and Lilia Prado, and *¡Buenas noches, Año Nuevo!* (1964), directed by Julián Soler and again starring Silvia Pinal alongside Ricardo Montalbán.

El León was convinced that his Spanish-language television network would not only be a financial success for himself but also play a crucial role in the lives of Mexicans living in the United States. His vision was to provide a platform for broadcasting news, entertainment, and education in Spanish that would help the Mexican community stay connected to their roots and culture while simultaneously adapting to life in the United States. He believed that emigration to the United States would only increase because, in the wake of dictatorships and revolutions, Mexico's political and economic environment was deteriorating, and many people would be looking to escape poverty. And that's exactly what happened, though El León's prognosis—as audacious as it was—fell short of the actual scale. The same thing would soon happen with Fidel Castro's revolution in Cuba, the dictatorships in Central American countries, the violence sparked by the drug wars in Colombia, and the economic crises in Puerto Rico and the Dominican Republic, all of which triggered mass migrations of people seeking better lives to the north.

The Spanish being spoken by newly arrived immigrants exasperated many Americans. This frustration prompted a pattern of rejection that manifested itself in two ways: immigrants were either overtly attacked and forced to use English or they were ignored and marginalized.

The Treaty of Guadalupe Hidalgo, which required English-speaking residents of the United States to accept and respect the use of the Spanish language by their fellow citizens, was not embraced by all. Many immigrants from Mexico and other Spanish-speaking nations were still forced to assimilate as "white," renouncing the use of Spanish in order to obtain U.S. citizenship and forge ahead with improving their livelihoods. This was one of

An image inspired by "Uncle Sam," used by activist movements to promote linguistic and cultural assimilation in the United States.

the key triggers that gave rise to the Chicano activist movement, which staunchly opposed any attempt to reject Hispanic culture and the use of the Spanish language. It was an ongoing fight for economic rights that would enable the impoverished Mexican American community to flourish.

The English-only movement, also known as the Official English movement, advocates for the exclusive use of English in official U.S. government operations by establishing it as the country's solc official language. The United States has never legally declared an official language; however, at various times and places, there have been efforts to promote or even mandate the use of English.

Support for the English-only movement began in 1907, under President Theodore Roosevelt. But it remains clear that a significant portion of the American population chose to allow and even promote the proliferation of Spanish. And this was the population that benefited the most from SIN.

Control of SIN in 1962

In the fall of 1961, El León's company—in partnership with Fouce Amusement Enterprises—acquired control of the Spanish International Network. But just a year later, Fouce Sr. died suddenly of heart failure, and it wasn't long before his successors began to play a greater role, something that we'll explore later. But in 1962, El León's capital, René Anselmo's leadership, and Fouce Sr.'s absence propelled the company's growth, eventually establishing new stations in Fresno, Los Angeles, San Francisco, and Phoenix, along with the seed from which it all grew: KWEX in San Antonio.

Already in decline, El León gave Anselmo carte blanche. He paid himself an annual salary of $400,000 and positioned himself as the leader of Hispanic television in the United States. As we've noted, back in the 1960s, there were only three major, authorized TV networks in the United States: CBS, ABC, and NBC. But a fourth was only just beginning to emerge: SIN, a small network of Spanish-language TV stations.

As a business, SIN faced many challenges. One was that CBS, ABC, and NBC all broadcast on VHF (very high frequency) signals while SIN broadcast on UHF (ultrahigh frequency). Most TVs in the United States at the time had no way of decoding UHF frequencies. This technical limitation represented a significant disadvantage against the other networks. TV sets in the 1960s were predominantly equipped to receive VHF signals, which meant that UHF broadcasts like SIN's wouldn't reach most viewers without their modifying or upgrading their equipment. Not only did this reduce SIN's potential audience but it also posed a major hurdle in terms of visibility and popularity, especially when

René Anselmo, businessman Arturo "Art" Saavedra, and Emilio Nicolás Sr. (Photo: *La Prensa*, San Antonio.)

stacked up against its competitors, who were already enjoying a more established and easily accessible presence in American homes.

Anselmo and Emilio Nicolás Sr., with the support of the newly elected Hispanic congressman Henry Barbosa González, set about lobbying Congress to require television manufacturers to install receivers for both VHF and UHF signals in the United States. A bill was finally signed into law in 1962, the effects of which became noticeable toward the end of the decade, when many households were now able to buy TV sets capable of receiving both frequencies: a change that helped Spanish-language television to begin to thrive.

SIN's National Expansion

A few years later, in 1971, a year before El León's death, negotiations were underway to acquire TV stations in New York and Miami. By then, El Tigre was growing more and more covetous of his position as heir and questioned his father's efforts to purchase the station in Miami. El Tigre warned his father, in the presence of René Anselmo, that the Mexican government was an ally to Fidel Castro and supported his revolution, and because of that position, there was no love lost between Cubans in Miami and the Mexican community. El Tigre sensed that purchasing that station would bring trouble.

At that time, the Mexican government maintained a friendly diplomatic relationship with Castro and his revolution in Cuba: a stance that sharply contrasted with the views of Cuban expats in Miami. This community, comprised of those who had fled the revolution, harbored deep-seated disdain for anyone who supported or was otherwise associated with the Castro regime.

During the twentieth century, the Mexican government developed a foreign policy that often aligned with revolutionary leaders and movements around the world. This pattern of support reflected not only an ideological kinship with struggles for social justice and national autonomy but also a broader strategy of asserting sovereignty and leadership within the greater Latin American community.

Mexico maintained cordial relations with the Cuban regime from its beginnings, despite the tensions this generated with the United States and other nations during the Cold War. The influence of revolutionary figures like Castro also resonated with local movements and political parties in Mexico who saw the Cuban revolution as a model to follow, as a strategic ally in the fight against imperialism and for people's self-determination.

Support for these movements and leaders not only manifested itself through a pro-political asylum style of diplomacy but also through cultural understanding, education, and other avenues of international cooperation. Mexico had, by that time, become a crossroads for leftist intellectuals, revolutionaries, and artists from around the world, thus consolidating its image as a country committed to progressive and revolutionary causes.

That was the reason the presence of Mexican businessmen in Miami was seen as suspicious, if not outright hostile, by Cuban exiles. El Tigre, aware of these tensions, predicted that acquiring a TV station in such a polarized environment could trigger resentment and pushback that would complicate their efforts to establish a solid base of operations in the United States.

René Anselmo interjected himself into the father-son conversation, taking it upon himself to argue that if they didn't gain a foothold in Miami, they could never be considered a truly national Hispanic network in the United States. That's when El León gave Anselmo a blunt directive: "Buy the damn thing!" With that order, the meeting ended, and what happened next is now part of history. Anselmo immediately hired the McKenna law firm in Washington, DC, to apply for approval from the FCC to transfer the license of Miami-based WLTV.

The option to buy the station would expire in just seventy-two hours, at which point it could be sold to any other interested party. The situation in Miami was at a critical juncture: there was little time to act, and the pressure was mounting. In the world of communications and television broadcasting, opportunities like this were rare and highly coveted. If Anselmo failed to complete the purchase within this tight time frame, they risked losing a unique opportunity. And on top of that, the competition was lurking: other non-Hispanic media groups were interested and ready to strike if Anselmo wasn't able to close the deal.

The stakes were enormous. If the acquisition didn't go through, the future of Hispanic television in the United States could have turned out very differently. But, in the end, the Miami station became a crucial asset for the Spanish-speaking market in the United States, especially considering Florida's large Spanish-speaking population. If a different group had taken over, the history of Univision as we know it today would have been vastly different.

El León Dies, El Tigre Inherits

To add even more tension to the suspense, the senior partner at the law firm they had hired fell ill, so he delegated his duties to a twenty-seven-year-old attorney: Norm Leventhal from Brooklyn, New York. The FCC authorized the station's transfer in record time—on January 6, 1971—and Spanish International Communications Corporation (SICC), a newly created company in Delaware, acquired WLTV, Miami's Channel 23. From that point on, René Anselmo would have no further business meetings with El León. The boss's health was in sharp decline, and he would be dead within months. El Tigre, for his part, didn't return any of Anselmo's calls until after the funeral—when he'd become his new boss. During this period of intense activity and challenges, not only had El León passed away but just a year later, in 1973, Richard Nixon was facing impeachment proceedings that eventually led him to resign the presidency. This event marked a turning point in the history of Hispanic influence, which was just beginning to consolidate and solidify in the United States.

At the time of El León's death, SIN was already a platform of seven TV stations in the United States acquired through three different companies with various partners, having overcome numerous legal, political, and tax-related hurdles.

At the age of forty-two, El Tigre inherited his father's companies. His sisters, Laura and Carmela, also inherited part of Telesistema Mexicano and other family-owned businesses, but the new boss would be El Tigre by order of the late patriarch.

A few days after his father's death, El Tigre made two decisions, which El León never would have approved. The first was to marry Encarnación Presa Matute, the "weather girl" at Telesistema Mexicano. His father knew about his heir's relationship with that beautiful young blonde with light-blue eyes, but he had always insisted that he keep his romantic interests out of the public and family eye, especially when they involved women who weren't accepted in Mexican high society. The second decision was to fire René Anselmo for having bought the Miami station without speaking to his partners in the United States.

But after the roar came the meow. Anselmo would return just a few months later.

CHAPTER 2

From On the Air to Outer Space: René Anselmo and the Satellite Television Revolution

In June 1988, René Anselmo was at Mount Sinai Hospital in New York undergoing quintuple coronary bypass surgery. Days after this extremely delicate procedure came the scheduled launch of a rocket he had personally financed from a remote and almost completely inhospitable region of French Guiana on the northeastern coast of South America. René had bet nearly all of his money on that launch; it was one of the Ariane series of rockets developed by the ESA, the first European space corporation dedicated to launching satellites into space for private companies. It was the first time in history that an individual had, in a personal capacity, invested in such a rocket.

His wife, Mary Morton Anselmo, entered his luxurious room at the Madison Avenue hospital, pulled a bottle of champagne from her purse, and said to René, "My love, Berta just called to tell me the rocket didn't blow up! ¡Salud, mi amor!"

Mary was referring to Berta Escurra, René's longtime personal assistant, who had called with the news that the rocket had launched successfully early that morning and its extraplanetary mission was underway as planned.

In just seventy-two hours, René Anselmo had won two extremely risky bets: emergency surgery resulting from cardiac failure that nearly took him away from this earthly world, and an investment in the nascent space and satellite business, which, if it had failed, would have led to instant bankruptcy.

Although he wasn't Mexican, Reynold Vincent "René" Anselmo became president of the Spanish International Network in its new expansion phase.

Anselmo's Beginnings

Curly-haired and short in stature, Anselmo was born in January 1924 in Bedford, Massachusetts. His father, an Italian immigrant with no college education, had a respectable career in the U.S. Postal Service. Young Reynold was highly intelligent, astute, serious, and feisty. His childhood was plagued by inner turmoil due to his solitary lifestyle and the distance he placed between himself and his parents and schoolmates. He disliked traditional Italian festivals and the religious obligations his mother imposed in the home. He was, however, fascinated by art, literature, the stars, the planets—by knowledge in general. At an early age, he took delight in reading books by Jules Verne over and over again. And while Boston has some of the world's greatest universities, he saw them as beyond his reach.

Reynold wanted to escape from the monotonous and traditional daily routine experienced by other kids around him. He had big ambitions and didn't want to lead the life his father had. The only pathway young Reynold found to get out, to see the world, and to expand his horizons—without needing to ask for his parents' permission or help—was through the military. In 1942, after his first year of high school, he decided to enlist in the United States Marine Corps. Although he was only sixteen at the time, he declared himself an eighteen-year-old man ready to fight for the United States in World War II. He was trained as a tail gunner and flew thirty-seven missions in the Pacific Theater.

Lying about their age in order to enlist was common among disaffected teens who saw the military as a way to leave home, experience other cultures, and lead a more exciting, less stagnant life than what the country had to offer its civilian youth. Anselmo, a creative dynamo who was constantly coming up with new ideas, felt trapped in the monotony of Boston's Italian American community, where he felt misunderstood.

The Gringo Arrives in Mexico

World War II came to an end in 1945, yet Reynold Vincent Anselmo didn't want to return home. Thanks to the G.I. bill, he earned a scholarship to study literature and theater at the University of Chicago. He was an excellent student who also proved to be an excellent comedic actor. Anselmo participated in early performances by the now- renowned Second City comedy theater group. While in college, he entered the Great Books program, which offered exchange opportunities in other countries. One of these was the chance to go and work in a theater group in Mexico. Between 1936 and 1956, the Golden Age of Mexican cinema, the country had established itself as the undisputed epitome of the Latin American film industry, having become the top producer of Spanish-language films in the world, driven in part by the impact World War II had on international filmmaking.

Reynold's arrival in Mexico was magical. He clicked instantly with the culture, the food, the humor, the freedom, and the safety. Through his University of Chicago connections, he hooked up with a theater group owned by El León Azcárraga. Though his Spanish was rather limited, it was in that group that he met El Tigre, who often hung out around the theater scouting out talent for his father's television stations. Over the next few months, Anselmo dedicated himself to learning how to read and converse in Spanish, a time during which he also developed a friendship with the future heir, with whom he could speak comfortably in English. El Tigre, meanwhile, took advantage of his role as a talent scout in order to get closer to the group's aspiring actresses, many of whom were willing to accept his advances in hopes of increasing their chances of starring on the silver screens of his father's film and television empire.

Anselmo tried his hand at Mexican theater, but his thick accent and limited command of the local language prevented him from accessing any real opportunities. On several occasions, El León would stroll through the theater group's facilities, then sit and chat in English with his son and Reynold. It was then that El León recognized Anselmo's great talent for communication and considered him the ideal person for another project he already had underway: distributing his media empire's content across other latitudes, including the United States. El Tigre, however, felt uncomfortable with Anselmo growing closer to his father, who had welcomed him with admiration. René agreed to stay in Mexico, work for Telesistema Mexicano, and collaborate directly with its owner. Thus began a complex relationship marked by the ups and downs of brotherhood among El León, El Tigre, and Anselmo—a relationship that would last throughout the rest of their lives.

Tireless in his ambition to crack the American market, Azcárraga Vidaurreta often shared with his closest colleagues a strategy he saw as essential for success in the States. His approach was based on an astute observation he made about the prevailing imperialist mentality in the United States: Americans, particularly Anglos, would never accept being colonized or otherwise dominated by foreigners. Therefore, in order to integrate and succeed, it was essential that they believe control remained firmly in the hands of one of their own: a white, English-speaking American.

El León had a very particular way of describing and using the term "gringo" in his conversations with Anselmo. He explained that, while it might sound derogatory to some, given the right context, "gringo" could have a more neutral or even affectionate connotation not unlike the colloquial use of "cabrón" among Mexicans. In Mexican Spanish, "cabrón" can be offensive in certain situations, but among friends, it's often used in a casual, informal manner to indicate camaraderie or even brotherhood. El León wanted Anselmo to understand that "gringo" could also be used to refer to Americans in a way that, while perhaps rather blunt, didn't necessarily have to be offensive if handled with the proper mix of familiarity and respect.

He understood full well the cultural and economic dynamics at play in the United States and suspected that a Mexican would face significant barriers that could compromise the success of his project. His vison was clear: he needed someone who represented the best of both worlds. A gringo who, while born in the United States and considered to be an American, shared his values, remained loyal to his mission, and was deeply connected to the essence of all things Mexican.

Only someone with this particular set of characteristics could carry out "self-colonization": leading operations and negotiations in the United States in a way that appeared to be completely controlled by Americans while being under a strategic directive that served the exclusive interests of the Azcárraga family in Mexico. It was a smart and calculated move. This "ideal gringo" had to have the appearance and accent that would make him acceptable to the English-speaking public, while at the same time remaining a loyal ally who understood and shared the objectives of El León's media empire.

René was the perfect candidate for this position. He'd demonstrated an admirable capacity for adaptation in Mexico, where he had not only learned how to navigate a complex cultural terrain but also earned El León's trust. With this strategy, Azcárraga ensured that his empire would cross borders without him losing any control, laying the foundation for an expansion model that, while ostensibly led by Americans, always served the interests of his business vision. This approach sought not only to adapt to local sensibilities but also to guarantee the successful penetration of Azcárraga's operations into a market that was reluctant to accept direct foreign influence.

The Front Man

This is how René Anselmo, through his legal advisers, signed loans convertible into shares and acquired a stake in the Spanish International Communications Corporation in Los Angeles. This was El León's strategy to ensure that the majority owner of his TV stations was an American.

The convertible loans provided to René Anselmo by the Azcárragas played a crucial role in this ingenious arrangement. These weren't conventional loans, because they had a special feature: they could be converted into shares of company stock at any time. This meant that if Anselmo was unable to repay his loan in cash, El León (and later El Tigre) had the right to convert the debt into an equity stake in SICC. As such, while Anselmo was the nominal holder of the shares, in reality, the Azcárragas held significant leverage over them. This arrangement not only provided Anselmo with the necessary funds to begin investing in SIN, it also established an indirect form of control, which was essential, given the regulatory context of the previously mentioned 20 percent rule requiring media outlets to remain in the hands of American citizens.

Anselmo had studied Spanish-language literature and loved acting, while at the same time he had a firm grasp of electronics, was good with numbers, and had a passion for innovation. But most of all, he really liked money, which is something he didn't have much of when he moved to Mexico. Another of Anselmo's important traits—and one that played a key role in his personal and professional relationships with the Azcárragas—was his deep loyalty to the family. And thus René Anselmo's career in American broadcasting began with initial financial backing from the Azcárragas. Under El León's tutelage, Anselmo gained experience in the business of Mexican media, developing skills that would later prove essential to his future role as CEO of SIN. He depended on the Azcárragas financially, and this bond of loyalty and service cemented him as the key figure for carrying out El León's vision in the U.S. market.

In order to reduce costs, Anselmo had set up an audiovisual production center in San Antonio out of which he shipped to various stations all the prerecorded footage arriving from Mexico as well as newscasts produced in the United States, using the same style as the other major networks. Because his eldest daughter, Pier, was married to a young engineer, Fred Landman, he convinced his son-in-law to work on a special project for him: disseminating video via an alternative method already being tested by the big networks: data transmission line spaces operated by the telecommunications monopoly American Telephone & Telegraph (AT&T).

Before the advent of satellites, AT&T had almost total control of the data transmission infrastructure in the United States. This included telephone lines and microwave networks that were essential for broadcasting audiovisual content. The major TV networks and media conglomerates relied on AT&T's technology to distribute their programming nationwide. This was done by sending video and audio signals through copper wires. Using these interconnections was extremely expensive and subject to fees and conditions imposed by AT&T, limiting the ability of smaller companies to compete in the sport of long-distance data transmission.

Eventually, the FCC approved the use of land-based microwave transmissions. These networks utilized a series of relay towers to send signals over long distances, allowing for live broadcasts of content to different corners of the country. The equipment was not only costly but risky as well, because even after the hardware had been purchased, the FCC still had to authorize the use of microwaves. Companies wishing to broadcast their content via AT&T's lines would not only have to pay higher fees but also adhere to a set of rules and requirements put in place by the FCC.

As such, AT&T had significant control over both costs and the quality and reliability of its transmission services. The lack of competition in the telecommunications market left little room for negotiation or a search for cheaper options.

During the months when he was no longer working with El Tigre, owing to the much-discussed purchase of the Miami TV station, Anselmo chose not to continue arguing with him. Instead, he dedicated himself to studying, financing, and developing a project that had long been an obsession of his: broadcasting television via satellite. It was a technology that had already been successfully tested by the governments of Canada, the United States (through the nonprofit Public Broadcasting Service, PBS), and the Soviet Union. He named this venture the PanAmSat Corporation.

It was Anselmo's firm belief that the future of content transmission would be via satellite and that VHF and UHF frequencies would become obsolete. He also believed that AT&T's monopoly on content distribution had to be challenged and that he wouldn't allow himself to remain chained to its expensive service. René was starting to become an antitrust crusader, first battling against AT&T and later against Intelsat, the company that controlled access to satellite space.

During his time in Mexico, René Anselmo was deeply impressed by the strong sense of nationalism and pride that permeated Mexican culture. He observed with fascination how Mexicans so passionately embraced their culinary traditions, generally preferring regional food over any foreign option. This preference wasn't simply a matter of taste; rather it was a reflection of their love and respect for their heritage. Anselmo found himself particularly captivated during the celebrations of the Grito de la Independencia, or "Cry of Independence," where the effusiveness and patriotic fervor of the people overflowed into every plaza and every home across the country.

He was further struck by the way Mexicans wouldn't hesitate to raise their voices and cause some ruckus when it came to expressing their grievances or demands. It was an attitude that reflected their own combative spirit and refusal to remain complacent... something that deeply resonated with Anselmo. These experiences in Mexico shaped his own worldview and strengthened his resolve to speak up when it came to his beliefs, instilling in him a more passionate and committed outlook. On one occasion, he joined a group of Irish friends on a hunger strike in defense of the universal human right to food in Ireland. He also became a vocal and even controversial critic of government bureaucracy, especially when it came to domestic telecommunications and satellite regulations.

While Anselmo was evaluating the feasibility of launching a company to broker satellite space for TV stations in the United States, the station in Miami that had sparked his conflict with El Tigre was consolidating its position with great success. Channel 23, still operating under the call sign WLTV, was successfully broadcasting Mexican telenovelas (which was Anselmo's idea), forming a deep connection with the Hispanic audience in Florida and solidifying its popularity in the market.

Anselmo and El Tigre had to reconcile. There were so many potential interests to discuss. The minority shareholders in SIN wanted Anselmo back. The Miami project was thriving. And Anselmo wanted to sell El Tigre on the idea of Telesistema Mexicano and Spanish International Network broadcasting their content via satellite. El Tigre had never had a problem with accepting blame—which is exactly what he did in order to formalize An-

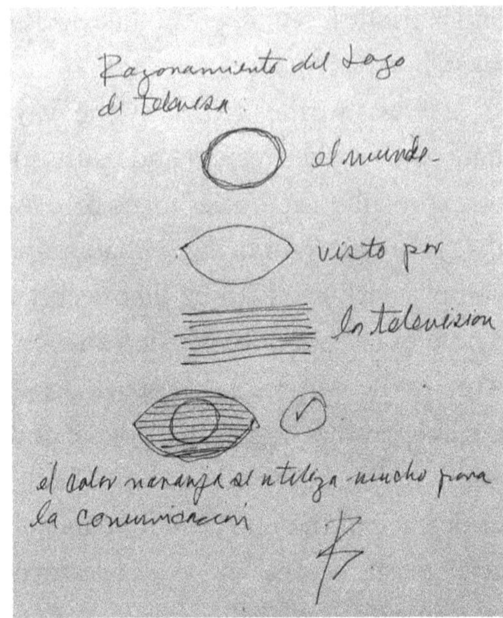

Televisa logo, designed by Mexican architect Pedro Ramírez Vásquez.

selmo's return to SIN. From that point on, they maintained an excellent friendship. Anselmo ran the U.S. side of the business, though always with Azcárraga money.

Fast forward now to 1973, one year after El León's death. El Tigre agreed to have Anselmo return to the company and assume the role of president not only of Spanish International Network Corporation (SINC) but also of the company that purchased content from Telesistema Mexicano for broadcast on SIN. Between the dual roles, Anselmo would earn an annual salary of $650,000. At that time, the CEO of CBS was being paid approximately $850,000.

El Tigre decided to invest in satellite video transmission. Telesistema Mexicano and SIN were recognized as pioneers in the private television industry—both in the United States and in Mexico—for implementing satellite transmissions of audiovisual content. This technological leap began in Mexico, marking a turning point in how television content reached its audiences. Aware of the magnitude of this change, El Tigre both embraced this new technology and decided to reflect this evolution in the company's very identity. Thus, Telesistema Mexicano became Televisa (short for "televisión vía satélite"), a name that captured the company's transmission capabilities, which were cutting edge at the time, and also symbolized an era of modernization and expansion unprecedented in the history of Mexican television. This decision was a milestone not just in terms of infrastructure and reach. It also helped situate Televisa as the brand it is today.

Satellite Television in Spanish

In 1976, Spanish International Network distinguished itself by being one of the first private television networks in the United States to adopt satellite transmission for all of its content. SIN's adoption of this technology allowed the network to significantly expand its reach and audience throughout the United States while keeping costs reasonable. This technology made it possible to distribute programming more efficiently and on a much larger scale, connecting with homes across the country. The transition to satellite broadcasting meant not only greater flexibility when it came to content distribution but also a reduction in transmission costs, benefiting both the network and its viewers alike and marking a significant evolutionary stage in the history of private television in the United States.

El Tigre wanted Spanish International Network to change its name. He wanted a brand that would represent a union of words that reflected both the country (the United States) and the technology (satellite). He and René Anselmo came up with Univisa, but the other minority shareholders, Emilio Nicolás Sr., Frank Fouce Jr., Danny Villanueva, and Joaquín Blaya, refused to part with a brand name they had worked so hard to establish.

René Anselmo negotiated space on the Westar II satellite, owned by the Western Union financial services company, paying out $1.5 million in 1976 to transmit video files from Mexico to Los Angeles and from the U.S. West Coast to the East Coast, thus making the dream of revolutionizing the future of TV signal transmission a reality. This change had such a positive impact on SIN's intrinsic value that, by 1980, advertising sales had practically doubled.

That same year, the Port Authority of New York and New Jersey authorized the relocation of antennas and transistors used by TV stations from the Empire State Building to their new home atop the World Trade Center. Much to Anslemo and El Tigre's astonishment, the authorization included only affiliates of CBS, ABC, and NBC, leaving SIN on the outside looking in. No matter how much Anselmo discussed and debated with everyone from local authorities to congresspeople in Washington, the decision to exclude Spanish-language television remained in place. The matter escalated to such a degree that Anselmo decided to rent one of those trailers used by construction companies as an on-site office and parked it at the foot of one of the Twin Towers. There, he set himself up with a folding chair and a banner denouncing government discrimination against Hispanics. He announced he was beginning a hunger strike to protest the racial, social, and economic discrimination against SIN, the Spanish-language channel that had not been allowed to install its antenna atop the World Trade Center as other television stations had.

Anselmo's lawyer, Norm Leventhal, visited René during his hunger strike and tried to convince him to give it up. Leventhal later spoke with me about that episode: "René didn't look healthy. All he did was smoke Winstons and drink orange juice. He confirmed to me that he truly hadn't eaten anything. He was incredibly stubborn and refused to give up protesting what he saw as a grave injustice."

This was one of the things about Anselmo that El Tigre admired. The Mexican magnate flew to New York with his star Televisa host, Raúl Velasco, to visit René and document his activism on behalf of Hispanics and his company. El Tigre got the media as stirred up as he could and instructed Velasco to record a special program for New York's Channel 47, which would show Anselmo's physical deterioration after having been on a hunger strike for ten straight days. The Latino newspaper *El Diario* ran the headline "A Millionaire Goes on a Hunger Strike." Support from both SIN and Televisa, alongside coverage in the Hispanic press, helped the news reach major radio and television outlets in New York.

Anselmo's odyssey would not be in vain. His solitary struggle against unbending bureaucracies captured the attention of both the public and the media, turning him into a symbol of perseverance. In the end, his tenacity bore fruit when the Port Authority, in a dramatic turnaround, bowed to the pressure and granted permission for WXTV, a SIN affiliate, to install its antenna on the roof of one of the World Trade Center's towers.

In 1986, Anselmo was legally forced to step down and sell his shares in SIN: an event we'll discuss in greater depth later. At the time, he was convinced he no longer wanted to be involved in content creation; rather, he wanted to make his mark through innovations in content distribution. And thus began his battle against the monopoly that was Intelsat, the only company offering satellite service for audiovisual content, which was owned by the governments from several countries, including the United States.

One day, he received a call from his lawyer, Norm Leventhal, who told him that the Reagan administration had opened the door for private companies to apply for a satellite operating license, therefore shattering the monopoly he had fought so hard against. Anselmo was thrilled with this news, and yet also skeptical about whether the authorities would actually ever approve his proposed satellite venture. Leventhal insisted that Anselmo apply, especially considering his status as the only satellite operator dedicated to serving the Hispanic audience in the United States.

The PanAmSat company was registered with a single shareholder: Reynold Vincent Anselmo. He'd followed Leventhal's advice, and—indeed—the FCC authorized the company to own and operate satellites. At the time, Anselmo offered Leventhal a 5 percent stake in PanAmSat, but Leventhal declined for ethical reasons, maintaining as he did a strict attorney-client relationship. "If I'd accepted that offer, I'd have had one hundred million dollars in my bank account from those shares right now," he told me in a conversation prior to this book's publication.

Anselmo created a mascot for his battle against Intelsat's monopoly. It was a dog named Spot that he promoted in the halls of Congress, in newspaper ads, on posters at international conferences, in letters to the FCC, and on the streets surrounding the U.S. Capitol. It was a bold message: Spot had his hind leg raised and was urinating... presumably on monopolies. Accompanying this eloquent image was an equally eloquent message: "Truth and Technology Will Triumph over Bullshit and Bureaucracy."

René Anselmo, creator of Spot.

In many corporate and political circles during the 1980s and 1990s, René Anselmo was considered something of a folk hero. According to former FCC chairman Mark S. Fowler, he was "the Indiana Jones of the communications business, a real swashbuckler who had an idea and put a large part of his personal fortune on the line. René was a fighter and a scrapper. He was crazy like a fox."

Fowler presided over the 1985 FCC decision that authorized private international satellites, ending a government-sponsored monopoly that had lasted a quarter of a century. And it had been Reynold "René" Anselmo's fight. As an increasing number of countries moved toward deregulating telecommunications, Anselmo became the symbol of a new order. Today, one can only imagine what René Anselmo would have been like with a Twitter account and billions of dollars in his pocket with which to launch his own rockets.

René's triumphant launch of the rocket carrying his own communications satellite was a monumental event in his career. He chose to name the satellite *Simón Bolívar* in honor of the iconic Latin American independence hero. Bolívar would have wanted all of the Americas to be one great nation, from Canada to Patagonia, and PanAmSat was born of a very similar dream: to connect the entire American continent through the transmission of satellite-based audiovisual information.

Despite facing extreme adversity, recovering from open-heart surgery at his Connecticut home with a $66 million personal bet on the line and a rocket launch hanging in the balance, Anselmo defied all odds. With a boldness that bordered on recklessness, he not only became the first person in history to own his own communications satellite but he also put an unmistakably personal stamp on it. In a move that was as mischievous as it was original, Anselmo insisted that the image of his virtual dog, Spot, be placed on the nose of the rocket: a playful nod that reflected his indomitable spirit and determination to leave a distinctive and memorable mark on this historic event. His was not only an astonishing technical achievement but also a bold statement about his unique personality, about his ability to overcome even the most daunting of challenges.

In 1990, Czech journalist Frank Kuznik met with the sexagenarian billionaire René Anselmo. In this interview for *The New York Times*, he wrote:

> In person, the 64-year-old Anselmo seems not so much swashbuckling as brooding as he gazes out his office window through a misty gray drizzle at the Tudor-style outlines of downtown Greenwich. To ward off the chill, he is wearing

two sweaters, a green cardigan over a navy blue pullover, and he walks with stooped shoulders and a shuffling gait. Had he been disappointed about missing the satellite launch, four years in the planning? He dismisses such romantic notions with a wave of his hand and a scowl: "I had no interest or desire in banging around the tropics." Then the veteran of two heart operations, who smokes three packs a day, lights another Winston... "Maybe I was born never to be bouyantly happy or something," he says.

The Creation of PanAmSat

Launching the rocket in French Guiana was a highly significant event in the history of the space industry. It originally had been scheduled for March 29, 1988, but it didn't actually take place until September 8 of that same year. It's worth noting that the European aerospace company had eleven successful launches out of eighteen in all. With that success rate, there was a nearly 40 percent chance that the launch would result in a catastrophic failure for Anselmo.

The *Simón Bolívar* satellite was launched from the Kourou space station using an Ariane 4 series rocket. It was designed to provide telecommunications services, including television, radio, and long-distance links, for all of the Americas. This was a major step forward for businesses and governments; until that point, satellite telecommunications services were provided solely by Intelsat, which maintained a monopoly across the industry and prioritized corporate, government, financial, military, and English-speaking media interests.

Like most modern communications satellites, the *Simón Bolívar* operated twenty thousand miles above the equator. At that distance from the earth, it orbited at the same speed as the earth rotated on its axis, making it appear stationary. Positioned over the easternmost tip of Brazil, the satellite could transmit television programs and other types of video, audio, and data signals to the United States, Latin America, and Europe. It was capable of broadcasting up to thirty-six television channels simultaneously. Since its launch in 1988, it was predicted that, by 2002, the satellite would be out of range of the rockets launched periodically to keep it in its celestial place, and that *Simón Bolívar* would eventually become space junk, which is exactly what it is today.

By 1989, Anselmo's clients for the newly created PanAmSat included companies such as Reuters, ESPN, and Ted Turner's Cable News Network (CNN), as well as several Latin American governments. As such, the corporation reported gross revenues of $17 million during its first year.

On PanAmSat's first anniversary, Anselmo stated that he would need "approximately $160 million to recover my investment in this project over the satellite's lifespan. I have twelve years to generate and grow that number."

PanAmSat, with Anselmo as its sole owner, faced an imposing competitor in the global consortium: Intelsat. Headquartered on Connecticut Avenue in Washington, DC, the company was incorporated in the Communications Satellite Act of 1962 and signed into law by President Kennedy to promote international connectivity. In the 1990s, Intelsat had 118 member nations and operated a network of satellites that circled the globe. More than half of the world's international telephone calls and satellite TV programming were carried by Intelsat. Peter Marshall, former deputy director of the company's broadcast services said, in 1990, in response to Anselmo's venture and the creation of PanAmSat, that "the world into which Intelsat was created has changed."

Six months after the launch of *Simón Bolívar*, a commercial consortium in Luxembourg deployed their own television satellite, and a few months after that, a Hong Kong based–group announced plans to launch another satellite with similar aims.

In order to expand, René Anselmo needed investors, and in 1993, he flew to Mexico to speak with El Tigre and invite him to invest in PanAmSat. El Tigre didn't hesitate and offered to provide the necessary capital to fund the launching of three more satellites.

The relationship between El Tigre and Anselmo was marked by a mix of camaraderie and hardball negotiations: a reflection of their deep friendship. Anselmo knew how to handle business and brotherhood the Mexican way. They didn't mince words when discussing key terms, nor did they halt talks in order to consult with legal counsel. The deal in question not only promised an excellent return on investment but also involved crucial technology for the operation of the TV channels themselves, increasing its strategic value.

El Tigre was interested enough to offer up the necessary capital, but the lone condition he placed on his involvement was that he become the majority shareholder: a position that would guarantee his control over business decisions. For his part, Anselmo had learned to value his independence in order to retain operational control and resisted any arrangement that might compromise his leadership and vision for the company.

The impasse between the two was clear: Anselmo needed the investment in order to expand the business but was unwilling to relinquish control, while El Tigre required certain guarantees to protect his investment and ensure himself a dominant position in management. The negotiations were fraught with tension as each side defended their interests fervently, aware that the project's success depended as much on collaboration as it did on mutual respect for their respective visions and concerns.

Finally, they were able to reach a pragmatic agreement, one that incorporated a particular clause: Anselmo would retain control while he was alive, but his controlling vote would be discontinued in the event of his death. This arrangement not only resolved the immediate dilemma but also demonstrated a deep trust between the two friends who, despite their differences, managed to find common ground on which to build a prosperous future for PanAmSat. This commitment reflected their mutual recognition of both the importance and the potential for this business, and ensured the much-needed and impressively powerful technology for Televisa and SIN.

El Tigre invested in exchange for 50 percent of PanAmSat, while Anselmo retained the other half. Anselmo, however, would control 51 percent of the voting power when it came to company decisions, though only in his personal capacity. In the event of Anselmo's absence, the company would have no majority shareholder.

Meanwhile, Spot (remember that little pup?) continued to be emblazoned on the nose of the Ariane 4 rockets carrying the next PanAmSat satellites into orbit.

Reynold Vincent "René" Anselmo died on September 20, 1995, at the age of sixty-nine from a massive heart attack that took him within minutes. It was two days before the announcement of PanAmSat's initial public offering (IPO) on the Nasdaq stock exchange. And while only a minority portion was sold, it was another triumph that Anselmo never got to enjoy. News of René Anselmo's death left El Tigre Azcárraga devastated. His own cancer was spreading, and he never thought his friend and business partner would die before he did.

At the time of Anselmo's passing, PanAmSat had four satellites orbiting the globe, transmitting channels like CNN, HBO, and MTV to more than a hundred countries. PanAmSat was one of the crown jewels in the elite world of global satellite networks. The company had a market capitalization of $2.9 billion, and a number of investment bankers estimated that, if the Anselmo and Azcárraga families decided to sell, the company could fetch a price somewhere between $3 and $4 billion.

Mary Morton Anselmo, his widow, had been by her husband's side during those intense years at SIN and, later, during the development of PanAmSat from a misbegotten concept to a publicly traded company valued at more than twenty-five times its revenue in 1995.

Months after Anselmo's death, El Tigre decided to personally visit Mary. El Tigre typically traveled with an entourage befitting the most powerful media mogul in Mexico. But this time, he traveled alone to meet with the woman who was now his partner in PanAmSat. El Tigre was already ill, and Mary was one of the few people aware of his condition.

Some time later, Mrs. Anselmo would recount this meeting to *The New York Times*, summarized as follows: On a cold, bright morning, Emilio Azcárraga Milmo arrived alone at Mary Anselmo's home in Greenwich, Connecticut. El Tigre had shared a friendship and professional relationship with Mrs. Anselmo and her late husband for four turbulent decades. Through his company,

Grupo Televisa S.A., he had backed Anselmo's bold endeavor. Now, though, El Tigre wanted Mrs. Anselmo to sell her husband's creation, PanAmSat, which had become the world's largest private satellite network, so he could liquidate his investment.

After a brief, subdued conversation in front of a crackling fireplace, Mrs. Anselmo acquiesced. She confided she had been in agony ever since her husband's death.

Mr. Anselmo's son-in-law, Frederick A. Landman, had worked for PanAmSat since 1973 and was appointed president and CEO shortly after Anselmo's death. Landman, forty-eight, and Pier Anselmo were recently divorced, but he retained close ties to Mary. Mary's two granddaughters, Rissa and Chloe, further strengthened the close ties between him and Mary.

Upon learning of Anselmo's death, Rupert Murdoch, owner of News Corp., approached Mary to express his interest in acquiring PanAmSat. Other major companies did so as well, including Lockheed Martin, Hughes Electronics, General Electric, and the European Space Agency itself, which had granted the late Anselmo a major victory with the successful first launch from French Guiana years before.

In September 1996, PanAmSat was sold to Hughes Electronics, a division of General Motors, in a cash and stock deal worth $3 billion.

Mary Morton Anselmo would die a billionaire on August 14, 2013, at the age of eighty-four.

It's worth noting how certain details can be more revealing than they appear at first glance. The shares of PanAmSat, a company that made its mark on Nasdaq for years, had Spot as its logo, evoking the feisty activism of René's own creation. Oddly enough, today this same symbol represents another disruptive company in the entertainment world: Spotify. Those who were unaware of the hidden meaning behind Spot have likely never heard of René Anselmo.

René Anselmo: an individual whose curiosity, audacity, and conviction left a profound mark on the field of technology and also on the struggle between private enterprise and government bureaucracy. A figure whose temerity and vision challenged and changed the course of events in the media industry, Anselmo became a pioneer by trusting and investing in the transmission of audiovisual content via satellite, thus revolutionizing content distribution in the American private television industry.

It's true that the strategy of presenting René Anselmo as the "necessary gringo" worked for SIN when it came to keeping the network's true Mexican controlling hands in the shadows. However, this opaque way of hiding who was truly rocking the cradle eventually backfired. Anselmo will always be remembered for his colossal achievement with PanAmSat and his initial contributions to the Spanish International Network, but his complex duality highlighted him as both a success story and controversial figure in the history of television.

He was a man with "unflinching self-confidence and willingness to risk all in his fight to upend the status quo," as *SpaceNews* wrote in a tribute.

CHAPTER 3

The Rise of a Mexican Media Mogul and His Expansion into the United States

After his father's death in 1972, El Tigre Azcárraga quickly became a magnate who seemed to possess superpowers. He developed the personality of an autocratic boss, a staunch defender of his monopolistic position with a capacity for massive information distribution that no other business executive in Mexico could match.

From the mid-1970s through the early 1980s, media-owning families flourished, and the first Latin American media moguls emerged: Roberto Marinho of *O Globo* in Brazil, Agustín Iván Edmundo Edwards Eastman of *El Mercurio* in Chile, Ernestina Herrera de Noble of *Clarín* in Argentina, Gustavo Cisneros of Venevisión in Venezuela, Julio Mario Santo Domingo of Caracol in Colombia, and, alongside them, El Tigre of Televisa in Mexico stood out to some extent.

This generation of Latin American magnates wanted to emulate the power wielded in the United States by the Grahams of *The Washington Post*, the Sulzbergers of *The New York Times*, Henry Luce of the *Time* and *Life* publishing groups, the legendary William Randolph Hearst and his megamedia empire, and the new revelation in 1980s news media, Ted Turner with his CNN.

Around that same time, an Australian media mogul by the name of Rupert Murdoch, already approaching fifty years of age, was beginning to show interest in entering the U.S. market, though he was facing a significant obstacle: he wasn't a citizen.

The protection of media monopolies in the Americas by dictators and democracies alike helped concentrate the power of information in the hands of the elites who, in some cases, seemed more powerful than presidents. El Tigre's aim was to establish a monopoly in his own country, and he cleverly accelerated his omnipresence in the world of political and media power in Mexico, channeling it through his network of TV stations.

OTI: The Ibero-American Telecommunications Organization

In 1971, a group of television station owners from Latin America, Spain, and Portugal founded the Ibero-American Television Organization (later the Ibero-American Telecommunications Organization), or OTI, with the goal of unifying efforts and fostering collaboration between Spanish and Portuguese networks. The first meeting was held in 1972 in Madrid. While El León had shown great interest in having his station join the OTI, his illness initially prevented Mexico from signing on.

A source close to the events of that time revealed that the reason Telesistema Mexicano didn't join as a founding member was that Mexican president Luis Echeverría Álvarez had broken off diplomatic relations with the government of dictator Francisco Franco in Spain. El León, taking this political situation quite seriously, decided not to participate in the inaugural OTI conference. However, in a bit of a mischievous move intended to rile

Franco, Azcárraga proposed a bold tactic. In an act of defiance, Telesistema Mexicano sent Alberto Ángel, better known as El Cuervo, to appear as part of the OTI music festival that followed the meeting of the organization's members. El Cuervo performed the patently pacifist song "Yo no voy a la guerra" ("I'm Not Going to War"). This performance wasn't well received by Televisión Española, run by the Franco regime and the host of the conference, and El Cuervo was disqualified for violating the festival's rules. This move was especially provocative considering that it coincided with a time when the elderly dictator was nearing his eightieth birthday and growing ever more unwilling to tolerate such displays of pacifism. (If you're curious about this historic performance, I invite you to search YouTube for the original video recording of El Cuervo singing "Yo no voy a la guerra" at the 1972 OTI Festival. It's truly worth watching—much more effective than my simply transcribing the lyrics here.)

It wasn't until 1973, after El León's death, that his son took up his father's initiative and managed to become a member of the OTI. That same year, El Tigre participated in the organization's annual meeting, this time held in Belo Horizonte, Brazil, and again culminating in the renowned music festival bearing the organization's name and featuring artists from each member country. This decision marked El Tigre's first major independent political action, thereby challenging the perceptions of Mexican President Echeverría, who mistakenly thought the OTI was part of a Francoist strategy for gaining influence.

Televisa—or, rather, Mexico—took home the win with Imelda Miller's performance of her song "Qué alegre va María" ("María Moves with Such Joy"). The singer, whose real name was Imelda María Mézquita Pérez, was born in Mérida, Yucatán; her triumph resonated so deeply in Mexico that President Echeverría himself had no choice but to welcome El Tigre and Miller to the Palacio Nacional, where he offered them a warm welcome and congratulations for having represented Mexico with such honor and dignity on an international stage.

For El Tigre, the OTI represented a valuable opportunity to learn from and exchange ideas with his counterparts in the Latin American television industry. It was as a part of this organization that he first learned about Telemundo, an influential Puerto Rican TV channel run by Argentina Ramos, the Miami-based widow of Ángel Ramos, the company's founder and a renowned media entrepreneur on the island. And while El Tigre viewed Telemundo as a potential competitive threat, he was intrigued by the fact that it had registered with the OTI as the official representative from Puerto Rico and not the United States. In 1973, he convinced (or perhaps "ordered" is the more accurate term) René Anselmo to register SIN with the OTI as the representative from the United States, adding a new dimension to the power dynamics within the organization. This astute maneuver had profound significance in that it was the first time the importance of the Spanish-language audience in the United States was projected on a global stage.

El Tigre enthusiastically pitched Acapulco as the venue for the next conference and music festival, and in 1974, the OTI Festival was held in that popular port city. It was during that event that he met Gustavo Cisneros, the twenty-nine-year-old son sent by his father, Diego Cisneros, to represent Venevisión, the family's Venezuelan network. From that day forward, he practically adopted Gustavo as his pupil, admiring his education, his youth, and his fluency with English: skills Gustavo acquired during his time studying at Babson College in Massachusetts. The mutual admiration between the two cemented a friendship that would last for years, one that would, nearly two decades later, reveal just how significant a role Cisneros would play in Univision leadership.

At that 1974 festival in Acapulco, El Tigre was particularly impressed by the artist representing Venezuela, José Luis Rodríguez. His performance on this stage marked the beginnings of his international fame. That same year, Rodríguez also starred in a Venezuelan-produced telenovela titled *Una muchacha llamada Milagros* (*A Girl Called Milagros*). This production garnered him the nickname El Puma. El Tigre and El Puma had a brief yet fruitful professional relationship, one that we'll discuss in greater detail later.

During his twenty-one years at the helm of Televisa, El Tigre exercised significant control over Mexico's news and information narrative. This control not only influenced public opinion but also played a crucial part in keeping the Institutional Revolutionary Party (PRI) in power during the presidencies of José López Portillo, Miguel de la Madrid, Carlos Salinas de Gortari, and Ernesto Zedillo. During this era, Televisa became a pillar of support for the PRI through the favorable coverage it provided and for the systematic omission of certain critical issues and events that could have harmed the party's image.

Ernesto Zedillo marked the end of more than seventy years of continuous PRI rule. And while he wasn't the last PRI president of all, he was the last before the historic alternation of power in 2000. This political transition occurred shortly after El Tigre's death in 1997; he had led Televisa during a time when the PRI maintained a vicelike grip on the executive branch. With the death of Emilio Azcárraga Milmo and the subsequent defeat of the PRI in the 2000 elections, a significant chapter in the history of both politics and media in Mexico came to a close. The whisperings of the time were that the death of El Tigre Azcárraga foretold the death of Televisa's omnipotent power... and, by extension, that of the PRI.

Some Rule in Mexico, Others Do in the United States

In the United States, El Tigre's journey encountered a reality diametrically opposed to what he found in Mexico. Constrained by U.S. laws, El Tigre's imposing style at Televisa clashed directly with unyielding barriers. The aforementioned 20 percent rule stifled his ambitions for expanding, as his Mexican citizenship prevented him from acquiring a majority stake in any company. Furthermore, his attempt to replicate Televisa's success by broadcasting exclusively Mexican content was met with resistance from partners who advocated for programming that would resonate with the diversity of the Hispanic community as a whole, not just with Mexicans. This was evident in the failure of shows like *Siempre en domingo* (*Always on Sunday*), Raúl Velasco's popular musical variety show, which, while a phenomenon in Mexico, never found much traction with Hispanic audiences in the United States. "Too Mexican," a viewer at the time once told me, reflecting the disconnect between El Tigre's vision and the preferences of local audiences.

By 1980, it had become clear that Spanish-speaking people in the United States weren't just Mexicans. SIN's audience had grown to include all Hispanics. And this audience had two things in common: fluency in Spanish and the fact that almost all of them were immigrants.

Beyond that, El Tigre was attempting to impose a Televisa-style strategy of information manipulation on SIN in the hopes of shaping public opinion through news content. This tactic, however, not only failed to gain public acceptance but also sparked significant discontent within SIN's own news team, leading nearly the entire staff to take a stand against the practice. An example of this occurred during the 1985 Mexico City earthquake when SIN published the government's official figures stating that 5,000 people had died during the quake. English-language media, however, reported more than 10,000 deaths, in addition to 50,000 injured and at least 250,000 left homeless—with more than 770 buildings either collapsed or severely damaged. Viewers in the United States noticed and called out the discrepancy in the figures SIN reported, further intensifying public dissatisfaction with the network's editorial approach.

As he expanded operations in the United States, El Tigre faced challenges that went beyond the patent differences between doing business in Mexico and doing business with its neighbor to the north. One of the most significant obstacles was the overt discrimination against his company by the U.S. government, local governments, and businesses that refused to run their commercials on SIN. This bias manifested itself not only in direct dealings but also in the reluctance of large American corporations to partner with Spanish International Network, despite having established business relationships with Televisa in Mexico.

One example that illustrates this quite clearly is the case of Procter & Gamble, one of Televisa's main advertisers. In Mexico, the company didn't hesitate to invest heavily in advertising, but when it came to the United States, the company assumed a completely different stance. Procter & Gamble, along with other similar corporations, allocated only minimal amounts of their advertising budgets to the Hispanic audience, arguing that the audience's use of Spanish would limit the effectiveness of their marketing campaigns. El Tigre and Anselmo's proposals that P&G simply adapt their Mexican ads to fit the U.S. market were met with condescending smiles but no real commitment to investing.

This discrepancy in a willingness to invest advertising money in the two countries was not only frustrating to El Tigre and Anselmo but it also underscored a deeper disconnect in the appreciation and understanding of the Hispanic market in the United States. Despite their data showing the Hispanic audience was growing in both population and economic capacity, they faced constant reluctance from American businesses and the U.S. government when it came to recognizing this vast potential. For SIN, these nascent years, fraught with obstacles and frustration, tested its founders' resilience and ability to strategize in a market that was both hostile toward and distrustful of Spanish-language media.

Between 1976 and 1977, El Tigre and Anselmo argued in favor of changing the company name from SIN to Univisa, but this proposal was rejected by the minority shareholders who preferred to maintain the brand's already established identity.

La Hacienda

In 1977, as a means of generating interest in the United States, El Tigre Azcárraga bought a mansion in the Hollywood Hills overlooking Sunset Boulevard and the Los Angeles skyline. He remodeled it in the style of a Mexican hacienda. He also always made his presence known when arriving at private airports in Los Angeles, San Antonio, or New York aboard one of his three Gulfstream G-IV jets.

While he wasn't much of a tennis player himself, he would invite elite athletes like Mexico's Raúl Ramírez, who was world renowned in the 1980s, to play at his estate. Other regular guests included the Hollywood star Anthony Quinn. El Tigre was famously identifiable by the two cars he kept in LA—an elegant Rolls-Royce and a 1967 SEAT 850 Coupé imported from Spain—and he was well known for his afternoons of long, Mexican-style lunches attended by actors, actresses, sports stars, and other business magnates from California.

Being compared with his father was something that always affected him. El León was critical of his son's vainglorious purchases and playboy lifestyle. It's been said that El León would tell his friends that, though his son was an intelligent man, he would rather live the life of the idiot prince: a reference to one of Dostoyevsky's famous literary works. El Tigre never read that book because he was never that much of a reader, but it tormented him whenever someone described him as some sort of foolish boy czar. The best way to dispel that aura was to generate a new one of power and wealth that surpassed not only his own father but anyone and everyone else in his circle.

Achieving success in the United States by building upon his father's legacy was one way of demonstrating his superiority over him. Despite all the effort El León put into developing the first Hispanic television network in the United States, the company was hemorrhaging cash, generating barely $2 million in sales in 1972, the year of his death. At that time, SIN was, in fact, an accurate reflection of the state of the Hispanic community in the United States: poor, discriminated against, and unprotected.

Programming for a Different Audience

There was another company that was established in Delaware in 1962 called Spanish International Network Sales (SINS), entirely owned by El León and later inherited by El Tigre, which was responsible for selling content from Mexico to SIN. Eighty percent of the content broadcast by the group's channels had been sold by SINS at prices agreed upon with the partners. During the 1970s, the Golden Age of Mexican cinema had already come to an end, and many of the most-watched films from the theaters were being rebroadcast on SIN. A number of famous actors and actresses would visit SIN's studios in San Antonio, Miami, and Los Angeles to promote themselves, earn extra income, and keep their faces fresh in front of big silver screens.

Televisa also produced and broadcast a significant number of telenovelas, variety shows, newscasts, and other types of content. But not all Mexican programming was well received by Hispanic audiences in the United States.

This highlighted the differing cultural and media preferences between Hispanic audiences in the United States and viewers in Mexico. While programs like *Siempre en domingo* and Televisa's news broadcasts were established hits, the diversity of the Hispanic community in the United States required a more localized approach, one more representative of their varied experiences and backgrounds. This reality emphasized the necessity to adapt media content in order to meet the specific needs of particular audiences: a challenge that El Tigre was facing in his efforts to expand into the U.S. market.

SIN's Programming

And yet there were telenovelas and other shows produced in Mexico by Televisa that were, indeed, successful on SIN. There's *Chespirito*, for example: a sketch comedy series featuring a variety of characters, including El Chavo del Ocho and El Chapulín Colorado, both played by Roberto Gómez Bolaños. The show's name was a Spanish pun on Gómez Bolaños's nickname and meant "Little Shakespeare," or "Shakespearito."

Much to the surprise of SIN management, another cultural and market-based distinction had emerged, one that had to do with the way in which viewers responded to shows based on the characters El Chavo del Ocho and El Chapulín Colorado. While the former resonated strongly with Latin American audiences due to its depictions of the social strata and everyday life in working-class neighborhoods, the latter earned higher ratings from fans thanks to its unique sense of humor and by parodying characters like Batman and Superman. By offering a clumsy, comical take on the conventional superhero, *El Chapulín Colorado* captured the attention of American audiences, who appreciated and enjoyed parodies and reinterpretations of their own cultural icons.

As a result, *El Chapulín Colorado*, with its innovative visual effects and themes that challenged the traditional clichés of heroes, introduced Hispanic immigrants to a new form of comedy that contrasted with the simple, relatable charm of *El Chavo del*

Ocho. This represented yet another breakthrough discovery about the differences between the Spanish-speaking communities in the United Sates and Latin America: while they shared the same language, they differed in terms of their tastes and perspectives.

Another show that was very well received by the U.S. Hispanic audience nationwide was 1979's Televisa-produced telenovela *Los ricos también lloran* (*The Rich Also Cry*). Starring Verónica Castro, this show was a huge hit and helped consolidate the popularity of telenovelas worldwide.

In the years following the end of El León's era, El Tigre took over as the new owner, making decisions that generated tensions with his business partners. One of the most significant changes was transferring his shares in SINS, the company in charge of providing content to SIN, to Televisa. With control of SINS in Televisa's hands, El Tigre began implementing changes that no longer required prior consultation with other SIN partners in the United States. One of the most controversial changes was increasing the price for Televisa content that SINS sold to SIN. While the idea was to maximize corporate revenue, the partners had been left out of the decision-making process, which led to growing feelings of dissatisfaction and distrust.

The situation was further complicated because Anselmo—in his dual role as CEO of SINS (the content provider) and CEO of SICC (the company that managed the television stations)—was acting as the keystone intermediary in these operations. In theory, everything was agreed upon between El Tigre and Anselmo, but in practice, the adjustments being imposed by the Mexican businessman were perceived by the other shareholders as an abuse of power. El Tigre's unilateral decisions not only threw off the internal dynamics but also sowed the seeds of future conflicts.

Hostile Takeover

In 1976, SIN's situation was critical. Sales were stagnant, costs were rising, and the debt owed to Televisa was growing. Fouce Amusement Enterprises, founded by the late Frank Fouce Sr., a good friend and original partner of El León in their first U.S. venture back in the 1960s, was SICC's primary stakeholder, with 25.5 percent of the shares and who rarely discussed Anselmo and Azcárraga's corporate decisions. Neither the late Frank Fouce Sr. nor his widow ever disputed what came down from management led by Anselmo. The relationship between the partners was characterized by great respect and cordiality, maintaining a collaborative and mutually supportive atmosphere within the company. Frank Fouce Jr., who succeeded his father and represented his mother, assumed the role of chairman of SICC's board of directors.

On January 1, 1976, René Anselmo called a SICC shareholders' meeting for Wednesday, January 14, at the renowned Crockett Hotel in San Antonio, Texas. This unusual meeting took both the Fouces and the company's minority shareholders by surprise: they hadn't been expecting a meeting so early in the year and with so little time between the announcement and the date of the meeting.

On the day of that meeting, CEO René Anselmo arrived early with his lawyer, Norm Leventhal. While waiting for the appointed time, Anselmo stayed in the car, chain-smoking his Winston cigarettes. He watched Frank Fouce Jr. arriving while the other shareholders, Daniel Villanueva and Emilio Nicolás Sr., waited in the hotel conference room reserved for the important session.

Once all had gathered, Fouce Jr., as chairman of the board, instructed Leventhal to call to order the meeting that had been set up by René Anselmo, who continued smoking one Winston after another. El Tigre was not in attendance. Anselmo represented the Azcárraga family's vote and got straight to the point, announcing that the meeting's purpose was to solicit greater investment and to restructure the company. He explained to everyone present that the financial situation was unsustainable and that a $2 million outstanding debt owed to Televisa for content purchased had to be paid off. He then proposed issuing additional shares to increase the company's capital by $3 million and pay off the debt in full. If they couldn't raise the money that way, Anselmo explained that alternatives would be sought out for garnering the required capital, and that anyone who didn't would be diluted.

Frank Fouce Jr., who represented his mother, was his father's successor and served as president of SIN's board of directors. He frequently leveraged his relationship with the Azcárragas to hire Mexican artists and have them perform at the California theaters his family owned through Fouce Amusement Enterprises. But this time, stunned by Anselmo's proposal, Fouce Jr. opposed the scheme because his company didn't have the cash and it would dilute his position in SIN.

As night began to fall, and after many hours of negotiations, Anselmo left the hotel to buy another pack of cigarettes. He returned with a proposal that would change the course of history. With the audacity of the big, voracious players on the Wall Street–style capital markets, he presented an offer of $1 million to purchase Fouce Amusement Enterprises' shares in SIN: a dazzling sum in those turbulent times for the U.S. television station starved of both capital and patience.

In that dimly lit conference room, Frank Fouce Jr., a man carrying the weight of his family legacy on his shoulders, called for a recess. He was going to discuss the matter with his mother, though not before requesting a private space in which to make the phone call. Upon his return, with the determination of someone who knows his destiny is about to change, he accepted the sale for $1 million, demanding a signature and a cash payment in full within twenty-four hours. A handshake sealed the deal, marking the beginning of what would become a new and bitter era.

At noon the next day, with Leventhal and the shareholders gathered, everyone awaited the arrival of Fouce Jr. The air was thick with anticipation. When Fouce Jr. appeared, his immediate request for a private meeting with Anselmo cast a pall over the room. In a shocking twist, Fouce Jr. demanded an additional $250,000 from Anselmo as a fee for orchestrating the transaction and convincing his family to agree to the sale. The temerity of this move added a layer of tension and intrigue to an already dramatic negotiation.

The following exchange is based on the account given by Norm Leventhal, Anselmo and Azcárraga Milmo's attorney, who was present at this historic meeting:

Fouce Jr.: You can pay me this fee in installments if you like.

Anselmo (shouting): This is unacceptable! We shook hands to formalize the deal! The documents are ready, the money is ready.

Fouce Jr.: In honor of my father, who founded this company with Emilio Azcárraga Vidaurreta, I ask you to unders-tand our decision to conduct this transaction in a manner

> that's fair to both parties. My mother will accept the million dollars, but she also requires that I be paid an additional fee for completing the transaction.

Anselmo continued shouting so loudly that the other shareholders entered the discussion and tried to convince him to negotiate the fee down to something less than the $250,000 Fouce Jr. was asking for.

Villanueva agreed that Fouce Jr.'s demand for an additional payment beyond what had already been agreed upon was unfair, but he also understood the need to move forward. He believed Fouce Jr. was willing to negotiate and that the initial $250,000 was merely a starting point. He suggested offering $100,000 and haggling until a mutually acceptable agreement was reached.

But Anselmo wouldn't budge. He believed the deal should be honored under the original terms of the agreement and saw no reason to entertain Fouce Jr.'s new demands. Resolute in his belief that negotiations had come to an end, Anselmo decided that there would be no agreement after all. Instead, he resolved to proceed with a capital increase through the issuance of new shares, a measure he saw as the only path forward.

Alarmed by the potential dilution of his family's stake in SIN, Fouce Jr. reacted swiftly. Determined to protect his family's interests, he began exploring legal avenues for ensuring his position would not be weakened. As chairman of the board, he insisted that no decisions would be finalized that day, believing that more time was needed in order to fully assess the situation and consider all possible options.

Enraged, Anselmo called for a recess and asked Fouce Jr. to wait for a moment. He stepped out to make a call, presumably to El Tigre, and returned to the hotel conference room with two proposals for the board to vote on:

1. Remove Frank Fouce Jr. from his position as chairman of the board of directors.
2. Appoint himself, Reynold "René" Anselmo, as the new chairman of the board of directors while continuing to serve simultaneously as CEO.

In that climate where the tension was palpable, and with a calmness that contrasted sharply with Anselmo's fiery obfuscation, Fouce Jr. said his goodbyes and announced his formal resignation from the board without casting a vote. The other members, while clearly perturbed, did not confront Anselmo and instead quietly left the scene. In a document that appears to have sealed the company's fate, Anselmo was named the new chairman of the board.

Ten months later, Fouce Jr. unleashed a legal firestorm, accusing Anselmo and Laura Investments of diverting business opportunities and exercising unfair control over the company, violations of their fiduciary duties. Furthermore, Fouce Jr. attacked Anselmo and El Tigre's management of SIN, alleging that they were putting the renewal of the FCC license in jeopardy by ceding operational control to Televisa, a foreign group.

Additionally, in a strategic move that came months later, Fouce Jr. revived the Spanish Radio Broadcaster Association which, while founded in 1970 by radio station owners in the United States, had been inactive for several years. His idea was to use it as a legal roadblock with which to thwart any attempt by the Azcárragas and Anselmo to encroach into U.S. radio territory, thus sparking a very sensitive issue in the country. The association accused El Tigre and his sisters of being foreign investors attempting to violate the 20 percent rule through the use of a front man: Anselmo. This caught the attention of the FCC, triggering an investigation that plunged all involved parties into a decade-long legal battle that consumed millions of dollars and culminated in an outcome that absolutely no one could have anticipated on that January morning in 1976, when Anselmo and Fouce Jr. arrived at the meeting in San Antonio.

In the game of power and ambition, Anselmo and El Tigre had learned a crucial lesson: in the United States—unlike Mexico, where El Tigre seemed to pull the strings at will—the playing field was different. There, the rules of the legal and corporate game strongly favored the minority shareholder not because they were in the minority but because they were an American asset demanding justice from a foreign entity. The Azcárraga family didn't wield the same power in the United States as it did in Mexico.

The outcome of this war was a surprising one. Later we'll take a look at how this situation led to the renaming of SIN as Univision.

SIN and Ronald Reagan

By 1983, seven years had passed since the pivotal shareholders' meeting that sparked the conflict, and both the FCC and the Justice Department were keeping a close watch on SIN. In a bold display of influence, El Tigre and Anselmo chose to organize the annual meeting of the Ibero-American Television Organization and its accompanying music festival at DAR Constitution Hall in Washington, DC, a venue located near both the White House and the Capitol and just a few blocks from the headquarters of both the FCC and the Department of Justice. Representing the United States, the host country, SIN took center stage during this international festival, which left an indelible mark on the recognition of the Hispanic community in the United States.

The event featured a special performance by the renowned Spanish opera singer Plácido Domingo, and during the opening ceremonies, President Ronald Reagan addressed the attendees and TV audience via a three-minute video in which he improvised a few words in Spanish On that day, Reagan proclaimed the first-ever National Hispanic Heritage Week, an event that would eventually evolve into what is now known as National Hispanic Heritage Month, celebrated annually between September 15 and October 15.

This is what President Reagan said:

> Bienvenidos. I am very happy on behalf of the American Government and people to welcome all of you to this Twelfth International Song Festival of the International Television Organization, OTI. I am also pleased to greet the 200 to 300 million people in Latin America and Europe who are watching this important event via satellite.
>
> This festival vividly shows the power of music to cross frontiers and bring people of diverse backgrounds and traditions closer together in harmony. Henry Wadsworth Longfellow, the nineteenth-century U.S. poet, once remarked, "Music is the universal language of mankind." What we are about to see tonight is living witness to those words. However, Longfellow in his time could not have possibly imagined how satellite technology would give people everywhere

almost instantaneous communications through radio and television, and our common musical idiom.

I thank OTI for designating our capital, Washington, DC, as this year's festival site. This is the first opportunity we in the United States have had to host this magnificent event. It is appropriate that the United States should serve as a host. We are extremely proud of our Hispanic heritage, a heritage that has meant so much to our country from earliest colonial days to the present. Hispanic Americans have worked shoulder to shoulder with their compatriots of other ethnic backgrounds to make our nation what it is today. In recognition of this substantial contribution, I was proud to proclaim the week beginning September 11, 1983, as National Hispanic Heritage Week.

I would also like to congratulate the Spanish International Television Network for its significant public affairs role in our nation and for bringing this telecast to millions of viewers here and in other countries. SIN has, for the last twenty years, helped give Hispanic Americans the recognition they so rightly deserve. It has been a catalyst for the great strides made by Hispanic Americans during that period.

It is very reassuring to me that, despite whatever grave economic and political problems face the Americas, twenty-three nations will be united together tonight for the next three hours via satellite television. This is a remarkable demonstration of the fundamental strength of the cultural ties which unite our people. This festival is proof to me once again that there is more that unites us in this hemisphere than could ever divide us. Together I know that we in this hemisphere can, with the help of our long-term friends in Spain, Portugal,

> and elsewhere, surmount the serious challenges of our day. I wish all of the contestants success. In fact, you already are winners of a larger contest. You are truly musical ambassadors of your countries who have conquered our hearts with your individual and collective messages of friendship. Buena suerte, y que Dios los bendiga a todos.

In 1983, Argentina Ramos, owner of the Puerto Rican channel Telemundo, decided to sell it to a group of American investors. This sale not only marked the beginning of Telemundo's aggressive expansion into the U.S. market but also established the Telemundo brand in the United States before SIN adopted the Univision name. This phase of Telemundo's growth was the prelude to an increasingly intense rivalry.

As Telemundo began its foray into the U.S. market, SIN was working to strengthen its own position in Hispanic television, organizing the OTI Festival in Washington, DC, and enlisting the support of the Reagan administration. And while consolidating its influence seemed like a sound strategy, these efforts failed to quash the ongoing litigation being relentlessly pursued by the Fouces. On top of all that, SIN was not only under the scrutiny of the Justice Department and the FCC but was also attracting attention from powerful economic and political interests. Figures like Rupert Murdoch, Ted Turner, and the rising Jerry Perenchio had emerged on the horizon, signaling the beginning of an era of transformation and challenges for René Anselmo and El Tigre Azcárraga.

CHAPTER 4

The Struggle for Control of SIN and the Rise of the Hispanic Audience

The 1976 shareholders meeting that began on January 14 and ended the next day, in which René Anselmo and Frank Fouce Jr. clashed at the Crockett Hotel in San Antonio, Texas, takes on an even deeper historical significance when you consider the context of the location. Built on land that was the site of the Battle of the Alamo in 1836, the Crockett Hotel evokes memories of a pivotal engagement during the Texas Revolution. From the Mexican perspective, this battle symbolizes the fierce resistance of the troops under the command of Antonio López de Santa Anna against the Texas volunteer soldiers. For Americans, though, the Alamo represents a decisive moment of heroism and sacrifice that was necessary in order to achieve final victory in the war.

The site has become immortalized as a rallying cry in both the fight for Texan independence and the ensuing Mexican-American War. Ironically, the hotel is named after Davy Crockett, one of the Texan defenders who fell during that very battle: a permanent reminder of converging histories. Here, Anselmo represented the interests of the Azcárragas (Mexico) against Fouce Jr. (Texas). It was Anselmo who chose the meeting's location, perhaps with some symbolic intentions in his mind. More than a simple business meeting, this encounter at the Crockett Hotel reflected an ambitious attempt by the representative of SIN's Mexican interests to assert himself on American soil.

René Anselmo, whose vision always saw beyond the present moment, was convinced of SIN's bright future. His demeanor during the two-day meeting at the historic hotel radiated confidence, a sense of absolute control over situations and events. His vision would prove to be correct, as the Mexican television station's future would indeed be a bright one, but what he failed to foresee was that this brilliance would ultimately shine without him as its beacon. His stubbornness in refusing to give in and negotiate with Fouce Jr. would come at a massive economic and emotional cost. This episode didn't just drain resources while adding anxiety and stress. It strained the relationship—both personal and professional—between Anselmo and El Tigre.

Silence reigned in the wake of the Crockett Hotel meeting. When Fouce Jr. bid his farewells, Anselmo was flooded by feelings of fear, rage, powerlessness, and the determination to act despite innate feelings of guilt. Frank Fouce Jr. was also awash in anguish as he went to inform his mother, the legal representative of Frank Fouce Sr.'s estate, about what had just happened.

Anselmo knew he'd made a unilateral decision without consulting either El Tigre or the other minority shareholders. This act not only jeopardized the harmony within SIN's ownership but also unleashed the wrath of Villanueva, who would never forgive Anselmo's aggressive and volatile refusal to negotiate with Fouce Jr.'s unexpected request for an additional fee. With the intense atmosphere bearing down on him, Anselmo would have to face the consequences of his actions and tell El Tigre what had happened. He wasn't afraid of taking this step; his self-confidence made him the master of his own truth. A phone call wasn't enough for a matter of such magnitude, and El Tigre, understanding the gravity of the moment, asked Anselmo to fly back to Los Angeles and meet him at La Hacienda.

During the meeting, El Tigre chose not to browbeat Anselmo with any further recriminations. Instead, he demanded loyalty along with a redoubled effort to transform SIN into the project they'd both fought so hard for. SIN had to be transformed into Univisa, the name he'd long been wanting for the network but that had always been rejected by the other partners. Despite the adversity, El Tigre was determined to defend the legality of his position to the bitter end. He was convinced that the aggressors—in this case, Fouce Jr. and his mother—could eventually be worn down to the point where they'd return to the negotiating table. This approach reflected his resolve, his determination to stay the course without letting any concerns he might have about the Fouces' actions distract him from his plans. Deep down, he knew this would be a trial by fire in the United States: a country where, unlike Mexico, he still had to learn how to navigate the turbulent waters of politics and power.

For El Tigre, the battle wouldn't be fought solely in the courtroom, with high caliber attorneys, big money, and political sway, but also in the arenas of internal loyalty and trust. This crisis represented a pivotal moment that would come to define the future of SIN. Jimmy Carter's days as president were numbered. It was widely felt that he wouldn't be winning reelection, and that California Governor Ronald Reagan stood a significant chance of becoming the next president of the United States.

Reagan's Debt to SIN

On August 29, 1970, a march protesting the Vietnam War drew more than thirty thousand African American and Hispanic activists to the streets of Los Angeles. This was an unprecedented mobilization for local authorities. Reagan was governor of California at the time, and intelligence reports reaching him concluded that the demonstration had been primarily organized by a TV station with the call sign KMEX, a SIN affiliate, which aired a Spanish-language newscast and had promoted the march for quite some time. This activism was in coordination with Spanish-language radio stations across Los Angeles as well as the newspaper *La Opinión*, which reported in detail on the logistics of the SIN-announced march and published invitations to participate. The march took place, and the brutally repressive response by the Los Angeles Police Department followed swiftly. In what was, allegedly, a freak accident, one of the tear-gas canisters fired by an LAPD officer struck Hispanic journalist Rubén Salazar in the head, killing him instantly. Salazar was a journalist for the *Los Angeles. Times* and also coordinated SIN's local news broadcast in Sacramento. Worried that the impact of this tragedy could lead to further social unrest among LA's Hispanic community, Governor Reagan asked to meet with SIN's owners.

The general manager of SIN in Los Angeles was Danny Villanueva, who was also a minority shareholder in the company, while the chairman was Frank Fouce Jr. They both answered the governor's call. Reagan urged caution when it came to reporting on Salazar's death and asked that only official statements regarding the incident be broadcast. At the same time, the Chicano movement was demanding justice. In response, SIN's management, under the leadership of Villanueva and Fouce Jr., and with the influence of René Anselmo and El León, decided to oblige the governor's request. They chose not to openly join in the public outcry and cut back on judicial coverage of the killing, focusing instead on the news station's internal mourning of Salazar's tragic death. While Hispanic activists wanted to use SIN's Los Angeles platform to denounce Salazar's murder, the station redirected its attention toward covering international news. This decision to silence activist discourse deeply disillusioned not only the Chicano movement activists but the community in general, which saw SIN as having betrayed the seeking for justice and recognition of Salazar assassination, who became a journalistic martyr within the Hispanic community.

Before his death, Rubén Salazar was noted for his incisive coverage of the tensions and challenges faced by the Chicano community in Los Angeles. Throughout his career at the *Los Angeles Times* and SIN television, Salazar documented emerging social and political dynamics, becoming a critical voice in the civil rights movement. His focus was always on issues of injustice and the struggle for recognition of Mexican Americans' rights. His killing on August 29, 1970, by a tear-gas cannister fired by a sheriff's deputy, symbolized the violent repression faced by Chicano activists at the time.

While within the Hispanic community Salazar's killing was compared with the assassination of Martin Luther King Jr., the American press, with the exception of the *Los Angeles Times*, failed to report on the incident. It's important to note that the *Times* ran the story on the front page above the fold the very next day, August 30, and unlike the official report, which described the weapon as a tear-gas canister, the paper headlined its first edition as follows: "One Dead, 40 Hurt in East LA Riot: Times Columnist Rubén Salazar Killed by Bullet."

The article was accompanied by a photograph of a smiling Salazar, along with another of the riots. The front-page columns were written by veterans Charles T. Powers and Jeff Perlman:

> An East Los Angeles parade and rally that attracted about 20,000 persons to demonstrate Mexican-American opposition to the war in Southeast Asia erupted into a riot Saturday, claming the life of one of the city's leading spokesmen for Chicano rights.
>
> The dead man was Rubén Salazar, 42, award-winning Times columnist and news director for television station KMEX (Channel 34).
>
> Deputies found him sprawled on the floor inside the Silver Dollar Café, 4945 Whittier Blvd., with a bullet wound in the head.

The Chicano Moratorium (formally known as the National Chicano Moratorium Committee Against the Vietnam War) was an antiwar activist movement that built a broad coalition of Mexican American groups to organize opposition to the Vietnam War. The movement was led by local college activists and members of the Brown Berets, a group stemming from the high school movement that organized walkouts in 1968. They called their struggle La Causa (The Cause).

The effectiveness of street mobilization, patently visible though this demonstration, led Reagan to want a better understanding of SIN's reach among the Hispanic community, both in California and beyond. Grateful for SIN's restraint following the

Brown Berets emblem,
La Causa.

tragic death of Salazar, the governor began to publicly acknowledge the network's influence and importance. This event demonstrated the relevance of the local Spanish-language newscast, capable of covering crucial events for the Hispanic community that weren't necessarily of interest to the English-language or international media. While this connection between SIN and Reagan is seen as a step toward greater understanding and political recognition of the Hispanic community, some critics see it as the moment when the Anglo-American establishment recognized the need to more closely monitor and manage Spanish-language communications. To these critics, this recognition was not a friendly gesture of inclusion but rather a more sinister strategy for exerting more effective social control over the growing Hispanic population.

In 1976, six years after Salazar's killing and following the deadlock between Anselmo and Fouce Jr. in San Antonio, El Tigre recognized the need to strategically consolidate his political alliances in order to strengthen his position in the U.S. market. Ronald Reagan had been governor of California from 1967 to 1975 and was already ramping up his presidential campaign.

Well aware of the power that could come from an inner-circle relationship with a potential Reagan administration, El Tigre and Anselmo set themselves about cultivating and deepening those ties. This tactic was not only an extension of their approach in Mexico, where their proximity to the political establishment had secured them a solid foundation and respect among competitors and rivals, but also a preventative strike in an environment where opposing interests were looking for any opportunity to challenge the men's leadership.

In the United States, maintaining a privileged relationship with the White House might buy them some time as they faced the ongoing litigation from Fouce as well as discourage those who sought to eradicate the power of Hispanic television in the country or other media moguls who might be licking their lips at the prospect of acquiring SIN, whether it be through hostile or friendly means. El Tigre and Anselmo were fully aware that all the key players in the television world were following the litigation and sensing the SIN shareholders' increasing vulnerability in light of their legal predicament. A political alliance with Reagan, then, would be a shield against their direct adversaries. It would also be a demonstration of power and stability in a business landscape that could turn even more stormy at any moment.

While SIN shareholders sought to leverage their relationship with Reagan in order to mitigate the pressure from ongoing litigation and ward off potential adversaries, Reagan himself also had very pragmatic reasons for strengthening ties with SIN. Across the electoral landscape, the Latino vote had become a decisive factor. This sense of mutual necessity between Reagan and SIN recognized a political and media symbiosis: one in which SIN offered an open forum to engage and communicate directly with Hispanic voters while Reagan provided SIN shareholders with crucial political support during times of legal and corporate turmoil. After losing the Republican nomination in 1976, Reagan persevered, eventually securing the nomination in 1979. In the following year's presidential election, he won a resounding victory over Jimmy Carter and became president of the United States. His inauguration on January 20, 1981, was a milestone in the history of presidential broadcast, because it was the first such event to be transmitted live via satellite with a simultaneous Spanish translation: a production carried out by SIN with technical support provided by Televisa, underscoring SIN's growing influence.

According to a *New York Times* article titled "Courting Hispanic Voters Now a Reagan Priority," the Republican strategy identified the Hispanic community as a "sleeping giant" in American politics. In fact, Reagan had captured more than 30 percent of the Latino vote: an unprecedented figure for a Republican presidential candidate.

On March 30, 1981, Reagan met with Hispanic leaders at the White House to thank them for their support during his presidential campaign: an event attended by René Anselmo. However, the media's focus would change drastically that same day when, just a few hours later, Reagan was shot in an attempted assassination while leaving the Washington Hotel a few blocks from the White House. This incident overshadowed coverage of the meeting, dominating the headlines and throwing the day's media agenda into utter disarray.

Six months into his presidency—and three months after miraculously surviving the attempt on his life—Ronald Reagan officially welcomed the president of Mexico, José López Portillo, to Camp David. Their summit was, in practical terms, organized by El Tigre. For the first time in history, a meeting between the presidents of both nations was broadcast live via satellite and aired simultaneously by SIN in the United States and Televisa in Mexico.

The Endless Trial (1976–1986)

In the legal battle between the Fouces and SIN's main shareholders, El Tigre and Anselmo, attorney Norm Leventhal made numerous attempts at reaching a settlement with the opposing party while insisting that his clients' fight to change the 20 percent rule, which, as we've mentioned, was the law imposed by the FCC to limit foreign ownership of U.S. television stations. Despite these efforts, the FCC continued its investigation with a growing determination to take action against SIN's primary shareholders: Anselmo and Laura Investments, the Azcárraga family company controlled by El Tigre.

Leventhal, relying on the strength of his network of contacts within the FCC and SIN's ties to the White House, urged René Anselmo to invest in lobbying to have the 20 percent rule repealed and allow foreign groups to acquire American TV stations. El Tigre and Anselmo, though, chose not to follow his advice and instead dug themselves in, ready to defend their position to the bitter end. Leventhal was convinced he could apply enough pressure to a number of senators and representatives sympathetic to the Hispanic cause to result in the repealing of Section 310(b)(3) of the Communications Act of 1934 (also known as the 20 percent rule). If Anselmo and El Tigre had opted to go with his initial strategy, the fate of SIN—and, therefore, Univision—could have been very different.

By 1983, the intensity of the litigation was taking a toll on everyone involved. In fact, the pressure had reached such a point that Carmela and Laura, El Tigre's sisters, were demanding that they be removed from the conflict in the United States. Anselmo, for his part, remained determined to continue with his business operations, both in the television sector as well as his satellite project, leaving the litigation in the hands of his lawyers, confident that everything would eventually be resolved. No one anticipated the tenacity of the Fouces, the growing importance that the FCC and the inherently political context would add to the confrontation, or the internal conflict that arose from within the Azcárraga family. Tensions were escalated even further as SIN's license—granted by the FCC—was up for renewal in 1987.

Business figures such as Jerry Perenchio, Rupert Murdoch, and Ted Turner were all following the developments in the United States District Court for the Central District of California, where SIN's future was being decided. Under mounting pressure, El Tigre proposed rebranding SIN as Univisa, attempting to project a new image that might distract the litigants. But this proposal wasn't taken seriously and was rejected by the minority shareholders. Yet despite it all, the perseverance and determination of Anselmo and El Tigre proved to be critical, for without their efforts to ensure SIN's survival, Univision never would have existed.

Hispanics Arrive in the United States en Masse

The wave of Hispanic immigrants to the United States was growing rapidly. The number had already risen from 3.5 million residents in 1960 to more than 9 million by 1970. By 1980, according to U.S. Census Bureau data, 14.6 million Hispanics were living in the United States, and by 1990, the country's legally registered Spanish-speaking community numbered more than 21 million. The perception of immigrants was no longer that of traditional day laborers with limited education in search of income they would later take back with them to Mexico and the families they had left behind.

During the 1970s and early 1980s, Latin American countries were facing profound economic crises that were exacerbated in part by economic instability in developed nations, particularly the United States. The recession there, which intensified during Jimmy Carter's presidency, marked a time of high inflation and slow economic growth. This situation didn't just destabilize the U.S. economy; it had repercussions that were felt around the globe, thus affecting Latin American countries' ability to garner investments in the international markets. High interest rates in the United States limited access to foreign credit and increased the cost of servicing external debt for these nations.

Meanwhile, the 1979 oil crisis was also playing a crucial role, triggering global inflation and reducing export demand from developing nations, many of which relied heavily on commodity sales. This combination of high financing costs and low export revenues pushed many Latin American countries into an unsustainable financial situation, precipitating an exorbitant debt crisis in the region. As the United States struggled with its own economy, its ability to serve as an engine of global growth diminished significantly.

As the decade of the 1970s gave way to the 1980s, and with the United States attempting to recover from its most severe recession since the Great Depression, Latin America faced a time of economic decline exacerbated by poor domestic policies and rampant corruption. These internal problems, combined with an adverse global economic environment, made the promise of a better future in the United States seem even more attractive to desperate Latin American immigrants. This changed the nature of migration from being predominantly labor-driven to an increasingly inclusive shift toward young students, professionals, and entire families seeking opportunity and stability.

SIN was the leading Spanish-language media outlet in the United States, one whose reach stretched across the country. Its newscasts had anchors based in Los Angeles, San Antonio, Washington, DC, and Miami, along with reporters based in other cities where SIN had coverage. By the early 1980s, the company could confirm that it was reaching 80 percent of the tens of millions of Hispanics living in the United States. Communication with this audience was direct and in Spanish. The powers that be were aware of this, and SIN was starting to relish its growing influence with politicians.

Runaway Hits: *El Chapulín Colorado* and *Los ricos también lloran*

In the early 1980s, during the years after its successful launch in Mexico, the telenovela *Los ricos también lloran* began resonating with SIN viewers. In the United States, it wasn't just a Mexican audience; it connected with all Hispanics, regardless of nationality. The plot follows the life of a young orphan living in the countryside who, after the death of her grandfather, moves to the capital where she's adopted by a wealthy and powerful man. Throughout the series, Mariana faces various hardships and challenges that include family intrigue, class conflicts, complicated romances, and the search for her own identity.

Around that same time, *El Chapulín Colorado*—a TV series about a hero who reflected his own struggles as a fearful yet daring human being—struck a chord with immigrants facing a new life in a new country filled with daunting challenges.

This Hispanic connection with El Chapulín Colorado is made clear in an interview with the character's creator, Roberto Gómez Bolaños, affectionately known as Chespirito. In the interview, Chesperito explained the essence of how the character came about, contrasting it with heroes like Batman and Superman. "They aren't heroes. El Chapulín Colorado is a real hero," he said to Argentine journalist and comedian Carlos Abrevaya. With a solemn tone to his voice and a raised index finger, he added, "I'm serious. Heroism isn't about the absence of fear. It's about the ability to overcome it. Batman and Superman are all-powerful. Fearless. But El Chapulín is afraid, and far from that being his weakness, it's precisely what makes him a hero. El Chapulín Colorado is scared to death. He's clumsy, weak, stupid, and yet, despite these limitations, he's still able to bravely confront his challenges. That's what makes him a true hero, and his catchphrase—"¡Que no panda el cúnico!," which is a spoonerism that could loosely be translated as "'Pobody nanic!'" —resonates as a message of calmness and courage amid chaos. A ninety-year-old viewer who migrated across the border with Texas once told me that "when we arrived and settled down here, we were like Chapulínes Colorados."

The viewership of these programs was in the millions. Even so, advertisers weren't reaching out en masse to SIN because Nielsen, the company that held a near monopoly when it came to reporting TV show ratings through its Nielsen Television Audience Measurement system, wasn't tracking Spanish-language viewership at the time. Advertising revenue at SIN, which was growing ever so slowly, depended on direct contact between SIN's owners and executives and the advertising agencies themselves. El Tigre and Anselmo managed to convince Procter & Gamble, already one of Televisa's most important clients, to pay more attention to the Spanish-speaking audience in the United States. As such, SIN's advertising revenue gradually began to climb, eventually reaching nearly $15 million in the early 1980s.

Anselmo, an antitrust activist by nature, refused to negotiate with Nielsen when it came to measuring the Hispanic viewership in the United States. And El Tigre either downplayed or outright ignored the issues of ratings altogether. In Mexico, he didn't need to measure audience share, because he owned the only major entertainment and information channel in his country. In the United States, he was the leader in Spanish-language content, but this audience was, at the time, being ignored by companies looking to buy ad time.

In 1980, a Cuban man named Roberto Goizueta was appointed CEO of The Coca-Cola Company, and one of the immediate changes he made at the soft drink giant was to open the first Hispanic marketing department at a major U.S. corporation, encouraging other major ad agencies to consider Spanish-language advertising. The experiments began. By 1985, the tobacco company Philip Morris was among the top advertisers, investing $7 million in Spanish-language advertising. Not far behind were Procter & Gamble and Anheuser-Busch, with investments of $6.5 million each, and the McDonald's Corporation, which invested $6.3 million that same year.

The Fiesta Hispana at the Garden

In 1981, El Tigre organized a massive concert he dubbed the Fiesta Hispana at Madison Square Garden in New York City. He invited executives from Coca-Cola, Proctor & Gamble, and a number of advertising agencies. Tickets for the concert, held over a weekend, Saturday and Sunday, October 10 and 11, sold out, resulting in an impressive event featuring performances by José Luis "El Puma" Rodríguez, Rocío Durcal, Juan Gabriel, Lupita D'Alessio, Camilo Sesto, José José, Armando Manzanero, Roberto Carlos, Miguel Bosé, and Lola Beltrán. The emcee of the event was Raúl Velasco, host of the Mexican variety show *Siempre en domingo*.

Part of the concert was broadcast live via satellite by Televisa in Mexico and SIN in the United States. It's been difficult to measure the full impact of this performance, which should have been major news, as it appears to have gone largely unnoticed by the media at the time. In fact, very little exists, even in Televisa's own archives, apart from a brief note published in *The New York Times*:

> GRAN FIESTA EN EL MADISON, a three-hour Latin American variety show Saturday and Sunday in Madison

Square Garden, brought together a multinational cast of Spanish-speaking pop stars in an unprecedented display of Spanish-speaking talent. [. . .]

The sleekly produced program showed just how little rock-and-roll, one of America's great cultural exports of the last three decades, has penetrated Latin American culture. Only one out of the 10 acts that appeared—Miguel Bose, a Spanish pop—put on a real rock performance, and it was an odd mixture of aggressive singing and coy, teen-idol mannerism performed with a laser light show.

It was the more conventional male singers who evoked the most hysteria, however. The sensation of the day, Jose Luis Rodriguez, is a star of Venezuelan soap opera, with the nickname El Puma, and the tiniest swivel of his hips sent the arena into a frenzy. Mr. Rodriguez's Anglo-American equivalents are booming balladeers like Tom Jones and Engelbert Humperdinck, except that Mr. Rodriguez is younger, better looking and can out-sing them, with his dramatically intense pop tenor.

Camilo Sesto, a Spanish pop star, was greeted with almost equal excitement by a younger contingent of female fans. Mr. Sesto, who once starred in a successful European production of "Jesus Christ Superstar," is more flamboyant than Mr. Rodriguez, but he has a powerful tenor, like Barry Manilow's, to match his theatricality.

The Fiesta Hispana at Madison Square Garden, organized by El Tigre, was a landmark event in the history of the Hispanic community in the United States. The concert represented much more than a simple weekend of music and celebration: it was an opportunity for cultural identity that, unfortunately, never received the recognition it deserved from the English-speaking media.

Despite the concert's resounding success in front of a sold-out Madison Square Garden crowd, the English-language mainstream media (with the lone exception being the aforementioned article in *The New York Times*) failed to cover it, showing a lack of interest in or understanding of Hispanic culture.

Despite having witnessed firsthand the power and passion of the Hispanic community, the lukewarm response by the corporate executives in attendance highlights another disconnect in how this vital segment of the market was understood and valued. This two-day performance, while ignored at the time, proved crucial in laying the groundwork for what would eventually become a broader recognition of the importance and influence of the Hispanic community within American culture and the economy.

José Luis Rodríguez, also known as El Puma, confided in me that, during the Fiesta Hispana, El Tigre was not only promoting the show but also making logistical decisions about the order of the performances. At one point, El Tigre approached El Puma with a special request, hoping for his help in maintaining peace between the artists. The businessman calmly expressed his concerns: "Puma, I need you to help keep things calm backstage. Do you think you'd be willing to give up your set time and not be the one to close out the show?"

"Sure, brother, don't worry," the Venezuelan star said with a nod before offering an alternative. "If you want, I could open the concert."

That gesture strengthened the bond between El Puma and El Tigre, who treated him with the greatest respect from that night on. In 1985, this relationship led to El Puma being offered a starring role in the Televisa telenovela *Tú o nadie* (*You or No One*), alongside Lucía Méndez. Rodríguez accepted the offer and traveled to Acapulco to begin filming. During the first few days of production, however, an impasse arose involving the actress, El Puma's manager, Televisa producers, and El Puma himself, allegedly regarding some sort of romantic relationship. This incident led to El Puma's decision to withdraw from the show, which later starred Andrés García.

On his way back to Venezuela, during a layover of a few days in Miami, El Puma felt the need to personally explain the situation to El Tigre, so he called him. The conversation had barely even begun before he cut to the chase. "Emilio, let me tell you what happened..."

But El Tigre cut him off with a few sharp words, "Don't tell me anything. You messed with me, so now you can go and fuck yourself!"

From that moment on, El Puma found the doors to acting or performing in Mexico closed to him. It was a situation that endured until after El Tigre's death.

The story of El Tigre and his interactions with José Luis Rodríguez is a clear example of the power and influence that certain media moguls can wield over an artist's career. Accustomed to having total control over the media and entertainment worlds, Azcárraga not only decided who appeared on his TV screens and when, but he also had the ability to influence and determine the fate of a famous Latin American artist's career in Mexico. In the wake of this impasse, El Puma made the decision to further his international career farther south on the continent.

SIN's Growth

Meanwhile, SIN's sales continued to climb. By 1981, the company had surpassed $25 million in revenue. However, the Fouces' lawsuit against SIN's shareholders was also intensifying.

In 1982, SIN acquired the television broadcast rights to that year's FIFA World Cup, which was being hosted by Spain. The games were broadcast in full color via satellite from Televisa's studios in Mexico. That year, SIN's sales hit $40 million. Once again, advertising agencies recognized the broadcast's success. It's worth noting that, although ABC and ESPN also held the rights, they aired only match highlights, and while ABC did air the final live, it did so with commercial breaks that didn't line up with the game's natural ebb and flow. Fans considered this a slap in the face, and many switched over to SIN, where they could watch the match uninterrupted. In doing so, however, English speakers couldn't understand the commentators or follow the action, so they were forced to turn down the volume on their TVs and turn on radio coverage in their own language. It was during the final match between Italy and West Germany that Andrés Cantor's now iconic extended cry of "Gooooooooal!" was first heard in the United States. Born in Argentina, the legendary sportscaster became a U.S. citizen in his twenties and was then already living in California.

In 1986, SIN became the epicenter of the soccer world by broadcasting numerous World Cup matches in Mexico, achieving unprecedented success in both viewership and commercial revenue, with Hispanic advertising sales approaching $91 million: an unparalleled figure in the United States. Unfortunately, along with this great triumph came an inescapable and grim reality for

SIN and its leader, El Tigre. While Diego Maradona led Argentina to glory on the pitch inside the colossal Estadio Azteca, owned by Televisa, El Tigre was staring down the beginning of the end of his reign as owner of SIN, having found himself at a crossroads that was beginning to consume him from within.

During the thrilling final in Mexico City, from his vantage point in the presidential box and surrounded by world leaders, El Tigre projected a triumphant facade. There, on his home turf, his expression reflected a victory that he knew would be fleeting. Meanwhile, hundreds of miles away, in his Connecticut mansion, René Anselmo was engulfed in rage and frustration. Isolated, consumed by remorse and anxiety, he was fully aware of the verdict about to be handed down from the federal court in California, which would tip the scales in favor of Frank Fouce Jr., ending a grueling, decade-long legal war.

This scene, charged with tension and contrast, marked the end of an era for SIN. El Tigre, despite his apparent World Cup victory, was about to surrender his stake in SIN, dealing a devastating blow to the media empire. The World Cup final was not only the culmination of an international sporting event but also the backdrop for a personal and professional defeat for one of the television industry's most powerful figures. Ironically, the triumph of Televisa and SIN—along with that of Maradona and FIFA—heralded the end of a feline reign.

CHAPTER 5

The Fouce Lawsuit and the Conflict That Transformed SIN into Univision

The Judge

In 1979, three years after Fouce Jr. filed his lawsuit against SIN and its shareholders, the trial was assigned to the United States District Court for the Central District of California. U.S. District Judge Mariana R. Pfaelzer, who would be presiding over the case, had been nominated by President Jimmy Carter on August 8, 1978. Her historic nomination as the first female federal judge in California was confirmed by the U.S. Senate on September 22, 1978.

Born on February 4, 1926, in Los Angeles, California, she received her bachelor's degree from the University of California, Santa Barbara, in 1949, and her juris doctor from the UCLA School of Law in 1957. She worked in private practice until 1978, when she was appointed as a federal district judge.

As part of his legal strategy, Fouce Jr. filed a lawsuit on behalf of his family's estate, and also—with the reactivation of the Spanish Radio Broadcaster Association—he managed to go after El Tigre and Anselmo and attempt to block their efforts to make any new acquisitions and expand SIN in any audiovisual format in the United States. Anselmo then began justifying the large sums of money being spent on legal defense and counterclaims. For ten years, the Fouce family persisted with their lawsuit. Fouce's mother made several appearances before the district judge, who began to sympathize with her.

As time went by, the Fouces' lawsuit against SIN began to stall, caught up in the tense calm that foreshadows a storm. The FCC was holding the sword of Damocles over the heads of all involved: a looming threat that could tip the balance of power toward a dangerous outcome. If the FCC were to decide not to renew SIN's broadcasting license in 1986, accepting Fouce Jr. and the Spanish Radio Broadcaster Association's claim that SIN was being controlled by foreign capital, the consequences would be devastating. Losing the license would not only cause SIN's value to plummet, seriously impacting the finances of all its owners, Fouce Jr. included, but would also jeopardize the future of Hispanic television in the United States, risking the demise of the leading TV network with Spanish-language content, leaving nothing behind but assets to be sold and liquidated.

This potential catastrophe attracted the vulture-like interest of other, previously mentioned industry moguls who saw SIN's collapse as a golden opportunity for one of them to apply for a new license, acquire SIN's equipment, and take control of a new but already established TV network—all at bargain basement prices.

Furthermore, the political and social struggle was intensifying, with groups both politically and socially opposed to the use of the Spanish language in the United States. For these groups, not renewing SIN's license would be a highly favorable outcome, one they'd surely been pushing for behind the scenes. This confluence of economic interests and cultural tensions fueled a climate of uncertainty and anxiety, leaving every move in this power game open to scrutiny, given its potentially consequences.

On August 13, 1986, in a formal and diplomatic setting, the president of Mexico, Miguel de la Madrid, went to the White House to visit his American counterpart, Ronald Reagan. This was not just another meeting on the agenda of international relations: it came with a topic to be discussed sent directly by El Tigre. Leading up to the meeting, Azcárraga, still optimistic, had asked the team accompanying President de la Madrid to intervene on his behalf and present the issue of SIN's license directly to the executive branch of the U.S. government, which he considered a strong ally. El Tigre believed he—and, by extension SIN—deserved protection.

The pressure was tangible among El Tigre's inner circle as they anxiously awaited news from the summit being held in Washington. The Mexican magnate was eager for an update, and it was Carlos Salinas de Gortari, serving as Mexico's secretary of planning and budget at the time, who was charged with relaying the conclusions regarding the SIN licensing issue and its broadcasting rights in the United States.

The lengthy recordings of the conversations between the two presidents show that Reagan dominated the talking; he barely allowed anyone else to speak. At his side during the meetings was Vice President George H. W. Bush, who wasn't there simply as a witness. Within the Mexican president's staff, it was rumored that Bush was starting to assume a more active role in the administration and seemed to be the mastermind behind it all. With U.S. presidential elections on the horizon and the end of Reagan's term fast approaching, Bush's leading role was obvious, and El Tigre knew he had to redouble his efforts because the time to capitalize on the current administration's influence was quickly running out.

The Mexican presidential team's return to Mexico City did not bring with it the news that El Tigre and his circle had been hoping for. On the contrary, the atmosphere was charged with a tension that indicated drastic changes were coming and that SIN's days as an independent entity were numbered. El Tigre was forced to rethink his strategy, viewing the swift and decisive sale of shares as the only viable option for avoiding a financially catastrophic outcome for the Azcárraga family's interests. This conclusion, while not officially confirmed, was easy to deduce: the message from the meeting between the presidents was clear, and the Reagan-Bush administration was imposing a single solution that had to be executed quickly. SIN had to be sold, and the sale had to be coordinated by the Justice Department. There were no other alternatives. If it wasn't executed in this manner, a decision regarding SIN's future would be left in the hands of the FCC, which, in all likelihood, would not be renewing the current owners' license.

In the days following the historic meeting between Reagan and La Madrid, Judge Pfaelzer, known for her skills as a mediator and her effective resolutions, summoned all parties involved in the Fouces' lawsuit to a meeting that promised to be decisive. Her intention was to propose a settlement that, while not ideal for either side, offered a practical solution that would avoid a major scandal and preserve some semblance of dignity for SIN's current shareholders. This urgent summons to federal court in California's Central District added more tension for the litigants.

SIN's future hung in the balance, leaving up in the air the question of whether it would continue to be a bastion of Hispanic language and culture or be absorbed by the insatiable Anglo-American media market, which was clamoring for a fourth major television network.

In this high-pressure atmosphere, the judge proposed a solution that seemed to balance out the competing interests: the complete sale of SIN's shares to a third party. Under this agreement, both Fouce Jr. and the other shareholders would receive fair compensation for the license. The plan the judge put forward was somewhat like an expropriation without an executive order, more of an out-of-court negotiated settlement. Anselmo, the company's CEO, vehemently rejected this proposal, convinced that SIN could still reverse the situation without sacrificing the company's independence. However, he didn't have majority support.

El Tigre Sells SIN

In what must have been an unexpected turn of events for Anselmo, El Tigre decided to back the judge's proposal. With a firm mandate to his lawyers, El Tigre informed the court of his intention to accept the sale of his shares and requested that a committee be formed as part of the sale process that would include three current SIN executives to discuss proposals for the purchase. The Mexican businessman's decision to suggest René Anselmo as part of that committee not only changed the dynamics of the case but also intensified the pressure on Anselmo himself.

Anselmo felt betrayed when he saw his longtime ally pulling away at the most critical moment. Meanwhile, El Tigre's lawyers carried out their mandate, informing the judge that the majority of shareholders had agreed to sell SIN to a third party. While this was a bitter resolution, it promised to be less painful than the alternative. The company was on the cusp of surpassing $100 million in sales, projecting a successful close to the decade. Legal advisers on El Tigre's side of the aisle estimated the potential sale would reach at least $300 million. Eventually, El Tigre found a moment to speak with Anselmo, during which he tried to explain that there were no other viable options. The Azcárraga Milmo sisters, who were also still involved in the family business, strongly supported this decision, joining the consensus that left Anselmo in an uncomfortable minority position.

After a period of deep reflection, El Tigre had come to understand that SIN's situation in the United States went beyond mere business: it had become a symbol of cultural and political resistance. Pro-immigrant leaders had turned SIN's success into a rallying cry in their fight against anti-immigrant sentiment rising across various parts of the country. This added an emotional and political dimension to the situation, bolstering support for the Mexican businessman. This broader perspective allowed El Tigre to view the sale not only as a desperate solution in the face of impending financial devastation but also as an opportunity to reaffirm the channel's relevance as a voice for the Hispanic community in the United States—and potentially keep Televisa as a key content provider.

His strategic vision led El Tigre to look beyond the imminent sale, to see it as something other than a failure. He understood that, although the channel's ownership would change, the importance of maintaining programming that reflected and supported the Hispanic community would allow him to maintain a certain level of influence within the channel—enough, perhaps, to one day buy back some shares. El Tigre bared his claws once again to make this sale a tactical move rather than a total surrender.

Selling SIN was a tactical retreat for Azcárraga, still convinced that his long-term vision would prevail in the end. He was determined to leave his mark and pave the way for a possible return. The key was to leave a mysterious aura that would keep anyone from suspecting that he might come back one day. El Tigre never appeared defeated. In fact, this wasn't even a defeat; it was rather a necessary transformation.

While Anselmo wrestled internally with the decision to give in to pressure from his partners and the uncertain fate this would hold for SIN's legacy, circumstances forced him to acknowledge the direction being taken by El Tigre and the other shareholders. Despite his fierce opposition and the years he spent defending the company's original vision, his battle seemed to be coming to its inevitable end.

Within this context, El Tigre began to mobilize in an effort to demonstrate the vital importance of the Hispanic immigrant community in the United States. He appealed not only to economic arguments but also to political and cultural ones. Convinced that this strategy offered both dignity and the best chance at a comeback, he prepared to negotiate both the terms of the sale and also the conditions that would ensure SIN's continuity as an essential channel for Hispanic audiences, regardless of who its next owner might be. And beyond that, he was focused on maintaining the possibility of returning to the U.S. Hispanic market with a different format from broadcast television.

In addition to protecting his legacy, El Tigre also saw a strategic advantage for his own business. If he could ensure that the network's new owner would keep the business dedicated to the Hispanic and Spanish-language community, he could maintain Televisa as the primary content provider and preserve its strong influence and presence in the U.S. market. His company, Televisa, would be as indispensable as ever, achieving a perfect balance between continuing his legacy and strengthening his market position.

It was at that point that René Anselmo decided to fly to Mexico and meet with El Tigre. In a tense but decisive conversation, Azcárraga candidly laid out the fact that selling their shares was the only option that remained. He explained that, in spite of it all, Televisa could benefit financially from the sale and either continue selling content to the new owners or perhaps even start fresh with a new cable television venture. He also suggested that Anselmo could always find himself in a valuable new role, leveraging his extensive knowledge and innovative ideas regarding satellite technology, which was emerging as an effective new way to distribute audiovisual content. This technology, still in its nascent stages, promised to significantly reduce transmission costs while increasing reach and efficiency, thus presenting Anselmo with a unique opportunity to profit financially and also to significantly contribute to and maintain his influence in the industry.

A Lack of Transparency Between El Tigre and Anselmo

This situation was far more complex than a simple business transaction. El Tigre had uncovered crucial information and confronted Anselmo with his findings. During a thorough review of SIN's financial accounts, he discovered that Anselmo had used some of the company's expense accounts to finance his own ambitious foray into the world of satellite technology without informing the other shareholders.

Despite these somewhat murky irregularities, El Tigre wasn't looking to stir up a scandal. Instead, he used this information to bolster his argument for the need to sell SIN. He explained to Anselmo that the funds obtained from the sale would not only cover the financial shortcomings but leave a substantial surplus. That capital would be enough for Anselmo to continue developing his satellite project. As such, El Tigre was looking to ensure a transition that, while forced by difficult circumstances, promised a viable future for both SIN and Anselmo's personal ventures.

What was even more urgent, however, were the concerns bearing down on them from the FCC, which was taking an increasingly firm stance against SIN's majority shareholders. El Tigre added that his communications with political contacts had left it all quite clear: without a quick resolution, SIN ran the imminent risk of losing its broadcasting license. The gravity of the situation was tangible, and the business endeavor had reached a point of no return. Confronted with the reality of his increasingly compromised situation and the weight of the FCC's impending decisions, Anselmo accepted the proposed terms, a decision that marked a turning point in his career and SIN's future.

In October 1986, Judge Mariana Pfaelzer ruled that, with the consent of all its shareholders, SIN should be sold, without any penalties or exceptions, at market value. The judge also agreed to the formation of a committee—one that would include René Anselmo—to assist in the technical analysis of SIN's valuation. In her unprecedented decision, the judge relied on the 20 percent rule to explain that, due to shareholder conflicts related to the number of effective foreign beneficiaries, there was an agreement between the parties for SIN to be sold immediately.

Following this decisive, mutually agreed-upon ruling, Judge Pfaelzer assumed an even more active role in the process of selling SIN, a rare course of action in cases of this type. Apparently not satisfied with having simply presided over the case, she took it upon herself to call for potential investors interested in acquiring SIN's license. This unusual step demonstrated her commitment to an efficient and equitable resolution of the case, ensuring that the process was transparent and fair to all parties involved.

Utilizing the authority of her position, the judge established a strict protocol for selecting the new owner, inviting investors to submit their proposals. She would personally review each offer, reserving the right to make the final decision as to who would be most suitable to take over the reins of SIN, and ensuring that the channel's future was in capable, committed hands. There was a lot of apprehension—along with a bit of hope—in both the Hispanic community and within Azcárraga himself that the California judge's decision would reflect his understanding of the channel's cultural and social importance, which went beyond its commercial value.

The race to acquire SIN involved a number of major players in the media landscape, but not all of them showed a genuine interest in continuing the channel's original mission of serving the Spanish-speaking market. Rupert Murdoch and Ted Turner, two of the most prominent suitors, had ulterior motives and other strategies that appeared to diverge from Hispanic-themed content.

Murdoch, born in Australia, became a naturalized U.S. citizen on September 4, 1985. His strategic interest in SIN was more aligned with his desire to expand his own media empire. On the other hand, Turner, the visionary behind CNN, was focused on consolidating his twenty-four-hour news project, which was revolutionizing the way the world consumed information. His interest in SIN's assets could be interpreted as a move to diversify his media portfolio and take advantage of any potential synergies, though not necessarily an explicit focus on Spanish-language content.

The Network Remains in Spanish

This lack of commitment to maintain Spanish-language content was a significant concern for many activists, who urged the judge to select a pro-immigrant group in order to avoid a radical shift in SIN's programming and the possible loss of its identity as a network dedicated to the Hispanic community. It was still unclear whether Judge Pfaelzer's decision would be based not only on the financial offerings but also the cultural and social impact of selecting a new owner who could divert SIN from its original mission and affect both the network and its audience.

Back in the 1960s, the American businessman Andrew Jerrold "Jerry" Perenchio was one of the candidates for acquiring SIN. Perenchio rose to prominence as Ronald Reagan's artistic manager when the future president was a Hollywood actor, and became a major contributor to his political campaigns, first for governor of California and then for the 1980 presidential election. Through his friendship with Reagan, who, by 1981, was already occupying the Oval Office, Perenchio came to understand the growing power and influence of the Hispanic audience in the United States. This knowledge would shape his future strategies and businesses, a topic we'll discuss in a later chapter. Perenchio had owned WNJU, a TV station in New Jersey, since 1979, and in 1982, he began exploring the acquisition of Spanish-language content.

Potentially influenced by his access to privileged information owing to his connection to the White House during the Reagan administration, Perenchio made his first move by initiating litigation against SIN shareholders, attempting to secure a leading role in the case. Perenchio saw SIN as an opportunity to replicate his previous success in other media projects, potentially transforming the channel into a key player in the U.S. Hispanic market. He was considered a strong contender to take over SIN.

Hallmark Cards, Inc., led by Irvine O. Hockaday Jr., was looking to expand beyond its traditional business of printing and marketing holiday cards and other gift products. Headquartered in Kansas City, Missouri, a region historically marked by racial tensions and a limited Hispanic presence, Hallmark appeared to be an unusual candidate to take over a network like SIN, which catered primarily to a Spanish-speaking audience.

Hockaday's interest in entering the media sector through the acquisition of SIN might at first appear to be a significant departure from Hallmark's traditional market focus. The move raised questions about the card company's ability to adapt to a new audience, but also how a company rooted in such a different context could effectively manage a TV channel that served a community with needs and expectations that differed so significantly from its original consumer base.

Moreover, Hockaday's endorsement of the Republican Party and his donations to George H. W. Bush, then vice president, added another layer of complexity to the matter. These political ties could be seen as strategic during a time when policies and positions on immigration and minorities were at the center of the national debate. Added to this were persistent rumors that Bush was playing an increasingly dominant role in the administration, particularly amid speculation about the possibility of Reagan's declining mental health. These questions fueled the notion that, in effect, Bush was wielding considerable influence over decision-making in the White House, intensifying the relevance of his business endorsements and the potential implications of his domestic policy on major commercial decisions like the sale of SIN. What was true was that Reagan was on his way out and that Bush was the favorite to remain in the White House, this time as president.

In addition to these giants of media and business, also expressing interest were a number of groups with Hispanic leaders and businesspeople associated with both the Democratic and Republican Parties in various states where the Latino vote was becoming increasingly influential. These groups saw SIN as a potential tool for gaining influence and support within the Hispanic community, something that could prove crucial for future electoral battles. These players not only recognized SIN's commercial value but also its political potential as a means to connect and mobilize the Hispanic community, which could then translate into significant electoral power.

The influence of these groups wasn't limited to mere expressions of interest. It also increased the pressure on Judge Pfaelzer. This pressure sought to ensure an outcome that wasn't only financially favorable but also one that reflected and supported the political and social interests of the Hispanic community.

Months before deciding who would buy SIN's shares, Judge Pfaelzer regularly convened the parties involved in the lawsuit as well as potential buyers. One day, René Anselmo and Jerry Perenchio, who had been one of the more persistent suitors, were called to a meeting in her chambers. Anselmo and Perenchio knew each other as competitors in the tristate area, but they didn't understand why the judge wanted to interview them both at the same time. Before her stood two men whose decisions would make history of Hispanic television in the United States: René Anselmo, forced to sell, and Jerry Perenchio, an ambitious buyer and friend of the Reagans. The air was laden with tension and expectations.

After a pause, the judge expressed her concern for the interests of the country's Hispanic community. Anselmo was tacitly accused of favoring a foreign partner, Emilio Azcárraga Milmo, who had refused to appear before her. Although Anselmo contested the accusations, the judge ignored his evasions. She had thoroughly investigated Anselmo and Azcárraga's rise in the world of Hispanic television in the United States, knowing full well that Anselmo had used El Tigre's money to further his own success. Anselmo defended his collaboration with El Tigre, arguing it had benefited the Hispanic community, driving it toward progress.

The judge then focused her scrutiny on Perenchio, whose interest seemed to be much more about power and profit than the Hispanic community's cause. Perenchio, triumphant and arrogant, coldly replied that television was simply a business, nothing more. The judge clarified that this particular business had the potential to change lives, that this transaction was more than a simple exchange of money.

The political and cultural pressure of that time was evident. Threats from white supremacist groups who wanted to limit the use of Spanish on television darkened the skies even more. The opportunity to acquire a network in the United States was very attractive to investors who saw it as the potential fourth major network in the country. Neither Turner, nor Murdoch, nor the owners of ESPN, nor Disney was thinking about such a thing. Judge Pfaelzer knew that granting the sale to one of these groups could mean the end of Hispanic television in the United States, at least for a time. Hallmark, for its part, swore its intent was to maintain the network's Spanish-language content if it were granted ownership of SIN.

There was another Hispanic figure who had shown interest in acquiring SIN: Tirso del Junco, a Cuban-born doctor and executive director of the Republican Party in California. Del Junco rallied thirty-two businessmen behind his bid to purchase SIN, but his coalition failed to convince the judge, possibly because he presented an improvised and rather unprofessional proposal.

Judge Pfaelzer rarely refused to accept comments and suggestions through letters, visits, or even phone calls at odd hours. In those days, well before the advent of social media, sensitive and even offensive information was leaked through anonymous calls from pay phones, letters with no return addresses, or posters distributed by young canvassers. She was pressured and even threatened, usually anonymously, not to include any clause in the sale of SIN requiring the network to maintain 100 percent Spanish-language content after its sale. However, Judge Pfaelzer was not an easy woman to intimidate. In this particular part of the saga, the Fouce family matriarch—the mother of Frank Fouce Jr.—played a key role. Despite the adversity, her determination and charisma resonated with the judge, and this connection would prove crucial in the course of events.

A struggle for cultural identity in the United States was in full swing, and these protagonists were smack in the middle of it, even if they were as yet unaware of the importance of their roles. Each person played their part in the drama that was Hispanic television and the use and importance of Spanish in the country. Every decision—every stage of the negotiation—would have profound repercussions for millions of lives.

In the end, only two finalists were chosen to present their best offers for acquiring SIN. And the political maneuverings and machinations between the two opposing sides were swift: the Hallmark Cards/First Chicago/Warburg Pincus conglomerate, representing the institutional approach closely linked to Vice President Bush, and TVL Corp., a legal entity created specifically for this acquisition and led by the charismatic Diego C. Asencio, a former ambassador with strategic connections among Hispanic political circles.

Court documents from the proceedings show a secret meeting between Asencio and Hockaday in which the former put forth an audacious plan: use his political influence to secure a 25 percent discount by designating the transaction as a "crisis sale" for Hispanic buyers affiliated with Hallmark. Hockaday not only rejected the proposal but also denounced Asencio's offer to the judge as a morally questionable strategy to secure benefits outside the scope of guidelines imposed by the court. Hockaday's refusal and accusation set the tone for the final confrontation.

The narrative takes an even darker turn when other court documents reveal that representatives of Asencio's group threatened to use their political clout to block Hallmark from acquiring the network.

TVL exploited ethnic identity as a weapon for delegitimizing its non-Hispanic opponents, while Hallmark, in a splendid move of its own, negotiated stock participation agreements with SIN's general managers, including Joaquín Blaya and Daniel Villanueva, who were key to maintaining the stations' operations. In the words of a contemporary journalist, "From that point on, Hallmark gave in to everything the managers wanted, which turned out to be a brilliantly opportunistic move."

Hallmark's initial offer was $276 million, including key incentives such as job offers and stock options for key executives like William Stiles, Andrew Goldman, Joaquín Blaya, Emilio Nicolás Sr., Daniel Villanueva, and Blaine Decker. It also included a programming agreement with Televisa.

For its bid, TVL submitted a higher initial offer of $311 million. What it failed to do, though, was secure any programming deals with Televisa or establish any trust with SIN's top management. In fact, TVL reportedly did the opposite, creating uncertainty among employees through hints that some could lose their jobs after the sale was finalized.

In mid-July, Hallmark increased its offer to $290 million, removing certain financial conditions in order to strengthen its position. Meanwhile, TVL struggled to raise the necessary funds, with its own lack of experience as an organization hampering its efforts. On July 16, TVL finally submitted an offer of $320 million, but it still contained some unresolved issues.

Hallmark raised its offer yet again, reaching $301 million on July 15. However, one of the partners, Warburg Pincus, decided to withdraw from the bidding group, considering the price too high and that the company's conditions posed significant risks.

On July 18, the decision was left to the court. That same day, Judge Mariana Pfaelzer issued her ruling.

Hallmark Cards

In September 1986, one year after the judge's decision and the parties' agreement to sell SIN, and with FCC approval and the blessings of the Reagan-Bush White House, which was one year away from the end of the second term, the company was sold to Hallmark Cards, a family-owned company controlled by the Hall family. Founded in 1910 by Joyce Clyde Hall and primarily known for its greeting cards, they had already made public their desire to have a presence in the media and entertainment industry.

Surprisingly, despite all the aforementioned factors, Hallmark emerged as the winner in the bidding war over the acquisition of SIN. This decision left many wondering how a company whose roots and practices seemed so far removed from the realities of the Hispanic audience could manage a network that was, in many ways, its complete opposite. Intrigue and skepticism surrounded this decision, leaving observers and the Hispanic community in suspense when it came to SIN's future. The fear that the network would stop broadcasting in Spanish became even more tangible, as Hallmark was perceived by many Hispanics as a company with no knowledge or understanding of their community.

But when the judge's decision was announced, it explained that the acquiring company had agreed to:

1. Pay $301 million for SICC (the owner of SIN).
2. Pay $115 million for 100 percent of the shares of SINS (the content provider owned by Televisa).

And, clearly and decisively, the judge required that, for the duration of the license:

3. The stations would continue to produce and broadcast content in Spanish for at least fourteen more years, which was the term of the new license, now under Hallmark's name.

The forced sale of SIN for more than $400 million was a wake-up call. This transaction was more than a simple change in ownership. It was a testament to the value of the Hispanic market inside the world's largest economy. Indeed, that was the vision behind the transaction as presided over by the California Democratic judge Mariana Pfaelzer. And the lengthy and trenchant investigation by the FCC regulators, which was led by the Republican-occupied White House, supported the judge's ruling.

After balancing the books, El Tigre and his sisters earned just over $300 million, Anselmo netted $80 million after paying off his debts to El Tigre, and more than $35 million was distributed among the minority shareholders, some of whom were allowed, if they so wished, to remain onboard as Hallmark shareholders.

For the Fouces, instead of receiving $1 million for their shares in 1976, they ended up with $75 million in 1986. This sum of money leads many to wonder whether the course of SIN's future (not to mention its shareholders) was a good or a bad thing. Was it simply a stroke of luck or the inevitable consequence of decisions made a decade before?

Judge Pfaelzer, the compass throughout this storm, would become one of this narrative's central characters. Her role in SIN's transition of ownership and its transformation into what is now Univision was equal parts formidable and indispensable. She not only presided over the case with steadfast conviction and an even keel, she also remained true to her belief that the Hispanic audience deserved authentic media representation.

When it came to dealing with outside stakeholders from the bench, Judge Pfaelzer was unfazed. She stood firm against political leaders and activists who opposed the growth of a television network whose content and culture differed from the Anglo-American mainstream. Her ability to balance conflicting interests while maintaining the integrity of the legal process was unquestionable. Her contribution to the progression of the Spanish language and the Hispanic community in the United States is worthy of significant recognition and the deepest respect.

Some years later, in 1995, Judge Pfaelzer made headlines when she struck down Proposition 187, which had been approved in 1994 by nearly 60 percent of California voters. Proposition 187, also known as the Save Our State initiative, or S.O.S., proposed establishing a statewide citizenship verification system and prohibiting undocumented immigrants from using non-emergency health care, access to education, and other services in the state. While understanding that Californians were frustrated with the federal government's ineffective enforcement of immigration laws, Judge Pfaelzer ruled that "the authority to regulate immigration belongs exclusively to the federal government, and state agencies are not permitted to assume that authority." This decision paved the way for future court rulings that struck down state and local laws still attempting to deny housing and other benefits to undocumented immigrants, as well as laws that allow state police to arrest people simply under the suspicion that they're in the country illegally.

Meanwhile, in SIN's studios and offices, nothing was known about the proceedings in California's district court about their employer's future until Judge Pfaelzer's decision was released to the public. Rumors abounded, yet no one imagined that Anselmo and El Tigre Azcárraga would no longer be running the show.

A former SIN employee shared with me their immediate reaction to the news: "When we heard, we immediately thought a bunch of cowboys would never be able to run SIN, that they'd surely change the network's identity into something more English."

From SIN to Univision

The financial transaction that led to the purchase of SIN was unusual for the time, if not outright opaque. Hallmark had partnered with an innovative investment firm, First Chicago Venture Capital, which was responsible for structuring a $270 million bridge loan to complete the purchase. In other words, SIN's purchase was leveraged almost entirely through short-term, temporary financing. Shortly after the purchase was finalized, in 1988, the partners—Hallmark Cards, with 78 percent, and First Chicago Venture, with 22 percent—changed SIN's name to Univision and formed a holding company called Univision Holdings. Immediately after its creation, the company issued $270 million in long-term bonds with a yield of just more than 13 percent annually. These funds were then used to pay off the bridge loan.

It's fair to wonder how Univision emerged without much in the way of announcements or fanfare, and how a Missouri-based card company with no apparent ties to the Hispanic community was behind its creation. But the fact of the matter is that Univision's birth as the chosen channel for Hispanics was fraught with uncertainty. The decision to launch the brand was likely a hasty one designed to form a company that was in debt from its very inception and facing major financial challenges. Some might even have been already justifying its failure as a means of later converting it into an English-language network. However, like an unwanted child, Univision counted on the loyalty and passion of its employees as well as its audience, both of whom ensured that the network would not only survive its formative years but actually thrive.

The mystery surrounding the creation of the Univision brand adds yet another layer of intrigue to the story. According to Norm Leventhal, it was first conceived by El Tigre and Anselmo. Ever since inheriting his father's companies, El Tigre had been looking to change the name of the U.S. operation from SIN to Univisa, but his partners, Fouce Jr., Nicolás Sr., and Villanueva, had refused to accept the change. According to Leventhal, Anselmo and El Tigre had previously come up with the name Univision for a company that would sell joint advertising between Televisa and SIN. The endeavor ultimately failed, leaving the name collecting dust under SIN.

It was in Hallmark's legal department where the idea emerged of using the Univision brand to break with the past without completely disconnecting from it. Initially, its launch was perceived as a financial vehicle for justifying the acquisition of SIN, but Hallmark subsequently decided to promote Univision as the channel's new image, thereby marking the beginning of what would become the Hispanic media giant.

And, with that, Univision—the channel for Hispanics—was born. "Uni" was a subtle homage to the United States, where the network had its base of operations and its primary audience. The other part, "vision," without an accented *ó* in order to maintain uniformity of pronunciation in both English and Spanish, conveyed two ideas: TV and vision.

But who would be interested in buying bonds from a brand-new company that owned a Spanish-language TV channel with a barely known brand and a whopping $100 million in annual sales? Well, they were purchased almost entirely by Continental Illinois Bank, which had been bailed out by the Reagan administration just two years earlier. A bailout that gave rise to a phrase now common during any financial crisis: "Too big to fail."

After Univision Holdings was formed, already in debt thanks to the aforementioned bonds, Continental Illinois Bank (still under government receivership) also authorized an additional $300 million loan to fund the acquisition of SINS (the company that purchased content from Televisa) and to inject working capital into the newly formed Univision, now owned by Hallmark. In short, Hallmark borrowed money to buy Univision and then borrowed from Univision to repay the loan. Later we'll take a closer look at how those bonds and loans were repaid.

The list of buyers for these unusual bonds was very short, which isn't surprising considering the unorthodox nature of the transaction. However, it's worthwhile to note a subtle yet striking detail: the buyers included not only the government-controlled bank but also a company by the name of Chartwell, owned by none other than Jerry Perenchio. Shrewdly, Perenchio had acquired a small number of these bonds in order to keep abreast of what was going on at Univision Holdings, the company he had wanted to acquire himself before being denied by Judge Pfaelzer.

Univision Holdings was required to maintain a level of transparency and disclose information that allowed all bondholders, including Perenchio, access to the same financial and operational data as shareholders of a publicly traded company. This move allowed Perenchio to maintain a strategic position and closely monitor Univision's operations, demonstrating his ongoing interest and ability to maneuver effectively in a complex financial environment.

An American named J. William Grimes, who just weeks before the sale of Univision was the CEO of a fledgling sports television station called ESPN, was hired by Hallmark as president and CEO of Univision. His first decision was to appoint Chilean Joaquín Blaya, who had been station manager of WLTV in Miami and a minority shareholder in the company since the days of El Tigre, as the new East Coast director. Blaya was tasked with erasing the SIN brand from the viewers' collective memory and promoting the company's new image under the Univision name. On the West Coast, minority shareholder Danny Villanueva remained in his leadership role.

At the end of this chapter—and not without a touch of irony—it was minority shareholder Blaya who took the helm when it came to Univision's future. El Tigre was gone, Anselmo was gone (though certainly against his will), while Blaya stayed. And that was something El Tigre never forgot.

CHAPTER 6

1986: The Year That Revolutionized Televised News

On March 14, 1986, just months before sweeping changes were about to hit SIN, El Tigre, doing everything possible to strengthen his relationship with the White House, decided to accept a request made to Televisa by his friend, John Gavin, the U.S. ambassador to Mexico at the time. His given name was John Anthony Golenor, but his birth name had been Juan Vicente Apablasa Jr. Gavin, born in Los Angeles, son of a Mexican mother and a Chilean father. When he was two years old, his parents divorced, and it was then that his American stepfather changed Juan's name to John. He was a renowned Hollywood actor who had a degree in philosophy and literature from Stanford. After his acting career, he chose to pursue a career in politics, which led to a position at the Organization of American States, and later in diplomacy, serving as the U.S. ambassador to Mexico from 1981 to 1986; he was always accompanied by his wife, Constance Towers, herself a prominent Hollywood actor as well.

The request was for a live interview of President Reagan from the White House, with the condition that only one topic be covered. It would be an interview for the purpose of disseminating information about the administration's strategy in Nicaragua at a time when Daniel Ortega's socialist Sandinista movement had become a threat to democracies in Central America and the Caribbean. No other topics were to be addressed.

El Tigre had wanted to recruit his Televisa newsman Jacobo Zabludovsky for the job, but René Anselmo convinced him to use Noticiero Nacional SIN's staff instead. Cuban American Gustavo Godoy, then director of SIN's Miami-based *Noticiero Nacional* and host of the weekly program *Temas y Debates*, assigned the task to his Washington, DC, correspondent, a Peruvian named Guillermo Descalzi.

The full video of that interview is available at the Ronald Reagan Presidential Library and Museum in Simi Valley, California. In it, you can hear how, after the formal meeting ended, and unaware that the mics were still live and recording their personal chatter, Reagan asks Descalzi in English, "Did I sell you?" to which Descalzi replies, "You definitely did, and let me tell you one thing, you didn't need to sell me. I'm sold, and as I told Luis Acle here, whatever we can do for you on *Temas y Debates* and on SIN in general, we're at your disposal."

This interview was very important for El Tigre, Anselmo, and Godoy. The first two knew that the future of their control of SIN depended on a crucial decision by a judge who might buckle under pressure from the White House. For the third, this interview also represented a sign of his network's power. Godoy had already convinced Anselmo to turn *Noticiero Nacional SIN* into a powerhouse on par with CNN, which was already making waves with its continuous, real-time coverage of global events.

The CNN Revolution

Television underwent an unprecedented transformation in June 1980 with the arrival of CNN, the first channel in the United States dedicated exclusively to broadcasting news twenty-four hours a day. This innovative project revolutionized the way viewers access information, offering continuous, real-time coverage of global events. The creation of CNN not only altered the media landscape but also set a new standard for television journalism.

Ted Turner had always showed interest in experimenting in the Hispanic market as a globalization strategy. He'd been interested in the idea of buying SIN, but his offer was never made official, and there were doubts as to whether the innovative entrepreneur was truly committed to maintaining the network's Spanish-language content focus.

Turner quickly became a news mogul, taking a significant bite out of the market share previously held by traditional newspaper owners. Many believed that TV and radio stations were media outlets aimed solely at the masses, who required only entertainment, with the occasional breaking news story. But CNN revolutionized the landscape by offering in-depth analysis and real-time news that included live images. Turner had long aspired to owning a fourth network, but his efforts to purchase SIN were thwarted by Judge Mariana Pfaelzer. He then focused on expanding CNN through cable television, doing so with great success, especially once René Anselmo's first satellite entered into orbit. In fact, one of Anselmo's very first clients for international audiovisual transmission was none other than Ted Turner himself.

With the launch of CNN, the first twenty-four-hour news channel, and ESPN, the first twenty-four-hour sports channel, there was an explosion in demand for cable television among American viewers. The magnates of the three major broadcast networks didn't anticipate the impact cable television would have on the viewing public. To understand the magnitude of this change, in the 1960s and 1970s, broadcast television was all that existed, and only a privileged few had access to closed-circuit TV systems for special events, conferences, movies, and live transmissions. These circuits became cable broadcast channels, available only in select cities and in affluent areas. It wasn't until CNN and ESPN entered people's homes that the need for cable TV became apparent to a broad audience. It's worth noting that, even while Turner lorded over the industry, his reign was actually under threat. A ten-year monopoly on information was shaken when Rupert Murdoch, the Australian-born media mogul, decided to launch Fox News in 1996. Turner, as shrewd as he was vigilant, convinced the giant Time Warner to acquire CNN for $7.2 billion. He knew the competition from Murdoch was significant and decided it was time to sell.

The emergence of cable news through CNN and ESPN marked the beginning of a new era in the way we consume information and entertainment: a change not unlike what would happen decades later with the arrival of the internet and its impact on print newspapers. Before the internet, newspapers dominated the news landscape with daily editions being delivered to millions of homes. But the dissemination of online news radically transformed access to and distribution of information. Readers no longer needed to wait until tomorrow morning to learn about today's events; instead, they could get real-time updates with just a click of a mouse.

In much the same way, cable television, with its uninterrupted and specialized programming, forced broadcast television networks to reconsider their business models and innovate if they hoped to stay relevant in an increasingly fragmented and competitive media market. Furthermore, cable television operated under a less stringent regulatory framework than broadcast networks did. This deregulated environment is comparable with the internet, where content freedom and the lack of restrictions have allowed for an unprecedented variety of information and entertainment. This transformation illustrates how technology and deregulation can reshape, in a profound and long-lasting way, audience consumption habits, which set new paradigms in a number of industries.

The First Hispanic National Newscast in the United States

In the early 1980s, the idea of producing a national newscast for a Hispanic audience took root at WLTV studios in Miami: *Noticiero Nacional SIN*, the only Spanish-language news program in prime time broadcast across the United States. Until the late 1970s, SIN had two sources of news: the local source in each of the cities from which the broadcast originated and the Televisa newscast coming out of Mexico. The new idea was that, through satellite transmission, they could centralize content and reach millions of screens with national information. But what content would be acceptable to all Hispanics in the United States?

René Anselmo had come to understand the power and influence that a well-produced national newscast could achieve. He also recognized that the one broadcast by Televisa presented a very clear editorial line that supported the Mexican government and didn't connect with Hispanics in the United States—not even with Mexicans who had come seeking a better life, fleeing the economic disasters that were blamed, organically, on the poor governance of politicians in their country of origin. Finding the ideal news content for Hispanics in the United States was Anselmo's primary challenge.

SIN's Miami director was the Chilean Joaquín Blaya, who, before being promoted and relocating to Florida, had worked for René in the sales department at SIN's New York station. It was there, in that city, that Blaya and Anselmo first heard about a Hispanic journalist with production experience working at the CBS affiliate: Cuban American Gustavo Godoy. Godoy reached out to Blaya to express interest in working at SIN to produce and present news in the style of CNN. Anselmo and Blaya decided to hire him on the condition that he move to Miami.

Florida would become the center of power for Godoy, who, in addition to beginning his work at SIN, decided to join a group of Cubans who were engaging in anti-Castro political activity from the American peninsula. Godoy helped transform the meetings held at the legendary Versailles Restaurant—still located on Calle Ocho—from conspiratorial gatherings for ranting against Fidel's dictatorship into spaces where business, religious, and community leaders felt they could build political clout and promote prosperity and influence among Cubans already living in Florida. Godoy dedicated much of his life to promoting Cuban power not only there but throughout the United States.

Godoy persuaded Anselmo and Blaya to develop a different sort of newscast from the one being broadcast by Televisa. Anselmo, thinking of CNN's success, agreed. And with that, Noticiero Nacional SIN was born. In the early stages, there was significant disconnect between the East and West Coasts. The question of immigration, for example, was extremely important to journalists in California and Texas, while Cubans and Puerto Ricans working in the newsroom in Miami didn't see it as relevant, considering the fact that their compatriots didn't have to face the same documentation or legalization issues to work in the United States. It's important to note that, ever since November 2, 1966, when President Lyndon B. Johnson signed the Cuban Adjustment Act, a path to legal permanent residency was provided for Cubans arriving in the United States after Castro's revolution. This law specifically allows Cuban nationals and their immediate family members to apply for a green card after being physically present in the United States for at least a year.

SIN executives in California and Texas believed that the Hispanic immigrant day laborer audience would be engaged in content centered on humor, education, and everyday life. El Tigre Azcárraga often said that his audiences in Mexico and the United States tended to ignore and reject content that was overly serious or filled with "big words," but Godoy disagreed with that notion and insisted on journalism dedicated to educating Hispanics both politically and economically, covering both national and international events. Watching some of the early episodes of *Noticiero Nacional SIN* that aired in the early to mid-1980s (still available on YouTube), one can see the heavy focus on economics, politics, and international affairs from the reports out of Miami, New York, and Washington, DC, whereas the stories coming out of Los Angeles and San Antonio were centered more on local issues related to Hispanic life, whether it was the intense heat and high cost of electricity in Texas or a serial killer wanted in California. *Noticiero Nacional SIN* grew and improved year after year while also increasing its audience.

In 1986, SIN's promotional materials claimed it reached more than six million viewers in the continental United States. This same marketing tool included a list of the country's most-watched programs, which included *Noticiero Nacional SIN*.

Gustavo Godoy also hosted the program *Temas y Debates*, which featured interviews and editorial opinions on the American political climate straight from the news director himself.

The differences between Godoy and his Miami team and others in SIN's West Coast offices were clear. By the summer of 1986, Godoy realized that his primary advocate, René Anselmo, was losing power. Joaquín Blaya, the Miami director, was intent on achieving a leadership position among SIN's ranking executives, suspecting that a power struggle among the owners could implode at any moment. Godoy was well aware that he had to prepare for the future, and that that future might lie somewhere other than SIN.

El Tigre admired Ted Turner's vision, which had led CNN to such success. In his never-ending search for innovation, Azcárraga tasked his most trusted newsman, Jacobo Zabludovsky, with finding a way to replicate the CNN model, but in Spanish, for a global launch. Zabludovsky presented him with a project called ECO, though with little information beyond its metaphorical meaning of "echoing" the world's news. El Tigre gave it a literal, American-style acronym: Empresa de Comunicaciones Orbitales. The channel would be dedicated to broadcasting news in Spanish twenty-four hours a day with worldwide satellite distribution handled by PanAmSat, the company founded by Anselmo in partnership with El Tigre. The content would then be redistributed via cable in regions of Latin American and Europe where this technology was available. El Tigre had the brilliant idea of offering ECO's signal to all Ibero-American Telecommunications

Organization (OTI) affiliates. ECO's first retransmission order was made through SIN with clear instructions that the international newscast, which Televisa produced and broadcast from Mexico, would now be hosted by Zabludovsky and would go by the name of *Noticiero ECO*. As such, it would air in prime time on the West Coast of the United States, while on the East Coast it would air immediately after *Noticiero Nacional SIN*. This development was not well received by the newsroom led by Godoy in Miami.

Godoy Versus El Tigre: Rebellion and Ambition in Miami

Like an ominous sign of a coming storm, a rebellion was brewing among the news staff in Miami. At the center of the controversy was Godoy himself, who first tried speaking with Anselmo—whose position had already been significantly weakened by the impending and unfavorable resolution of the long-standing litigation against the Fouces—but who ultimately rose up with his team against the imposition of ECO.

Once again, Miami had become a problem for El Tigre—recalling the premonition discussed in chapter 2, when El Tigre reproached both Anselmo and his own father for buying the station in Miami, saying it would bring only headaches and trouble.

Godoy didn't wait for the outcome of the aforementioned trial, or for the subsequent announcement of the sale of SIN. In November 1986, he used the news of the purported arrival of Zabludovsky—the charismatic anchor of Televisa's national newscast in Mexico—as global head of ECO to announce his departure from SIN. This decision was seen by the channel's executives as an early exit, but the truth of the matter is that Godoy never anticipated El Tigre being ousted from SIN or that Joaquín Blaya would take on a much more important role in the company. He couldn't have imagined that ECO would be excluded from programming in Miami or that SIN would change its name to Univision within the short span of a year. What Godoy did have was a well-developed plan for independence.

He explained to his team members—many of whom had fled Cuba under Castro's regime—that they'd never be able to work with Zabludovsky, who was seen by many as the voice of Televisa and, therefore, the subservient voice of the Mexican government that had treated Castro's Cuba favorably. But this wasn't simply a matter of professional pride. There was a deep cultural and political conflict at play. At that time, Mexicans were seen as having taken a soft stance on Castro, even going so far as to applaud him and welcome him with open arms. This perception contrasted sharply with that of Cuban expats in Miami, for whom Castro was a criminal communist dictator who had driven them from their home country. In the words of the renowned journalist María Elena Salinas, who chronicled some of the events of this period in her book *I Am My Father's Daughter*: "Before the sale to Hallmark Cards was finalized, a cultural shock reverberated through Miami." And so the rebellion began: with the same passion and determination that had driven them to leave their homeland, Miami journalists prepared themselves to stand up against El Tigre.

It was at that moment that Gustavo Godoy and his team staged a daring move, taking to the airwaves of Spanish-language radio stations in Miami like WAQI, sounding the alarm to the Cuban expat community: "We're hearing that Jacobo Zabludovsky, the voice of the Mexican government, is coming to Miami to take control of our newscast."

In the eye of this storm, two critical decisions by Godoy would come to define the future of SIN. Televisa denied that it would send Zabludovsky to Miami, but Godoy intuitively ignored this memo and, along with a group of fourteen other people, including journalists as well as editorial and production staff, decided to resign effective immediately. Godoy had already set up his own news platform in Miami, the Hispanic Broadcasting Corporation, funded primarily by Amancio Víctor Suárez, the owner of Miami radio station WAQI, who promised to raise $8 million for Godoy's new venture. The station, also known as Radio Mambi, was created by anti-communist Cuban expats led by Suárez. Those who didn't decide to join Godoy remained behind, waiting to see what would happen. After the schism, SIN's newsroom was left in ruins, understaffed and with no clear direction. And El Tigre didn't have the time to react to this cataclysmic event because the final blow had landed: the verdict in the famous trial between the Fouce estate and SIN's majority owners.

Every Mexican telenovela, every comedy and variety show produced by Televisa was still beloved by viewers, but reporting the news had become a different matter altogether. It was a distinct, almost sacred domain where national interests and sensibilities clashed with heartbreaking intensity. Whatever SIN's fate, it had become a news outlet that served the common purpose of informing Hispanic immigrants.

The viewership numbers for SIN's newscast were significant. In 1986, everyone in the television industry dreamed of having their own CNN, and Godoy was no exception. Thus, Hispanic Broadcasting Corporation was born: a project conceived by Godoy to rival ECO and, obviously, SIN, which had been his home and the cradle of his professional career in Miami.

The media chessboard was fully stacked, with its pieces moving swiftly and cunningly.

María Elena Salinas and Jorge Ramos: A Transformative Alliance

Two news anchors happened to arrive in Miami from Los Angeles at the behest of SIN's vice president of programming, Rosita Perú. The executive wanted to launch a morning show that combined news with useful information for improving the quality of life for Hispanics in the United States, and so she decided to create *Mundo Latino*. Perú attempted to negotiate with Danny Villanueva, asking him to release María Elena Salinas. Initially, he refused to give up Salinas, who was anchoring the local Los Angeles newscast, but upon learning about what had transpired, Salinas was upset and frustrated enough to threaten Villanueva with quitting the network to pursue other opportunities. In fact, she had more than enough potential to be an anchor on any other channel, even an English-language one, so Villanueva had to concede and agree to the job change. With that, Perú convinced Joaquín Blaya, the station's director in Miami, and Danny Villanueva, who held that same position in Los Angeles, to produce the program with two talented Los Angeles natives: María Elena Salinas and Jorge Ramos.

María Elena Salinas, who would be one of the most prominent anchors in the news industry, was born in Los Angeles in 1954. Completely bilingual and with a firm dedication to pursuing journalism, Salinas was determined to build a career that would have a positive impact on her Hispanic community. Her media career began at a Hispanic radio station in Los Angeles, in the sales department—a field she already knew—though her true desire was to break into television.

At that time, El Tigre Azcárraga was prone to criticizing the physical appearance of SIN reporters and anchors in California, comparing them unfavorably with the talent in Miami as well as those at Televisa in Mexico. He insisted that Danny Villanueva hire "more attractive" people. In 1981, Villanueva discovered María Elena Salinas. She was initially put in front of the cameras to report on the weather, but she was soon sent out to cover local news on the streets of LA, despite having no experience as a journalist. Salinas's hard work and eagerness to learn on the job quickly led her to become a trusted anchor for the local Los Angeles newscast.

Meanwhile, across the country in Miami, Teresa Abate was the anchor of *Noticiero Nacional SIN*. In the wake of the upheaval following Godoy's resignation, she too decided to join the stampede. Several years later, Teresa would return to the channel, then renamed Univision, and she would do so with a new last name, presenting herself as Teresa Rodríguez, though no longer as the anchor of the national newscast.

Following El Tigre's instructions to hire more photogenic people, Danny Villanueva hired Jorge Ramos as a reporter for SIN in 1984. Ramos, a journalist four years younger than Salinas, was born in Mexico City and was studying at UCLA. He met all the requirements and, not looking to return to Mexico anytime soon, he accepted the modest salary offered by Villanueva. Within just a few years, Ramos was promoted to lead anchor for SIN's national newscast in Los Angeles. His desire to grow both professionally and financially led him to Miami, where, along with María Elena Salinas, he found an unexpected opportunity.

As *Mundo Latino* was launching, the staff exodus from the *Noticiero Nacional SIN* newsroom was also underway, and this striking and highly professional duo, Salinas and Ramos, quickly rose to stardom in front of the cameras, hosting the new news program that, within a matter of months, would be renamed *Noticiero Univision*.

In an interview with *The New Yorker*'s Stephania Taladrid, Jorge Ramos explained the situation upon his arrival in Miami: "There was a big protest in the United States, specifically in Miami, against [Zabludovsky's] presence." In the end, the company decided not to bring him. Taladrid then asked Ramos what people were worried about regarding the veteran Mexican journalist's arrival on the network's Miami broadcasts. Ramos replied, "Censorship. That [Zabludovsky] represented the Mexican government, that he wasn't going to deliver the news in a neutral and fair way." Taladrid then asked Ramos if he, personally, shared that concern, to which the Mexican American journalist replied, "I just didn't want to work with him. I would never have worked with him. So I ended up being the only male correspondent in the Miami office, and they offered me to do the newscast for a few days. I told them I would do it under the condition that I have complete freedom to report."

Jorge Ramos and María Elena Salinas rose to prominence as luminaries in the news world, becoming symbols of an era for the Hispanic community in the United States. Their presence on Univision's newscast not only informed... it inspired.

Noticiero Univision was launched in 1987. Its first director was Luis Nogales, Rosita Perú's husband, and everything grew quickly under the leadership of Joaquín Blaya, who played a crucial role in transforming the channel and establishing a standard that respected professional journalism.

Salinas and Ramos came to an agreement that they wouldn't be in competition with each other. Both would have equal screen time, and they would share scoops and exclusive stories. Even the side of the studio each one used was respected for the life of their careers together. María Elena Salinas anchored *Noticiero Univision* for thirty years, from 1987 to 2017. In December 2024, Jorge Ramos ended his four-decade term at Univision, though we'll discuss his retirement in greater detail later in the book.

Salinas earned the respect of several news directors and other members of the board at Univision during her lengthy tenure. Not even a highly anticipated pregnancy could stop her from conducting an interview with Subcomandante Marcos at the height of the Zapatista Army of National Liberation (EZLN) movement. The interview took place in an undisclosed location in Chiapas, Mexico. Along with Ramos, Salinas learned the best methods for conducting interviews, finding a format they both completely mastered. Presidents, dictators, governors, artists, and other celebrities were all interviewed by either Salinas or Ramos, who continued to share the most important interviews.

Outside of her time at Univision, Salinas has enjoyed a career filled with achievements and accolades. In 2012, she, along with co-anchor Ramos, received the Emmy Award for Lifetime Achievement in recognition of their contributions to journalism. She was also the first Latina to receive this honor. She co-founded the National Association of Hispanic Journalists (NAHJ) and was inducted into its hall of fame in 2006. Salinas has also been recognized for her philanthropic work, which focuses on empowering the Hispanic community and defending the rights of immigrants.

Jorge Ramos, for his part, has been an influential figure and is considered a titan of Hispanic journalism. His direct style and focus on issues relevant to the Hispanic community have made him a powerful voice in the media. One of his most notable interactions before a global audience came in 2015, when he confronted Donald Trump about his immigration policies. He did this during a press conference, which displeased the then-presidential candidate and resulted in Ramos's being forcibly ejected from the event.

Ramos has received numerous awards throughout his career, including multiple Emmy Awards and a Maria Moors Cabot Prize, which recognizes excellence in news coverage of Latin America, from the Journalism School at Columbia University. He has also been a staunch advocate for immigrant rights and used his platform to give a voice to marginalized individuals and communities.

Both journalists have published books reflecting on their own experiences and perspectives. In 2016, María Elena Salinas published *I Am My Father's Daughter: A Life Without Secrets*, an autobiography offering an intimate look into her life and career. Jorge Ramos has written several, including *Stranger: The Challenge of a Latino Immigrant in the Age of Trump* (2018); *17 Minutes: Interview with the Dictator* (2021), which chronicles his controversial meeting with Nicolás Maduro, president of Venezuela; and in 2024, his compilation of personal columns in the Spanish-language press titled *The Way I See Things: What I Never Told You.*

Salinas and Ramos weren't just news anchors. They were pioneers who transformed and shaped the way Spanish-language news was presented to the Hispanic community in the United States. And the bold, pioneering decision to elevate a woman to the same stage and professional stature as her male colleague is not only a milestone in journalistic history; it is a powerful message of equality and respect.

CHAPTER 7

Telemundo and Univision: Finance, Power, and the Battle for Viewership

In the 1950s, Desi Arnaz, actor and producer of "*I Love Lucy*," boldly used the Spanish language on TV. As Lucille Ball's charismatic Cuban husband, co-producer of the historic weekly sitcom that bore his wife's name, he ingeniously managed to integrate bilingualism into a successful show, creating a surge of enthusiasm for the use of Spanish on American television. The excitement, however, was short-lived.

Ricky Ricardo, played by Arnaz himself, proudly represented his Cuban roots with scenes in which he'd resort to speaking Spanish during moments of excitement or frustration while Lucy tried to communicate through comical misunderstandings. The show was revolutionary in the way it included Spanish dialogue without subtitles and musical numbers performed entirely in Spanish, which celebrated the richness of Hispanic culture and broke new ground at a time when such representations weren't common.

Although the use of Spanish in the show declined over time due to cultural restrictions and concerns about comprehension by mainstream viewers, the show left an important legacy. Beyond its humor, "*I Love Lucy*" connected with a diverse audience while addressing topics of cultural identity, integration, and the challenges of bilingual relationships.

October 3, 1954, was a historic moment. During the acclaimed *Ed Sullivan Show*, broadcast on CBS and watched by millions, a dinner was held in honor of Arnaz and his wife, Lucille Ball. This event, broadcast live, was attended by top CBS executives, corporate leaders, and prominent government figures. In his moving speech, Arnaz shared his poignant journey from his humble arrival from Cuba to the United States, where his first job was caring for birds. He recalled how, despite the doubts of some CBS executives (some of whom, we imagine, were present) about his ability to play Lucille Ball's husband, his real-life, twelve-year marriage became irrefutable proof of his appropriateness for the role. Nervous laughter rippled through the audience when he mentioned this detail. On that evening, the story of a Hispanic immigrant who achieved success was told on the nation's most popular show, generating a mixture of praise and rejection. In that tearful speech, "Thank You, America," Arnaz not only celebrated his personal success but also highlighted the complex dynamics of race and representation in American television at the time.

Desi Arnaz was a pioneer who helped establish the continued use of Spanish in television in the United States. After Arnaz, the lack of stories about Hispanics in the United States, largely ignored by mainstream networks during the 1960s and 1970s, contributed to the birth and growth of SIN.

The great awakening came in 1986, when political and financial interests fell in love with the Hispanic population's emerging electoral power. On the one hand, there was the controversial lawsuit that prompted the forced sale of SIN to Hallmark for more than $400 million. On the other, around that same time, financier Saul Steinberg announced the surprising news that he was investing a little more than $280 million to acquire John Blair & Co., which owned television stations in Florida and one in Puerto Rico, WKAQ, which operated under the Telemundo brand.

Steinberg, Silverman, Telemundo, Drexel, and More Junk Bonds

In the early 1960s, Saul Steinberg, a senior at the University of Pennsylvania's Wharton School, devised an innovative way to finance IBM computers for third parties with better terms than those offered by the technology giant itself. At the age of twenty-two, he convinced a bank to loan him the money needed to purchase the computers from IBM, which he then used as collateral with the bank and leased them out to clients, earning a profit between the bank's cost and the fees he charged.

With the money he accumulated at that early age, and by using an ingenious (for the time) means of issuing bonds with extremely high interest rates, Steinberg managed to acquire the insurance company Reliance. In 1969, he unsuccessfully attempted to acquire the giant Chemical Bank, and in 1984, he also failed to lead a hostile takeover of the Walt Disney Company. In 1986, he decided to promote Henry Silverman to CEO of his investment arm, Reliance Capital.

Steinberg, a pioneer in the use of high-interest bonds on Wall Street, was, along with Silverman, seeking investment opportunities using the funds from such bonds, which would later come to be known as junk bonds. They decided to explore the hotel market and Hispanic television, conducting coordinated transactions with the investment bank Drexel Burnham Lambert, known for its dominance in the junk bond market before its fall from grace in the 1990s. Silverman was known as the "asset stripper."

Reliance purchased the Days Inn hotel chain the same year they started acquiring television stations. In 1987, they purchased WNJU, located in New Jersey with a broadcast range that extended across the greater New York City area. WNJU aired Spanish-language content under the name NetSpan and had been owned by Jerry Perenchio and other partners who were themselves already experimenting with their newly discovered Hispanic market. Reliance paid $60 million for NetSpan, a company whose programming director was Cuban-born Carlos Barba.

Neither Silverman nor Steinberg had experience in the TV industry or the Hispanic market. Of all the stations acquired up to that point, Carlos Barba, who was born in Cuba, was the only executive who spoke Spanish. He had spent several years working for Gustavo Cisneros at the Venezuelan station Venevisión, always in the sales department.

If the lack of transparency surrounding the financing of the Hallmark acquisition of Univision was surprising, the financial maneuverings used to launch rival network Telemundo were no less questionable. An analysis prepared by experts at American International Group pursuant to filing a complaint against Henry Silverman, who was competing against them for the acquisition of an insurance company, with the Securities and Exchange Commission revealed the dark undertones of the operation.

On December 24, 1986, Reliance Capital Group LP. paid $283.5 million for 100 percent of the outstanding shares of John Blair & Co., which it later renamed Telemundo Group, Inc. The purchase was financed with $226 million in junk bonds issued by

Drexel Burnham Lambert. By August of the next year, Reliance Capital Group controlled 85 percent of Telemundo's outstanding shares; Henry Silverman served as the company's president from October 1986 through February 1990.

The aforementioned new owners of Telemundo immediately saddled the company with debt and began a financial juggling act, gradually acquiring broadcasting properties belonging to Reliance while also launching an aggressive program to dismantle and sell off all other assets inherited from John Blair & Co. By June 30, 1987, Telemundo Group owned and operated five Spanish-language TV stations; the following year, it acquired a station in Texas and another in Florida.

With debt totaling $189 million and the acquisition of Spanish-language television stations in Los Angeles and New York, the company lost $26.3 million in the first six months of 1987, prompting it to request a debt payment waiver from its bankers. In August of that year, in a transaction coordinated by Drexel, Telemundo issued two million shares of common stock and $220 million in junk bonds to the public.

According to an August 10, 1987, article in *BusinessWeek*, "Telemundo owes so much while earning so little that it's paying out more in cash for interest than it makes." As of December 31, 1987, the company had long-term debt of $240.7 million: more than three times its revenue.

Here is the list of Telemundo directors and executives in 1987, among whom only Carlos Barba had experience in Hispanic television:

- Saul P. Steinberg, Chairman of the Board
- Henry R. Silverman, President and CEO

- Donald G. Raider, Executive Vice President, Chief Operating Officer
- Peter J. Housman II, Senior Vice President, Treasurer, Chief Financial Officer
- Leonard P. Forman, Senior Vice President
- Thomas J. McKee, Senior Vice President, General Counsel, General Secretary
- Carlos Barba, Vice President, Director of Programming and Broadcasting
- Nancy R. Alpert, Vice President, Assistant to the General Counsel, Assistant to the General Secretary
- Kevin M. Sheehan, Vice President and Controller
- W. Gary McBride, Vice President, Director of Marketing and Sales
- George E. Bello, Director
- Robert V. Cahill, Director
- Martin J. Edelman, Director
- Lowell C. Freiberg, Director
- Andrew R. Heyer, Director
- Daniel Hirsch, Director
- Howard E. Steinberg, Director
- Robert M. Steinberg, Director

In 1986, Univision Communications and Telemundo Group, Inc., were ready for registration. On May 16, 1987, the Univision and, some months later, Telemundo brands were filed with the United States Patent and Trademark Office. In 1988, both trademarks were officially approved and registered. In 1987, however, both companies were heavily ladened with debt by their owners, who had used that debt to justify their acquisitions and make the investments they saw as strategically advantageous. The overwhelming rise of Anglo-Americans controlling the two corporations with the greatest reach and influence in the U.S. Hispanic community was astonishing, to say the least.

Telemundo's expansion came a bit later and with greater difficulty than Unvision's, as the latter had access to established programming from SIN, had Hispanic owners, and had a much more experienced staff. Telemundo, on the other hand, had only one high-ranking Hispanic executive, Carlos Barba, and was only just beginning to consolidate its content. Barba struggled to convince his colleagues, most of whom were from outside the industry and didn't speak Spanish.

Among the large group comprising Telemundo's board of directors and executive team, there were those who saw the channel as an opportunity to blend English with Spanish and foster the assimilation of Hispanics into the English-speaking world. Some even proposed experimenting with the use of Spanglish, and—why not—with English-language content aimed at English-speaking Hispanics, a growing segment of the population. This strategy had a dual purpose: to serve an audience that was gradually starting to forget Spanish or, at the same time, to induce them to forget it entirely.

While there were some exploratory trials of this troubling strategy, not only did the idea fail but the company's own programming director, Carlos Barba, was never convinced this was the right path for the company to take. While these trials were being implemented in the programming lineup, operational and financial costs began eating away at the coffers of the fledgling Telemundo. Attempts at attracting a bilingual audience failed to achieve the desired results, and the company was facing significant challenges in its efforts to find a clear identity and a programming strategy that would resonate with its audience.

In her excellent work "Mapping Latinidad: Language and Culture in the Spanish TV Battlefront," Arlene Dávila offers us an example of one of these bilingual experiments in one of the shows Telemundo aired in its early years:

> Rather than serving as a mainstay of some programs, English appears only in the form of Spanglish, which is used selectively as a "condiment" and mostly limited to comedy shows. In *Solo in America*, which revolves around the language and culture clash between a divorced Venezuelan, Spanish-speaking Latina and her two bilingual and bicultural teenage daughters in Brooklyn, one of the main comedic devices is the mother's scolding of her daughters' tainted Spanish. The mother constantly insinuates the evils of becoming too Americanized. Though the youths are supposed to be fully bilingual, they are only shown speaking short phrases and mostly single words in English or Spanglish. The actual meaning of their speech, however, is almost always conveyed by the context, by an immediate translation by their mother, or else by a deliberate rephrase in Spanish. The results are constructions like "Mom, I can't believe que tú a mí me mentiste" ("Mom, I can't believe that you lied to me") or "Mom, have you decided qué vas a hacer? Vas o no vas a Chicago?" ("Mom, have you decided what you're going to do? Are you going to Chicago or not?")

The Birth of Noticiero Telemundo

In January 1987, Barba was contacted by fellow countryman Amancio Víctor Suárez, owner of Radio Mambi WAQI and the primary investor behind a new newsroom crew led by Gustavo Godoy, who had just led the exodus of SIN's staff. Suárez and Barba reached an agreement, and Telemundo's first newscast was produced by the newly created Hispanic Broadcasting Organization headed by Godoy. With funding by Suárez's money and payments by Telemundo, Godoy believed he had the resources necessary to create and develop the equivalent of a CNN for Hispanics. His project began with a studio in Miami and bureaus in Washington, DC, New York, and Los Angeles, with future plans to open more in Mexico, South America, and Europe. However, the price Suárez wanted to charge Telemundo was so exorbitant that Barba asked to start with just a single half-hour newscast per day.

Godoy was determined to prove his ability to build a news network. He even tried, unsuccessfully, to persuade Barba to convince his bosses at Reliance Capital to invest in and acquire his Hispanic Broadcasting Corporation. Telemundo's relationship with Godoy lasted barely a year.

Amid the junk bond frenzy, one investment firm emerged as the leader in transactions utilizing this financial vehicle, which was used for the acquisition of Telemundo by Reliance Capital as well as MGM by Ted Turner. The name of that investment firm was Drexel Burnham Lambert, and the banker who earned the nickname Junk Bond King was Michael Milken. As any good banker would, he connected his client and friend Ted Turner with his other client and friend Saul Steinberg. Turner had already acquired Metro-Goldwyn-Mayer/United Artists in early

1986 on Milken's advice, and Steinberg had acquired Telemundo with Milken's help. Turner had unsuccessfully attempted to buy SIN and asked Milken to introduce him to Steinberg. From that connection came the decision to replace Godoy's venture with a newscast co-produced by Telemundo and Ted Turner's already famous CNN. Financially, it was much more viable to rely on CNN's production structure in Atlanta than paying for the entire infrastructure costs of Godoy's newly created project.

Barba's decision not to pursue Godoy's newscast meant the end of Godoy's project, forcing him to dismantle his team. In 1988, Godoy tried to convince René Anselmo to invest in and distribute his network, but Anselmo wasn't about to risk supporting what could be perceived as a betrayal in the midst of an already complicated situation. He wished Godoy luck while cautioning that he couldn't support such a move, advising Godoy to look for another satellite provider, as PanAmSat wouldn't be available. Gustavo Godoy would continue to have a successful career in journalism, but he never made another attempt at administration or entrepreneurship.

To host the new Telemundo-CNN newscast, Silverman hired a talented Uruguayan journalist named Jorge Gestoso. He convinced Barba, who in turn convinced Silverman, to hire former Miss Universe Cecilia Bolocco from Chile to join him on the newscast, which would then compete directly with the Univision duo of Jorge Ramos and María Elena Salinas.

The Telemundo-Viacom Alliance

Another endeavor Barba spearheaded was an alliance between Telemundo and Viacom Music Television, which resulted in

MTV International. This project featured a young Cuban American by the name of Daisy Fuentes, who, at twenty-one years of age, had barely two years of experience as a weather presenter at NetSpan, which later became Telemundo.

Born in Havana in 1966, Daisy Fuentes decided to try her luck at the fledgling Spanish-language TV channel headed by Barba and owned by Jerry Perenchio. Shortly after her stint as the weather girl, Fuentes took advantage of the fact that Barba, her former boss at NetSpan, was now the president of Telemundo and asked him to give her the chance to be the twice-weekly "veejay" that MTV International was looking for. Barba agreed, and Fuentes's career began to shine.

As Telemundo struggled along, learning from both its mistakes as well as its successes and adjusting its approach to better serve the Hispanic community in their native language, the financial storm stirred up by its own owners was fast approaching. And while debt and interest payments were already strangling Telemundo by late 1988, experimentation with content laid the groundwork for future growth and influence in the U.S. Hispanic market.

Noticiero Telemundo-CNN, which marked a landmark era in Hispanic television, came to an end in 1993. Similarly, the alliance between Telemundo and MTV ended that same year. This breakup came during a turbulent time for Michael Milken, the Junk Bond King. His empire collapsed when he pleaded guilty to six felony counts of securities and reporting violations, earning him a ten-year prison sentence. The junk bond market, once seen as an innovative source of capital, was exposed as a highly dubious practice. Milken cooperated with authorities, revealing details of the financing he had offered, including those to Steinberg and Silverman through Reliance Capital. This financial collapse directly affected Telemundo's funding structure and, as a result, ended the alliance between CNN's Turner and Telemundo's Steinberg. Milken managed to get his sentence reduced to twenty-two months as a result of cooperating with the authorities.

Despite these challenges, Ted Turner continued to rise, becoming a news and media tycoon. CNN, for its part, forged ahead with its Hispanic project, creating international news shows broadcast from its Atlanta studios. Jorge Gestoso, who had been a prominent figure at Telemundo, joined CNN to lead these new efforts, which continued to grow until they eventually became, in 1997, CNN en Español, a cable TV channel featuring twenty-four-hour Spanish-language news. MTV also continued to prove successful, launching MTV Latino, which broadcast music videos twenty-four hours a day, in October 1993. Daisy Fuentes remained the primary host of MTV Latino until 1997. Saul Steinberg's health deteriorated, and, in 1995, at the age of fifty-five, he suffered a stroke that forced him to step down from managing Reliance. Henry Silverman took over.

Amid these changes, Telemundo Group was facing a major financial crisis. On June 8, 1993, the company filed for chapter 11 protection after an involuntary bankruptcy petition had been filed in the U.S. Bankruptcy Court for the Southern District of New York. This move reflected the economic and structural difficulties faced by the company and its owner, Reliance Capital. It was a time fraught with both financial and strategic challenges for Telemundo. The network, though, managed to persevere and overcome them.

Why Don't You Learn English?

There's no denying the fact that the decade-long litigation prior to Univision's creation radically changed the trajectory of Hispanic television in the United States. During those ten years, from 1976 to 1986, Spanish secured its position as the second most spoken language in the country, with a Spanish-speaking audience that had already surpassed six million viewers. In 1986, the Immigration Reform and Control Act, also known as Reagan Amnesty, was passed, granting legal status and a path to citizenship to nearly three million undocumented immigrants, most of whom were Hispanic. Meanwhile, the dominating trio of broadcast television in the United States—ABC, CBS, and NBC—ignored the silent revolution brewing in the growing prosperity of the Hispanic community, both economically and in terms of population numbers.

This was a crucial time for the development of Spanish-language media as it laid the groundwork for creating programming that responded to the needs and preferences of an ever-expanding Hispanic audience. The major networks' collective failure to recognize and serve this emerging market allowed Univision and Telemundo to occupy the vital space they still hold to this day. The void left by the mainstream networks not only underestimated the potential power of the Hispanic market; it also underscored the need for authentic and committed representation in the media.

Oddly enough, the response of the three Anglo-American TV giants was not to adapt or otherwise appreciate the value of the Hispanic audience. Instead, they imposed a narrative that emphasized the supremacy of the English language and the need for Hispanics to assimilate into Anglo-American culture. Their argument to advertisers was that Spanish-language ads weren't worthwhile because Hispanics needed to learn English and adapt to the dominant culture.

This stance not only ignored the growing Hispanic population, but it also underestimated its purchasing power and cultural influence. While advertisers were being persuaded to invest in English-language channels, they overlooked the potential of a market that valued its own language and culture. Anglo-American networks maintained high advertising rates that they justified by their scope and prestige, while underestimating the importance of connecting authentically with Hispanic audiences.

This shortsightedness was the path by which Univision and Telemundo were able to capitalize on the opportunity to offer relevant, Spanish-language content and attract millions of loyal viewers. But the disparity in advertising revenue reflected persistent undervaluation: a commercial on Univision often went for a tenth of the price it commanded from any of the three major networks. This gulf reflected a lack of recognition of the Hispanic market's true value and it also presented an opportunity advertisers seized upon to effectively reach a growing and economically powerful audience with minimal investment.

The disparity continued until as recently as 2023, when a commercial slot on Univision cost approximately half of what it did on the major English-language channels in the United States. This difference in costs highlights the persistent underestimation of the power and influence of the Hispanic audience.

With Univision's satellite-connected networks, a new order had been established in the audiovisual media in the United States. It's remarkable how SIN paved the way for giants like CNN, ESPN, CNBC, A&E, HBO, Cinemax, Discovery, and

Fox to believe they could also position themselves to compete with the three giants. The regulatory framework that should have governed the growth and control of cable television came later in the game, which also contributed to the dizzying expansion of cable TV's reach right under the noses of the three giants.

The consolidation of Spanish and the growing influence of the Hispanic community ushered in a new era of American television that would be impossible to ignore in the years to come.

Progress and Setbacks

While it varied in strength and impact over time, there has always been a concerted effort to suppress the use of the Spanish language in the United States. In the 1950s and 1960s, there was mounting pressure on Hispanic children and families to abandon their native language. In some schools in California and Texas, the use of Spanish was prohibited, and students were severely punished if they were caught speaking it. Along the Texas-Mexico border, many students were forced to write "I will speak less Spanish" on sheets of paper that were buried in a symbolic grave marked with a cross that read "RIP Spanish."

"Why don't you learn English?" was the typical response René Anselmo and his SIN sales team were accustomed to hearing from advertisers in the 1960s and 1970s. But their persistence in demonstrating that there was a segment of the market that would always prefer Spanish continued. Instilling the notion of staying culturally connected through Spanish-language television was a winning strategy.

"Death Mr. Spanish." (Photo: Museum of the UTSA Institute of Texan Cultures, San Antonio, Texas.)

The local content being promoted by Danny Villanueva, SIN's director in California, and Joaquín Blaya, SIN's director in Miami, both of whom reported to Anselmo, resonated with the viewers, who began to recognize their potential and became more involved in American society. SIN was informing and entertaining people, and with real data to back up their claims, executives were beginning to persuade advertisers. The population was feeling its surging potential influence while economic and social interests began to recognize the profit potential and power of a growing social group. Recognition also intensified among local, state, and federal legislators who understood that the growth of the Hispanic community represented a growth in the total number of potential voters. Spanish-language media began to reflect a beneficial key position as the main channel of exchange between these groups. SIN had, in effect, rediscovered Hispanics in the United States.

And yet Frank del Olmo, the first Mexican American journalist to land a prominent position at the *Los Angeles Times*, wrote in 1989 that, while the decade had certainly been a notable one for

Hispanics, it had also left many (particularly Chicanos and Puerto Ricans) worse off than they were before. He wrote sarcastically that "the most evident impact Latinos had in the '80s was in the arts." Kenton Wilkinson, in his book about Spanish-language television in the United States, linked Del Olmo's view to Professor John Hoberman's argument that "Blacks are less threatening to dominant Anglo-American interests when they excel in popular culture and sports rather than business and politics."

The 1989 report by the Cuban American National Foundation stated bluntly that "progress and regress are two contradictory but nevertheless powerful currents that are transforming the Hispanic communities." The report's conclusion states:

> The increase in political empowerment, the rise of a Hispanic market and entrepreneurship, and the emergence of a national Hispanic agenda are powerful developments that can support long-term Hispanic progress.
>
> But sustained educational decline and the perpetuation and deepening of poverty are disturbing signs of long-term Hispanic stagnation.
>
> It is the clash of these forces that most accurately defines the fate of Hispanics in the 1980s, a decade perhaps best termed "The Elusive Decade of Hispanics."

The Consolidation of Spanish and the Adaptation of Programming to Anglo-American Models

It was obvious that J. William Grimes, Univision's first CEO appointed by new owner Hallmark, had no idea what it meant to lead a Hispanic media outlet. However, the executive had just transformed and grown the fledgling ESPN, itself a twenty-four-hour cable TV broadcaster of sports. Grimes rose to fame when he announced that ESPN had paid $153 million to the NFL for the rights to broadcast American football games from 1987 to 1989. When Grimes took over ESPN in 1981, it was bringing in just more than $1 million in revenue. Two years later, it had become the channel with the largest number of subscribers, totaling more than thirty million. And by 1987, the company reached its sales goal of $600 million. The difference between what he'd done at ESPN and what he was tasked with doing at Univision was that ESPN built capital as it grew while Univision was already saddled with massive debt, much of which had been used to purchase the company rather than fund its operations. Still, Grimes took on the challenge and immediately began a successful restructuring of the business.

In early 1988, Grimes was officially appointed president and CEO of Univision Holdings. His challenge (besides the obvious financial one) was noneother than replacing the duo of René Anselmo, the company's aggressive bilingual leader since its founding, and his partner and friend El Tigre Azcárraga. In July of that same year, Grimes announced the separation of his own two roles, explaining that, as CEO, he would be responsible for leading the business and its finances, and promoting Joaquín Blaya to president of Univision, entrusting him with the responsibility for managing programming and overseeing content production for the entire network. He retained Daniel Darío "Danny" Villanueva as head of Univision's operations in California and Texas.

Born in 1937 in a small town called Tucumcari, located in northern New Mexico, Villanueva was one of the first professional football players of Hispanic descent in the United States. He enjoyed a successful career from 1960 to 1967 as the kicker for the Los Angeles Rams and the Dallas Cowboys. He's affectionately known among fans as El Kickeador.

In an interview with ESPN, Villanueva recalled his experience with racial culture in the NFL. "We had a black bus and we had a white bus in those days. We were segregated." He then remembered how a teammate once told him, "All black guys get on that bus, white guys get on that bus, and Danny, you take a cab... I understood I was neither fish nor fowl."

In 1962, looking to supplement his income from playing football, Villanueva began working as a sportscaster for KMEX, then a little-known Spanish-language TV station in Los Angeles owned by SIN. He had to relearn Spanish, which he had distanced himself from in response to the pressure to assimilate.

"We were that transitional generation that thought that by distancing ourselves from our culture, our language, and our background and our roots, we were going to somehow magically be accepted by the general community," he said in a 1985 interview with the *Los Angeles Times*. "It didn't work."

After being traded to the Cowboys, Villanueva flew back and forth to his TV job in Los Angeles. Eventually, he became the news director at KMEX. Under Villanueva's leadership, KMEX became the flagship Spanish International Network station. He would go on to be co-owner and senior vice president of SIN until shortly after Blaya became CEO.

Grimes understood that, in order for Univision to succeed, he needed to leverage the knowledge and experience of Hispanic leaders like Daniel Villanueva and Joaquín Blaya, who had a profound understanding of the needs and desires of the Hispanic audience. While Grimes focused on stabilizing finances and optimizing resources, Blaya and Villanueva worked to enrich the programming and ensure that Univision remained relevant and engaging for its audience.

Another one of Grimes's moves was to explain, internally, to the entire staff that Univision was entering a new era, and that from then on, all corporate communications had to be conducted in English—a rule that's still in place to this day—and any programming issues had to include either Blaya or Villanueva or both.

On August 31, 1988, *The New York Times* ran a story by journalist Daniel F. Cuff about a key change in Univision's leadership: "Univision Holdings Inc., which is owned by Hallmark Cards Inc., yesterday announced the appointment of Joaquín F. Blaya as president of its Spanish-language television network." The piece describes how Blaya, forty-two at the time, had previously served as general manager of WLTV Channel 23 in Miami and manager for the eastern region of Univision Station Group, before being appointed to lead the Spanish-language network.

The article goes on to quote Univision spokespersons who claimed that the network reached 84 percent of Hispanic households in the United States through satellite broadcasts and cable affiliates. It also mentions that Blaya lived in Miami with his wife, Isabel, and their children. Blaya told the *Times* that he planned to split his time between New York and Miami. "We are really concentrating on the development of new programming," he said.

The article also recounts how Blaya began his television career in 1970 in New York as a sales executive for what was still SIN at the time. In 1972, he moved to the Miami station and was named general manager in 1974.

Weeks after this appointment, Grimes promoted the Cuban-born Ray Rodríguez to general manager of WLTV, Univision's Miami affiliate.

Under this new leadership structure, Univision began to experience sustained growth. The combination of Grimes's business acumen and Blaya's culturally informed vision enabled Univision to address the financial and operational challenges and build the foundation on which it would grow to become the media giant that it is today. Univision's transformation under Grimes's leadership was proof that, while the network faced considerable debt and operational hurdles, with a clear strategy and a committed team, significant and lasting change was possible.

However, at least financially, this wasn't enough to satisfy the goals and objectives set by Univision's parent company, Hallmark. Much to William Grimes's surprise, in the last quarter of 1990, Hallmark's board of directors called him into a meeting in which he was notified that they had decided to evaluate the possibility of selling the company. Univision's debt required capital contributions from its owners, who weren't inclined to provide them, preferring instead to sell off Univision Holdings. Grimes disagreed, but Hallmark's position was firm. There was no turning back.

Meanwhile, over at the competition, Telemundo was facing a financial crisis of its own. Carlos Barba foresaw a grim future for his bosses, Saul Steinberg and Henry Silverman, given the spectacular collapse of their primary financier, Michael Milken, and his firm, Drexel Burnham Lambert. During his career at Telemundo, Barba had reestablished contact with his former employer, Venezuelan businessman Gustavo Cisneros. Upon learning of Silverman's intentions to file for bankruptcy protection for Telemundo, Barba, well aware of his company's fragile state, decided to submit his resignation.

Just as the earlier description of the Hispanic community reflected both its successes and setbacks, Univision and Telemundo were also experiencing dizzying growth in both viewership and sales, but their owners could not—or perhaps were unwilling to—bear the weight of the financial burden imposed by the debt taken on in order to acquire both TV giants. In 1991, Hallmark Cards announced it would sell Univision, while Telemundo was preparing to file for bankruptcy protection.

These decisions would have lasting repercussions, shaping the landscape of Hispanic media for years to come. However, what nobody could have foreseen was how an unexpected twist of fate could forever change the rules of the game, setting off a series of events that would test the resilience of Univision and Telemundo and reveal secrets destined to shake up the future of these two giants.

CHAPTER 8

Rosita Perú and Don Francisco with Their *Sábado Gigante*

In his influential 1982 book *Megatrends*, John Naisbitt predicted that, by the year 2000, there would be three predominant languages in the United States: English, Spanish, and computer science. This prediction, which seemed quite futuristic at the time, underscored the growing importance of the Hispanic community in the country. For companies looking to capture this powerful emerging market, simply translating ads from English to Spanish proved insufficient and, in many cases, counterproductive. This superficial approach often caused confusion and failed to influence Spanish-speaking consumers but highlighted the need for advertising agencies that specialized in this demographic.

In the mid-1980s, well-known brands began to realize the Hispanic market's potential. Companies like Coca-Cola, Budweiser, and McDonald's, among others, began implementing strategies specifically targeted at this demographic. In 1984, a McDonald's ad campaign included the youth pop music group Menudo for promotional tours while the Coors beer company repeatedly declared itself "the beer for the Decade of the Hispanic."

The warming of corporate interest to the Hispanic market, sparked in no small part by the notable mention in Naisbitt's bestselling book, not only changed the way products and services were marketed but also had a significant impact on Hispanic TV programming. Univision, aware of the increasing advertising investment from major brands, saw the need to adapt its content to attract and retain Hispanic audiences in the United States, thus justifying its growing ad expenditure.

Rosita Perú played a pivotal role during this transformation. Having been a singer, host, and sales executive for SIN, Perú was a visionary when it came to Hispanic media. She understood the importance of offering relevant, culturally resonant content produced primarily in the United States to secure loyalty and connect with viewers.

The Rosita Perú Formula

Rosa Berruezo Granados, better known as Rosita Perú, was not only a successful singer in Spanish-language television during the 1970s but also one of its most influential architects. Her personal history is as rich as that of the entire Hispanic culture in the United States, something that she herself helped to shape. Rosita was a photogenic lady who captivated her audiences, including El Tigre, with her gaze. Born in Lima, Peru, on September 20, 1940, Rosita was the daughter of guitarist and flamenco dancer Asunción Granados and businessman Martín Berruezo. Her extensive career led her to explore various roles as a singer, producer, broadcaster, host, salesperson, and finally, television executive. She traveled across Europe and the Americas, excelling in the entertainment industry and leaving her mark with each and every step.

Her talents as a singer led to a record deal with the Odeón label in Madrid. An entire generation will remember how she sagely invited singer Tito Rodríguez, who was the leading symbol of Puerto Rican culture in New York, to appear on her show at SIN. Rosita Perú and Tito Rodríguez, also known as El Inolvidable, or "The Unforgettable," performed their greatest hits side by side. That show, which she created, was her triumphant entry into the hearts of the U.S. Hispanic audience. Perú was a visionary who left an indelible mark on the television industry with her wit and determination. In 1981, she joined the team at SIN in New York. Back then, executive positions in Hispanic media were dominated by men, but Rosita, through her talent and perseverance, broke through this glass ceiling by becoming the first woman appointed as executive vice president in the history of Hispanic television.

Rosita was in charge of programming and production at Univision for twelve years. But her leadership wasn't limited to these specific areas; she was also responsible for international sales, a role that allowed her to experience and understand the power that comes with financial success. From her early days as a singer in her homeland to her years in the United States, Rosita always knew that money wasn't the only element in living the life she wanted. Power and influence were equally important.

During her time as an artist, first in her home country and later in the United States, Rosita achieved a significant amount of fame. She hosted her own show and was bringing in money, though not at the level she'd aspired to. It was at this point that Rosita discovered her ability to attract clients and forge business relationships, something that allowed her to combine money and power effectively. SIN's owners at the time, René Anselmo and El Tigre, immediately had her on their radar.

Anselmo wanted her to stay in New York with him, but Rosita, ever strategic, decided to join El Tigre in Los Angeles, where SIN's headquarters was located. This decision proved pivotal for her career. There in LA, Rosita began to amass a fortune and understand finance on a much larger scale. Her role in the company became increasingly indispensable, especially when Hallmark took over the reins. Despite her ties to the previous administration, Rosita was able to maintain business relationships with major accounts, including the Ford Motor Company, Coca-Cola, McDonald's, and Barnett Bank, among others.

Even Joaquín Blaya, then president of Univision, advocated on behalf of Rosita. Instead of firing her because of her close relationship with Anselmo and El Tigre, he promoted her to executive vice president. In this new role, Rosita implemented a bold new strategy: to pitch SIN, now Univision, as the fourth major television network in the United States. She convinced clients that Univision wasn't competing with Telemundo, but rather with the three American giants: NBC, ABC, and CBS. This revolutionary strategy changed the opinion the industry had of the Spanish-language television industry.

In Los Angeles, she met the love of her life, Luis Nogales, who was executive vice president of news at SIN at the time. Nogales, a Stanford Law School graduate, co-founded MEChA, the Spanish acronym for the Chicano Student Movement of Aztlán, which promotes political and cultural awareness among Chicano and Latino students in the United States. In 1969, the day after he graduated from law school, Nogales became the first assistant to the president of Stanford University for Mexican American affairs. A student leader and member of the university's senior staff, he was instrumental in institutionalizing the enrollment and participation of Latino students, faculty, and staff at Stanford. He left the institution when he was selected as a White House fellow and from there pursued a career in communications while always staying involved in activism for the development and prosperity of the Mexican American community. Nogales fell head over heels for Rosita, and they became an influential couple, both at SIN under El Tigre and Anselmo and later at Univision under Hallmark.

Rosita had her finger on the Hispanic market's pulse and used her artistic sensibilities to collaborate with her superiors and take the network to new heights. She helped strike a balance among the fearsome El Tigre, the leader Anselmo, and station directors Joaquín Blaya on the East Coast in Miami and Danny Villanueva on the West Coast in Los Angeles. She was able to discover and promote new talent, creating new job opportunities for Hispanics. Among her most notable contributions are the modernization of SIN's programming, the opening of the U.S. market to Latin American producers, the creation of international sales for content created by Univision, and the promotion of new talent.

She admired the vision of Joaquín Blaya who, from Miami, pushed for transforming SIN into a channel that was less Mexican and more American in the sense that it embraced all the nations that make up the continent. Rosita is also credited with helping Univision gain relevance and recognition in Latin America. By the early 1990s, every TV actor and artist wanted to appear on Univision screens in the United States, and many behind-the-scenes studio professionals also hoped to one day work there.

Perú had another quality that helped her stand out from the crowd: her exceptional command of Spanish. Her Peruvian accent was perceived as neutral and sophisticated, which gave her a unique advantage when it came to communicating in the Spanish-speaking world. This type of Spanish, free of any marked regionalisms, not only made her easier to understand for a wider audience but also added a touch of elegance and clarity to her speech.

From Los Angeles, Perú supported the Chilean Blaya, director of WLTV in Miami, whom she'd known since her early days at SIN in New York. Rosita implored on-air talent to pay attention to their accents and try to create a more "neutral" voice. If you compare Jorge Ramos's early newscasts after arriving from Mexico with his more recent ones, you'll notice the change. María Elena Salinas is also recognized for being one of the first journalists to adopt a neutral accent in Spanish, something more in line with news anchors on American English-language networks.

Mario Luis Kreutzberger Blumenfeld, also known as Don Francisco, also introduced this circus-presenter accent in his megahit show *Sábado Gigante.* After several attempts, the Saturday program started to gain traction with audiences, finally finding just the right tone and formula that resonated with Hispanic viewers. This evolution is evident when listening to Don Francisco hosting *Sábado Gigante* alongside Rolando Barral in 1985 versus Don Francisco with Javier Romero in 1987. El Tigre credited Rosita Perú's almost obsessive insistence with bringing this new accent to Hispanic television.

In 1984, Rosita went to Villanueva and Blaya with a bold proposition. She suggested it would be worth refreshing the programming by exploring Venezuela's catalog of telenovelas. She knew of a Caracas-based production company called Coral Pictures that was already exporting its shows to other Spanish-speaking countries. She argued that the neutral accent with a Caribbean touch, the production quality, and the attractive Venezuelan actresses could be a perfect alternative to the Mexican telenovelas in SIN's lineup. This was something no one had dared to suggest to El Tigre, owner of Televisa and the sole provider of telenovelas in the United States at the time, and yet Rosita found a way to push the idea forward.

A former Televisa board member with whom I spoke recalls a production meeting in Mexico where the influence of Venezuelan telenovelas was discussed. During this meeting, the idea of exploring what was being done in Venezuela was brought up, along with the suggestion that Televisa might consider acquiring a telenovela production studio in that country in order to foster its own growth. The actress Lupita Ferrer and the positive impact she had on Mexican audiences was used as an example of the appeal the Venezuelan productions had. The growing popularity of Venezuelan women—including even in the personal lives of Mexican public figures—was also mentioned, highlighting the possibility of seeking talent in Venezuela who could collaborate with Mexican artists. The proposed strategy was to identify the best Venezuelan actors and actresses and find a way to integrate them with Televisa's stars.

At the time, Venezuela was already well known for the beauty of its women. Maritza Sayalero had been crowned Miss Universe in 1979 and, two years later, she married the outstanding Mexican tennis player Raúl Ramírez, who won multiple international tournaments including doubles titles at Wimbledon and Roland Garros. El Tigre joked that Raúl was one of the few people he envied, loudly proclaiming that it wasn't because of his talents as an athlete but because he married a Miss Universe, whereas he himself only managed to catch the eye of Miss Mexico contestants. The same year Ramírez and Sayalero married (1981), Venezuela won the Miss Universe title again with the beautiful Irene Sáez. The rights to the organization that trained and prepared women for pageants belonged to Venevisión, owned by the Cisneros family, with Gustavo Cisneros at the helm. As previously mentioned, Gustavo and El Tigre had already been building a strong friendship, with Cisneros eventually becoming a member of the board of directors at Televisa in Mexico. Incidentally, a former executive close to the media mogul confirmed to me that El Tigre offered Gustavo a rather hefty payment of $5,000 for each board meeting he attended at Televisa, though with the sole condition that he would deduct a thousand dollars for every question or comment he dared to make.

Venevisión was a major producer of Venezuelan telenovelas and competed fiercely with Radio Caracas Televisión, whose owners also controlled Coral Pictures, the international distribution arm of their telenovelas with whom Rosita Perú and Joaquín Blaya had already been negotiating. El Tigre gave the order to investigate the budding "Miss" industry and the Venezuelan telenovela scene. In 1985, Televisa hired José Luis Rodríguez, "El Puma," to star—or at least attempt to star—in the telenovela *Tú o nadie* alongside the very talented actress Lucía Méndez, who was a personal favorite and very much adored by El Tigre.

El Tigre had listened to Rosita Perú, but he didn't follow her advice. Not completely. Instead of buying a Venezuelan telenovela and broadcasting it in the United States, he wanted to control the entire process from the ground up, as he was accustomed to doing. And so he decided to hire Venezuelan talent like El Puma and test him out on his home turf. That attempt, as we've discussed, was a failure.

Despite this, Rosita's powers of persuasion were such that El Tigre asked her, in 1991, to personally help him modernize Televisa's production in Mexico. This turned out to be one of Perú's most notable achievements—her role in the launch of Anselmo's PanAmSat venture. She worked directly with René and succeeded in getting the government of Peru, her home country, to be the first nation to purchase satellite services. Rosita managed to oblige both El Tigre and Anselmo in their business dealings while also managing programming at SIN.

Rosita had always maintained a progressive vision when it came to the future of television. In one of the executive's few public speeches, which she gave during a ceremony where she received a lifetime achievement award, she said, "These days, when I'm watching TV, I think there's so much more we could do thanks to technological advancements, outreach with the Hispanic world, new talent, and most of all the potential for advertising agencies and buying Spanish-language ads."

After twelve years, from 1981to 1993, as the first female executive vice president of Univision, as well as playing a key role in building the network's successful prime-time lineup, Rosita Perú made the crossover into the world of public broadcasting, joining the board of directors at PBS.

During those years, the entertainment world was marked by a deeply unequal power dynamic, especially when it came to gender. In the 1980s and 1990s, machismo was a tangible and persistent reality in the industry. Women were often valued more for their appearance than for their talent or intelligence. This resulted in a veritable prison block of roles that exploited nothing but their image, rendering them little more than decorations on a stage dominated by male figures. In the executive offices of large television corporations, the female presence was rare if not entirely nonexistent. Women faced an almost unbreakable glass ceiling that prevented them from accessing positions of true authority and decision-making. This reality contrasted sharply with the richness and diversity of female talent that was evident on the screen but rarely reflected in positions of leadership. Rosita Perú's determination to be not just another pretty face in the crowd but a figure of power and influence was a revolutionary stance to assume in an environment where the rules were written almost entirely by and for men.

By 1985, Rosita already held the position of executive vice president of programming at SIN, though her true influence extended well beyond her formal title. With a beauty that captivated even El Tigre, Rosita became a valuable and respected adviser in the industry. Her ability to navigate a male-dominated world, combined with her charisma, allowed her to establish a network of influential contacts and strengthen her position within the company. Despite the speculation and gossip, Rosita always remained focused on her work, proving time and again that her true power lay in her ability to understand market dynamics and anticipate the needs of the Hispanic audience.

Rosita's acute understanding of power dynamics and the television industry was evident in several key decisions. She was the one who chose Jorge Ramos and María Elena Salinas to be the faces of Univision's newscast. She also advocated for the inclusion of English words in the programming: a revolutionary idea at a time when the purity of Spanish was the law of the land. She suggested peppering the newscast with Spanglish, incorporating words like "White House," "CEO," "small business," and "marketing," among other terms. Rosita also knew how to construct a successful program. She was the one who gave *Sábado Gigante* producer Antonio Menchaca the framework for captivating Hispanic audiences and suggested that he and the famous host of the Saturday prime-time show travel around the country and interact with its audiences. It was she who understood that Cristina Saralegui had the charisma to host her own talk show, and she was the one who saw, in Lili Estefan, a potential that would later materialize in her future with Univision.

But beyond her personal success, Rosita understood not only what was commercially viable but what wasn't. She knew a little vanity in the newscast wouldn't bother a working-class audience who, after a long day on the job, preferred coming home to pleasant faces delivering some light news. Univision was the first network in the United States to show female news anchors standing in short skirts—something that the controversial Roger Ailes later implemented (or copied) with his female anchors at Fox News.

Another one of Rosita Perú's great achievements was discovering a canned comedy show that came prerecorded from Venezuela called *Bienvenidos* (*Welcome*)—by "canned," I mean shows that were prerecorded and ready for distribution, rather than being produced live or locally. The rights to this show belonged to Venevisión, owned by the Cisneros group, but it was Perú who discovered it through Televisa México, which was already airing it on Canal 9 in Mexico. The show itself was unique in that it had two very talented screenwriters: Venezuelan Miguel Ángel Landa, the show's creator and main producer, and Mexican writer Raúl Zenteno, who was in charge of "internationalizing" the script so it wouldn't sound "so Venezuelan." "Hagan bien y no miren a quién" ("Do good for goodness' sake") was the phrase with which Landa closed each episode of *Bienvenidos*.

Although *Bienvenidos* had been a huge success in Venezuela since its premier on Venevisión in 1982, it wasn't until 1987 that the Mexican screenwriter managed to adapt the show for a more global audience. In 1988, the decision was made to give it a test run on Univision. The show proved to be as popular as the classic Mexican hits like *El Chapulín Colorado* and *El Chavo del Ocho*, quickly capturing the attention of Hispanic audiences in the United States. One of Landa's advisers commented that *Bienvenidos*'s arrival at Univision was an unexpected stroke of luck, thanks to negotiations facilitated by Rosita Perú and her connections at Televisa, by way of El Tigre.

Bienvenidos's success in the United States was such that its actors traveled annually to perform live shows in character in various cities.

Miguel Ángel Landa was often approached by numerous promoters from various independent production companies in Miami, offering him tempting sums of money in an attempt to get him to relocate to the city and produce the show there. Yet Landa always declined. His contract with Venevisión was good enough that he never even considered leaving his home country, which is where he also dedicated a significant portion of his time to producing films for the Venezuelan cinema.

Rosita Perú, the successful executive with a commanding presence and pragmatic approach to the Univision world, didn't just stand out. She sparked envy and controversy among her co-workers. One former colleague told me how female artists and backstage crew members would whisper about how Rosita seemed able to understand and manipulate male dynamics to her advantage: a talent that allowed her to move with an ease in a field dominated by men. "She got into men's heads," the colleague said, adding that this caused other women, suspicious and perhaps resentful, to complain about her ability to move effortlessly through such a competitive world. On the other hand, there were those who criticized her apparent conformity with the status quo, especially with regards to wage inequality and the objectification of women on camera: "She was like just another man," they said, alluding to her pragmatic and occasionally insensitive attitude toward the fight for gender equality.

Not all of Rosita Perú's suggested programs were successful. Always quick on the draw, she was willing to accept mistakes and cancel any programming experiment that failed to meet expectations. One of the network's major projects was the show *Estamos Unidos*, which featured celebrity interviews. Rosita, however, decided to cancel it due to its high production costs compared with the ad-sales revenue it generated. In its place, she opted for a music video program.

Rosita accepted and even promoted the idea that showing off legs and cleavage on-screen was an effective strategy for attracting audiences, both male and female. This position, while valid from a business standpoint, earned her criticism and even resentment in an environment where many women were fighting to change the narrative in pursuit of recognition that went beyond mere sensuality.

Rosita Perú stands out for her longevity and resilience in the ever-changing world of Univision, holding steadfast to her position through the reigns of three different ownership groups. She stayed under the dual aegis of El Tigre and Anselmo, then survived the Hallmark era, and finally continued to be a figure of authority until 1992, when she resigned from the company. That same year, she and Luis Nogales formalized their relationship. Through all of

"Rosita Perú," Rosa Berruezo Nogales. (Photo: The Hispanic Production Magazine.)

these ups and downs, Perú's position was never in doubt. There were no recriminations, no feuds; she was completely unshakable in her role. Nogales left the network in 1988 to join El Tigre in his international news project ECO. Rosita Perú dropped her stage name when she left Univision and started a new life as an executive media strategy adviser, supporting El Tigre on his projects as well as Anselmo and PanAmSat, among many other clients. From that moment on, Rosita was Rosa Berruezo Nogales.

The *Sábado Gigante* Phenomenon

In 1986, fate brought together two prominent Chileans in the Miami television industry: Mario Kreutzberger Blumenfeld, already famous as Don Francisco, and Joaquín Blaya, who was head of WLTV, the Spanish International Network's Miami operation, still under the leadership of René Anselmo and El Tigre. Kreutzberger had a vision: expand his iconic Chilean show *Sábados Gigantes* beyond his national borders, and he saw the Hispanic TV station in Miami as the perfect opportunity to realize his international ambitions. *Sábados Gigantes* was a Spanish-language variety show created and hosted by Don Francisco. It began broadcasting on August 5, 1962, in Chile under the name *Show Dominical* (*Sunday Show*), and later Saturdays, adopting the name *Sábados Gigantes* in 1963. The program was characterized by its marathon format, lasting roughly three hours, offering an eclectic mix of contests, humor, music, information, and constant audience interaction. And while in Chile the show didn't differ much from other similar Saturday musical revues in other Latin American countries, its reach and popularity made it an unprecedented television phenomenon.

At that same time, WLTV was broadcasting a talk show hosted by Rolando Barral, a respected Cuban American actor, television presenter, and radio personality known for his extensive career in telenovelas and for being the host of various music programs in Cuba, Venezuela, Puerto Rico, and the United States. Although Barral and Kreutzberger were the same age, forty-seven, and had similar industry experience, Barral's program hadn't done enough to convince key figures like Rosita Perú, René Anselmo, and El Tigre Azcárraga to expand it nationally.

It was then that Blaya came up with the idea of giving Kreutzberger the opportunity to record a few pilot episodes of *Sábados Gigantes* at SIN's studios on the condition that he be accompanied by Barral. The idea was for the charismatic and renowned

Cuban actor to benefit from the more sophisticated production level that Don Francisco brought from Chile. On April 12, 1986, the first U.S.-recorded episode of *Sábados Gigantes* hit the airwaves, co-hosted by Barral and Don Francisco. The show's debut featured the famous Venezuelan singer José Luis "El Puma" Rodríguez as the first guest. "Mario is very superstitious and always invited me to his shows when he needs just a touch of luck," El Puma remarked.

This first phase of the program, however, passed without much fanfare. The show, using a format identical to the successful Chilean version, was unconvincing. The production team was the same one used for Barral's talk show, and the frustration on set was twofold: on the one hand, Kreutzberger blamed the team's lack of experience, and on the other, Barral was annoyed at having to play a supporting role in the shadow of Don Francisco's dominant figure. Back then, an underperforming new show could quickly get the hook.

For most of 1986, the offices and studios of SIN were feeling mounting pressure from the legal battle Azcárraga and Anselmo were fighting against the Fouces, which (as we saw in chapter 5) ended with the company being handed over to Hallmark. These tensions led Rolando Barral to abandon the *Sábado Gigante* project at SIN and move to Telemundo. Barral convinced Carlos Barba, who was just then taking over the reins of Telemundo's expansion project, to hire him and his production team. *Súper Sábados*, the program Barral would host for Telemundo, wouldn't last a year. By the end of 1986, with Hallmark already the owners of the newly created Univision, Joaquín Blaya, now president of the network, decided to launch *Sábado Gigante* and was able to convince Hallmark to support him in this venture.

Blaya's decision to launch *Sábado Gigante* wasn't just a bold move. It was a clear vision for the future. Convinced by Blaya of the show's untapped potential, Hallmark injected significant resources, boosting the production quality to unprecedented levels. This influx of capital allowed for technical improvements when it came to equipment and recording technology and it helped significantly raise the salaries of host Mario Kreutzberger (Don Francisco) and its director and producer, fellow Chilean Antonio Menchaca.

Taking full advantage of the newly available resources, Menchaca focused his efforts on creating new, more elaborate, and more engaging segments for the audience. With renewed investment, *Sábado Gigante* not only managed to maintain its charismatic essence and connection with the audience, it also positioned itself as a benchmark for quality and entertainment on Hispanic television. Blaya's venture proved to be a great strategic success. The decision to change the name from *Sábados Gigantes* to *Sábado Gigante* was made by a network tech who eliminated the *s* in the character generator, arguing that "we don't pronounce the *s* here."

At first, some members of Blaya's team were skeptical of Don Francisco. However, despite their skepticism and underestimations, Mario—who was, in fact, an introverted and serious man, while at the same time ambitious and strategic—proved his work ethic, passion, obsession with success, and savvy in his pursuit of advertising revenue for his show. It was in that pursuit that Liliana Estefan came into play.

The discovery of Liliana "Lili" del Carmen Estefan and her commercial impact on *Sábado Gigante* is an example of how Rosita Perú's influence was clearly felt in Univision's executive offices. In 1986, Lili, just nineteen years old at the time, was introduced as one of the many models starting their television careers on *Sábado Gigante*, which was still struggling to gain traction in its attempt to reach U.S. Hispanic audiences on the new Univision network. Lili was the niece of Emilio Estefan, who, along with his wife, Gloria, created the band Miami Sound Machine. The group was at the peak of its success, having become one of first Latino pop bands to break through not just with Hispanics but with a multicultural, English-speaking audience. They had achieved what once seemed all but impossible: the crossover.

Lili confirms that, back then, she was making fifty dollars a show. For many, the arrival of this skinny, smiling teenager was what kickstarted *Sábado Gigante*'s surge in ratings. She wasn't your typical model. Lili had to endure bullying from both Don Francisco and the audience, both of whom mocked her for her slender frame and prominent teeth. This verbal abuse wasn't simply tolerated; in fact, it was an integral part of the show. At the time, bullying wasn't frowned upon as it is today. Instead, it was accepted as an added comedic touch that kept the viewers entertained. Lili understood that this behavior was part of the show, accepting it as a requisite of her role and, potentially, even as a boost for her career.

And yet it was Lili herself, with Rosita Perú's support, who stood out for her innovative ability to market the products that advertisers wanted to promote on the show. Unlike traditional Latin American variety shows, *Sábado Gigante* was beginning to separate itself from the pack and resonate with its audience.

There's a story told by Don Francisco, who was invited to appear in one of the very first episodes of *The Tonight Show* after Jay Leno took over as host in 1992. Leno and his wife lived in a Los Angeles suburb and employed a Hispanic housekeeper to manage their home. She was the one who suggested that Leno reach out to the Hispanic community and invite Don Francisco to be a guest on his show—and so he did.

Previously hosted by Johnny Carson, *The Tonight Show* was a huge hit for NBC for decades, becoming a mainstay of American late-night television since 1954. The show aired with Carson as host from 1962 to 1992, and solidified its stature as a cultural and entertainment icon throughout its lengthy tenure. Jay Leno took over in 1992, after having been Carson's standing guest host.

On a night filled with stars and surprises, Jay Leno's fourth show as host aired on May 28. And that episode became immortalized, at least for the Hispanic community. Among the guests was the iconic Hollywood star Sigourney Weaver, who was promoting the electrifying sequel to the movie *Alien*. But the night had an even more unique surprise in store for viewers. Don Francisco, the legendary *Sábado Gigante* host, brought his young star Lili Estefan along with him, adding a distinctly Latin flavor to the show.

Leno, as curious as he is witty and perceptive, couldn't help but be fascinated by Don Francisco's peculiar ability to sell products in the middle of his shows. In an unexpected and humorous twist, Don Francisco invited Estefan onstage to perform a parody commercial for a soap called Suavecito. It was a hilarious performance, with Leno comically repeating the slogan "suavecito," creating a truly memorable TV moment.

This episode, which blends Leno's spontaneity, Don Francisco's charisma, and Estefan's charm is a must-see TV gem. The video can be found on YouTube by searching "Don Francisco and Jay Leno," and it's guaranteed to bring a good dose of laughter and nostalgia.

From 1987 through the 1990s and beyond, Don Francisco hosted a show that reflected a distinctly patriarchal and sexist style. The program was a huge success, due to its entertainment-driven design and its host's appeal, ability, and skill in interacting with his guests and audience. It also served as a springboard for many female artists and models.

Miss Pechonalidad

In 1991, the year Hallmark sold Univision, the company's new executive team proposed organizing a Hispanic beauty pageant in the United States. The proposal was initially met with resistance from some executives. While they were fully aware of the success of Miss Universe, these executives saw this idea as an expensive investment for an event that would happen only once a year. They argued instead that it would be more strategic to invest in the Saturday show, *Sábado Gigante*, because it attracted a large and consistent audience.

The suggestion was then made to create a weekly pageant as part of *Sábado Gigante* that would highlight bold and provocative features in contests like "Best Butt" and "Best Breasts" but also one for "Best Personality." It was a daring concept designed to grab the attention of a larger and more regular audience and create a television phenomenon that no one could ignore. Advertising during the show would be subtly camouflaged through product placement and in-show purchases.

A few weeks later came the full proposal for "Miss Pechonalidad," a portmanteau of the words for "breasts" and "personality." The idea, while controversial, was seen as a strategy for appealing to both men and women, ensuring higher viewership and advertiser interest.

Most executives were in favor of investing in *Sábado Gigante* and including "Miss Pechonalidad" as one of the show's segments. The key was marketing and generating revenue, and "Miss Pechonalidad" promised to be a name that would be etched into the minds of viewers. With this bold proposal, Univision was aiming to aggressively consolidate its position as a leader in Hispanic television, captivating a broad and diverse audience.

In the weeks that followed the Univision decision, an audacious casting call for "Miss Pechonalidad" started to be promoted. It was a resounding success, attracting women of all nationalities, even those whose native language was English, because they too were convinced it was a brilliant idea.

The pageant ran for three long years, captivating audiences and becoming a true phenomenon. *Sábado Gigante* generated millions of dollars in ad revenue, and there seemed to be no limits to its success. Criticism, however, began to surface, with questions about the show's morality and ethical standards. In the mid-2010s, the show began to change, adapting to the times and leaving behind the machismo elements that were no longer socially acceptable. Beauty pageants were replaced by segments on health issues and advice for immigrants, though always accompanied by music and humor.

Don Francisco's contributions to how Latin American culture was represented in the United States were substantial. While his show did include bits that could be considered controversial or outdated by today's standards, it also highlighted the talent and diversity of the Hispanic community. During his travels across the United States, Don Francisco and his team focused on understanding the needs and aspirations of Hispanic immigrants. This insight allowed them to develop content that felt relevant and authentic to their audience. Many years later, Don Francisco acknowledged and accepted the criticisms that had been levied against certain aspects of his show, particularly its focus on women's physical appearance. Without any attempts at justification, he referred to the changing moral standards in television between previous decades and the present day.

Don Francisco's legacy also includes the promotion of many successful professionals. Despite her tragic and untimely death, Tex-Mex singer Selena Quintanilla left an indelible mark on Latin music and culture, and her performances on SIN and, later, on Univision's *Sábado Gigante*, played an important role in her rise to stardom.

The history of *Sábado Gigante* and its influence is a complex mosaic, the interpretation of which can vary significantly depending on the cultural and historical lens through which it's viewed. Throughout its history, *Sábado Gigante,* along with other shows on Univision, presented representations of women that might well be viewed as unacceptable today. These representations, however, met the social norms and expectations of the time. Meanwhile, Univision served as a launching pad for a large number of women who saw their professional careers take off, many of whom, thanks to their individual talents and charisma, achieved success in the world of entertainment and beyond. Notable examples include public figures such as Odalys García, Lili Estefan, Maty Monfort, Jackie Nespral, Sofía Vergara, Giselle Blondet, Nanci Guerrero, Isabel Fleitas, Rashel Díaz, Barbie Simons, Karol Rosa, Maribel Rodríguez, and Carolina Vielma, among many others. The impact of programs like *Sábado Gigante*, *Primer Impacto*,

Fuera de Serie, *República Deportiva*, and *Despierta América* was crucial in terms of shaping the trajectory and development of these celebrities' careers.

Despite the changes, Don Francisco and *Sábado Gigante* managed to remain relevant in the history of Hispanic television in the United States all the way through the show's final live broadcast on September 19, 2015, when Mario Kreutzberger was already seventy-four years old. He had proved to be a skilled and resilient figure. Throughout his decades-long career, he evolved and adapted to the demands of station owners, moral constraints, and censorship, all while keeping his show alive in the hearts of his audience.

CHAPTER 9

Hallmark Cards: The Hockaday and Blaya Era at Univision

Irvine O. Hockaday Jr. was an influential figure at Univision between 1986 and 1991. Those close to him called him Irv. Hockaday was the first CEO and president of Hallmark who wasn't a member of the Hall family.

Hockaday took over in 1981, beginning a leadership role that lasted until 2005. During his first three years in the position, he demonstrated a bold and strategic vision, which lead him to venture into the media market through the acquisition of SIN. His choice of William Grimes to lead SIN was no coincidence. Hockaday was looking for someone with deep experience both in television and in transforming media companies.

One of Grimes's first tasks upon taking over as head of Univision was to usher in a new era for the network, and in order to do so, he needed to shed the aura left by its former founders, El Tigre Azcárraga and René Anselmo. Under Grimes's leadership, Univision began to compete directly with the biggest names in television. Hockaday, for his part, continued to support the transition from Hallmark, ensuring that the initial investment in SIN would become a valuable asset and be able to manage the debt incurred from its acquisition.

Joaquín Blaya, President of Univision (1987)

When the news broke that Chilean Joaquín Blaya had been appointed as the new president of Univision, and therefore the person in charge of the company's editorial content, Danny Villanueva announced his retirement. Blaya was tasked with redefining Univision's programming and expanding its audience, ensuring that the network would be focused not only on telenovelas and news but also content that appealed to a more diverse, less exclusively Mexican audience.

In the 1960s, Blaya, who came from a family that published a political satire magazine, was one of the many young people who decided to emigrate during that turbulent time in Chile's history. His family's magazine ceased publication just before the leftist president Salvador Allende's administration took office. In 1970, looking for work, Blaya reached out to René Anselmo after having seen a newspaper ad seeking advertising salespeople. Anselmo offered him the opportunity to work for SIN in New York. (Anslemo himself had already moved to Connecticut by that time and was managing SIN from an office in the city.)

Blaya admits that the idea of a Spanish-language TV network seemed crazy to him, but he accepted the job because he needed the income. It seemed naive to him to think that advertisers would be interested in a channel broadcasting on a very weak UHF signal and in a language that was often marginalized and rejected. On this subject, Blaya recounts an experience during a meeting with a Colgate-Palmolive executive to whom he was trying to sell ad time on the channel. At one point, the exec snidely asked him, "Do Puerto Ricans brush their teeth?" Blaya also recalls how the ad buyer for a major New York supermarket chain once told him, "I'm not interested in talking to people like you!" On top of all that, in New York, he was the recipient of a lot of criticism regarding the channel's content, which he relayed directly to Anselmo. The main complaint among Hispanics was that the programming was all Mexican, while the majority of Hispanics in New York were Puerto Ricans, along with many Colombians and Dominicans.

But despite all these obstacles, Blaya wasn't a half-bad salesperson. He recalls how that same racist supermarket buyer called him back some months later to try out a small ad buy with SIN, and the ads paid off. This same buyer was later promoted to the head of marketing for the company, and from that position he continued to call Blaya and buy more ad space from SIN. As a result, Blaya gradually earned the trust of his boss, René Anselmo.

In 1972, Joaquín Blaya was transferred from New York to Miami to work at WLTV, the SIN station that had caused the earlier conflict between Anselmo and El Tigre (discussed in chapter 1). By 1974, Blaya was already the general manager of the Miami station, and it was during that time that he began interacting with Cuban audiences and talent. Before Fidel Castro took power, Cuban television was considered the most modern in of all Latin America, so much so that Cuban production engineers and journalistic talent in exile were highly valued by the three major U.S. networks: CBS, ABC, and NBC.

The acquisition and relaunch of Univision—and its subsequent control—by Hallmark generated significant controversy due to a perceived decline in the Mexican American community's influence in terms of decision-making. El Tigre's absence was acutely felt. The appointment of the former general manager of the Miami station as president instead of the head of the Los

Angeles station was seen as a de-Mexicanization of Hispanic television, causing concern among the community representing the largest number of viewers. Meanwhile, Telemundo was also facing criticism for the lack of diversity among its leadership, with Carlos Barba, a Cuban, being the only prominent Hispanic executive. This situation created serious tensions among Hispanic subgroups, particularly between Mexican Americans and people from Central American nations—Guatemala, El Salvador, Honduras, and Nicaragua—who tended to be more liberal and had lower incomes (and who were often grouped together with Mexicans). Mexican Americans also contrasted with Hispanics from Miami and New York, who tended to be from Puerto Rico, the Dominican Republic, Cuba, Colombia, or other Southern Cone countries (Argentina, Chile, and Uruguay, for example, whose people were often lumped together as Cubans) who were generally more conservative and had greater financial resources. This internal conflict reflected a struggle for representation and power within Hispanic media, and highlighted the existing socioeconomic and political differences. Mexican Americans, for their part, felt increasingly marginalized, while Cubans, with their growing influence, were seen as the new "owners" of the Hispanic media scene.

In addition to the internal struggle for power and representation, things were also complicated by the structural changes Hallmark was introducing at Univision. The departure of Danny Villanueva, an eighteen-year veteran of SIN, triggered a wave of resignations among station managers in California and Texas. The community saw his exit as a serious mistake by Hallmark and its new leadership. Despite not being Cuban himself, Joaquín Blaya was branded as the one promoting the "Cubanization" of Univision, sparking resentment, particularly on the West Coast. Blaya, aware of these tensions, appointed Emilio Nicolás Sr., founder of the station in San Antonio and a longtime figure at the network, as Villanueva's successor.

This strategic move was intended to appease disgruntled employees and take advantage of Nicolás Sr.'s strong ties to the political establishment in Texas, a key state for Univision and even more so for Blaya, who didn't want to rely solely on the political connections of his new bosses at Hallmark, who were staunch allies of the Bush dynasty, one of whom would soon be occupying the White House. The disconnect persisted, however, and many employees continued to feel the changes favored one particular group over their own. Blaya's leadership faced not only internal resistance but also external pressure from political and activist groups demanding more fair and equitable representation within the network.

Hockaday, Grimes, and Blaya deemed it essential that they distance themselves from El Tigre's influence and therefore decided to move their original headquarters. Univision's offices were located in Laguna Niguel, ninety minutes from Los Angeles, because that had been a prime location near the Orange County Airport in Santa Ana, where El Tigre could land in his private jets. Laguna Niguel was also home to the exclusive Waldorf Astoria Hotel, a favorite retreat for El Tigre when he wanted to escape from his work routines. Despite suggestions from Emilio Nicolás Sr, to move the headquarters to San Antonio, the choice was ultimately made in favor of Miami, driven by the need for better coast-to-coast news coverage due to the time differences. While strategically justifiable, the decision only amplified criticism from those who perceived a growing Cuban dominance in

U.S. Hispanic television, intensifying the controversy over representation and control.

Choosing Miami as the new headquarters represented not only a geographical shift but a culturally symbolic shift within Univision's organizational structure. With its large Cuban population and rising media influence, Miami became the new epicenter of Hispanic power in the United States. This relocation affected both Univision employees and executives and its audience, who watched these changes unfolding with interest and concern. The perception of this supposed Cubanization wasn't limited to Univision's inner circles; it was also evident in its programming and in the way the network handled topics worthy of and relevant to the Hispanic community.

The pressure to maintain fair and equitable representation of different Hispanic subgroups became a constant challenge for the network's leadership. Blaya and his team, which included Rosita Perú, had to balance internal demands with the expectations of a diverse and politically active viewership.

Villanueva's departure was followed by the resignations of Luis Nogales, national news director and Rosita Perú's husband, and Felipe Muñoz, news director in Los Angeles. At the same time, several managers were let go, and others in the California news department were forced to accept early retirement if they didn't agree to relocate to Florida.

In September 1990, *Los Angeles Times* staff writer Maria Newman wrote the following:

> The impending move, however, refuels criticism that Univision was "Cubanizing" the news. Since 1981, when the newscast first began and its owners debated where to locate its

headquarters, Latinos on the West Coast charged that taking it to Florida would give control of the news to Cubans and Cuban-Americans of Miami whom they said would slant the news to reflect anti-Castro and otherwise politically conservative views.

Her article continued:

> Local Latino leaders say they don't understand why the news operation has to move to Florida when most of its audience is in California, and is mostly Mexican-American.
>
> "It's a very strange thing in view of the population trends, with recent reports showing that California is not only the biggest state but the state with the biggest Hispanic population," said Esther Renteria, chairperson of the Los Angeles-based National Hispanic Media Coalition. "If you're going to serve your constituency, you need to be where they are."
>
> She agreed that the news program had presented a balanced view of Latinos nationwide but said this was only because "it's based here, and I don't see how you can be based in Miami, 3,000 miles away from most of your viewership. It's a very strange move."
>
> Said Raul Ruiz, Chicano studies professor at Cal State Northridge: "For them to get out of Southern California to go to Miami is a real slap in the face to their greatest supporters, the Mexican-American community."

After Nogales's resignation, Blaya hired veteran Cuban journalist Guillermo Martínez, who grew up in a family of reporters on his native island and came to the United States as a teenager along with his parents, who were fleeing Castro's revolution. Martínez studied journalism at the University of Florida and started working for the *Miami Herald* in 1975, where he proved instrumental in creating Spanish-language content that was included as a section of the paper from 1976 until the paper became *El Nuevo Herald*, a separate sister paper, in 1986. Blaya explained to Martínez that he needed to use his experience defending the Spanish language in the *Herald* and apply it nationally, thus empowering the Hispanic community at large by giving it an important role across the entire spectrum of news. And there was one other directive Blaya had for him: keep Jorge Ramos and María Elena Salinas as anchors of the nightly news.

Blaya didn't turn a deaf ear to the conflict with the Mexican American community. "We are not a Mexican, Cuban, or Puerto Rican channel. We are an American television station in Spanish," he repeatedly declared, both to Univision staff and the press in general. These were also the direct instructions he had received from Hallmark HQ in Kansas City: transform Univision into an American Spanish-language network.

Over the next three years, Blaya's work marked a milestone in U.S. Hispanic television. Together with Rosita Perú, and with a budget approved by the new owners, he set about the daunting task of Americanizing the network—although, to others, his efforts might have been better described as a "de-Mexicanization" of Univision's programming.

Jorge Ramos had to become the Hispanic Peter Jennings. From 1983 through 2005, Peter Charles Archibald Ewart Jennings (July 29, 1938–August 7, 2005) was one of the most famous news anchors in the United States. This Canadian American journalist was the primary anchor of *ABC World News Tonight*.

Despite never having formally studied journalism, Jennings is considered one of the most prominent journalists in television history. Today, Jorge Ramos is widely considered the Peter Jennings of Hispanic television.

On the suggestion from headquarters in Missouri, there would also be a daily show similar to Oprah Winfrey's, but in Spanish. With that in mind, Blaya hired Cuban Cristina Saralegui, well known as the editor of a major magazine and for standing out whenever she appeared as a guest on *Sábado Gigante* with Don Francisco. And, indeed, the subsequent *El Show de Cristina* (*Cristina's Show*) was considered *The Oprah Winfrey Show* equivalent in Spanish until the mid-2010s, when both programs aired their final broadcasts.

Blaya and the Hallmark executives also came up with the idea of creating a show similar to the famous *Entertainment Weekly* program that aired on Fox, only in Spanish. This led to the creation of *Primer Impacto* (*First Impact*), which continues to be one of the most watched programs on Univision to this day.

Additionally, there was a push to create a Hispanic version of the Grammys. Thus, Premios Lo Nuestro were born, which remain important awards given to the most beloved artists in Latin music. These awards later inspired the Latin Recording Academy to create the Latin Grammy Awards.

Hallmark executives also encouraged Blaya to create Spanish-language children's programming. Unfortunately, this initiative would fail. Blaya explains that they didn't take into account that school-age children primarily spoke English, and they already had their favorite programs being broadcast on English-language stations. At the time, there was still no strong motivation to promote bilingualism in children.

But aside from all of the above, it's important to note that the program that brought Blaya the greatest honor, satisfaction, and success in his professional career as a Hispanic television executive in the United States was still *Sábado Gigante*, hosted by his fellow Chilean Don Francisco. However, the relationship between these two didn't have a happy ending, leaving a swath fraught with mystery and tension behind. Details of this fallout will be revealed later.

Univision's Social Impact

From a business standpoint, one of the major accomplishments of Joaquín Blaya and the Hallmark executives was the negotiation of a multiyear contract with Nielsen, the corporate giant responsible for measuring television ratings and other data across networks. According to Blaya, Nielsen agreed to a $60 million contract to track Hispanic viewership. Once Univision began working with Nielsen, the network's sales surpassed the $200 million mark.

But something perhaps much more important for the penetration of Hispanic culture and influence in the United States occurred between 1990 and early 1992, when Univision succeeded in registering thousands of Cubans, who were already naturalized citizens, to vote. Miami experienced a political shift thanks to a number of factors, one of which was Univision, led by Joaquín Blaya and Hallmark. Blaya would appear on-screen, speaking on behalf of the network's owners, emphasizing the importance of becoming a U.S. citizen and exercising the right to vote in order to elect new politicians who would work for Florida's Hispanic community. The results were gradually becoming quite evident.

Today, Hispanic candidates are setting the tone in many places around the country, and we now see them serving in Congress as both senators and representatives: Bernie Moreno, Rubén Gallego, Alex Padilla, Catherine Cortez Masto, Ben Ray Luján, Pete Aguilar, Raul Grijalva, Juan Ciscomani, Adriano Espaillat, Darren Soto, Nydia Velázquez, Robert Garcia, Nanette Diaz Barragán, Tony Cárdenas, Joaquín Castro, Veronica Escobar, Sylvia Garcia, Teresa Leger Fernández, Nicole Malliotakis, Salud Carbajal, Henry Cuellar, Anna Eshoo, Lori Chavez-DeRemer, María Elvira Salazar, Linda Sánchez, and Alexandria Ocasio-Cortez, all of whom are leaders of steadily growing Latino caucuses. This is further reinforced by Supreme Court Justice Sonia Sotomayor and the recent appointment of Marco Rubio as secretary of state, further solidifying a Hispanic presence at the highest levels of the executive branch.

It's saddening to know that, even with all the transformation achieved by some of the Hallmark executives alongside Joaquín Blaya, the Chilean couldn't leave Univision through the front door.

CHAPTER 10

The Telenovela Business

As with any popular telenovela, the trials, joys, and rewards of the protagonists are key to understanding the essence of what Univision is today. The telenovela phenomenon has been a key part of the Hispanic television business. Unlike the endless soap operas of English-language TV networks, Hispanic telenovelas keep viewers, primarily women, glued to the screen, eagerly awaiting episode after episode until they reach the final one. In Hispanic telenovelas, unlike their American counterparts, there is a final chapter.

The First Telenovelas

As Professor Carolina Acosta-Alzuru of the University of Georgia, who specializes in the genre, explains, the first telenovelas were created in Cuba. Screenwriters emigrated from there, like Glória Magadan, who settled in Brazil, or Delia Fiallo, who traveled to Venezuela, or Inés Rodena, who first arrived in Venezuela before later making a great impact in Mexico. In that country, instead of promoting and crediting the telenovela's writer, only the adaptation by Televisa was advertised. This way, the network controlled any telenovela looking to break into the Mexican market. In the United States, the first telenovelas were broadcast on SIN and all were, for obvious reasons, Televisa products. Televisa is what drove the popularity of Mexican telenovelas on SIN.

El León Azcárraga knew that since the Golden Age of Mexican cinema (1936–1956), protagonists and their stories had resonated with audiences and influenced both Mexican culture and the nation itself. The success of Mexican Golden Age cinema demonstrated that the big screen was able to unite public sentiment and channel information to the masses. Social control through audiovisual entertainment was a given. With the arrival of television, that era came to an end, primarily due to President Adolfo López Mateos's decision to support the growth of television over cinema with greater resources.

The Mexican government was always the largest investor in the country's film industry, seeking to control content and, therefore, implement censorship to prevent the release of movies that expressed themes counterproductive to the power wielded by the current regime and its hegemonic party, the Institutional Revolutionary Party (PRI). El León was the first Azcárraga to realize that close ties with the government could serve as a first line of defense against potential competitors entering the arena, allowing them both to grow together and ensuring their grip on power. He was quite clever in convincing politicians of the time that it wasn't worth having more open TV channels if they could simply rely on corpoarate allies that understood the symbiotic relationship needed to consolidate power.

Unlike electricity, oil, metals, concrete, natural gas, and the national airline, television became the first industry that the government allowed the private sector to manage, albeit with a strong symbiotic connection that would allow them to control power and monopoly for years to come. Televisa and the PRI had something in common: the former was a monopoly reserved by the state, and the latter held the Mexican presidency for decades, propelled by Televisa. One protected the other.

The first telenovela broadcast Monday through Friday in Mexico began on June 9, 1958. Before that, this form of storytelling was known only through the radio. *Senda prohibida* (*Forbidden Path*) followed the life of Nora Valdez, a strong and independent young woman, and addressed social issues that broke the mold for its time. Though it was written by Fernanda Villeli, whose real name was María Ofelia Villenave Garza and who is considered the first Mexican telenovela creator, her role in the credits was reduced to "A Story by Fernanda Villeli." As Professor Acosta-Alzuru points out, unlike in Cuba, Brazil, and Venezuela, where the names of the writers were recognized and celebrated, this wasn't the case in Mexico. We all know who Delia Fiallo was, but few know who Fernanda Villeli was.

This was due to the fact that El León and, later, El Tigre sought to monopolize ownership of the telenovelas broadcast by Televisa in Mexico. This unique aspect of the telenovela business demonstrates how the Azcárragas' vision was one of commercial growth through control of the content they produced.

The case of Inés Rodena is one example of this phenomenon, which sought to diminish the importance of screenwriters in the credits so that rights to the intellectual property would remain with the Mexican broadcaster.

Born on April 20, 1905, in Havana, Cuba, Rodena was an influential writer of radionovelas and telenovelas. Before dedicating herself to writing, she worked as a nurse, and it was thanks to her experiences with patients and the stories told by those close to her that her passion for storytelling was born. In the 1950s, Rodena wrote her first radionovela, *La gata* (*The Stray Cat*), which was a huge success in pre-Castro Cuba. After the Cuban revolution, Rodena emigrated to Venezuela, where she was welcomed by telenovela producer Arquímedes Rivero, also Cuban, who recommended she go to Mexico, because he and Delia Fiallo were already active in the Venezuelan market.

Inés Rodena arrived in Mexico in 1970. There she met Valentín Pimstein, an important Chilean producer based in Mexico and a confidant of El León and El Tigre at Televisa. It was Pimstein who devised the legal strategy for acquiring the rights to Rodena's work for Mexico and the United States. That same year, *La gata* was released on Televisa; the credits read "Adapted by Pimstein" with no mention whatsoever of the true writer. *La gata* explored themes of social inequality, forbidden love, and the obstacles the main couple have to overcome in order to be together. Esmeralda, the protagonist, is illiterate until she meets Pablo Martínez Negrete, a rich young boy who teaches her how to read and write. Years later, Pablo realizes he's in love with Esmeralda, creating conflicts within his family. His mother tries to separate the couple by encouraging Pablo to fall for Mónica, a woman of higher social standing. Esmeralda becomes pregnant by Pablo, triggering a series of misunderstandings and more conflicts. Pablo's parents send him to study abroad, but before he leaves, he and Esmeralda marry in secret.

From that moment on, Inés Rodena's telenovelas began being produced in Mexico, with 1979's *Los ricos también lloran*, starring the young actress Verónica Castro, who became a standout success. The era of telenovelas either adapted or produced by Pimstein and owned by Televisa meant that Rodena's name went uncredited in everything broadcast by SIN in the United States.

In 1987, the telenovela *Rosa salvaje* (*Wild Rose*), based on an original story by Inés Rodena, became an unprecedented television phenomenon. Once again, Valentín Pimstein took sole credit as the producer, as the series captivated Mexican audiences before going on to conquer Hispanic viewers in the United States through Univision's broadcasts.

The plot, which developed over 198 episodes, revolved around Rosa García, a humble and impetuous young woman masterfully portrayed by Verónica Castro. Her life takes an unexpected turn when she falls in love with the wealthy Ricardo Linares. Guillermo Capetillo took on the challenge of playing a dual role, portraying both Ricardo and his twin brother Rogelio Linares, thus adding another layer of complexity and intrigue to the story. The success of *Rosa salvaje* was immediate and overwhelming. In Mexico, the telenovela reached historic viewership levels, doubling the ratings of other similar productions. The phenomenon was replicated when the series aired on Univision, consolidating its status as one of the most popular telenovelas of the era.

Telenovelas weren't simply entertainment. They also turned a lens on society, addressing relevant issues and providing a space for reflection and debate. The actresses who starred in these telenovelas, such as Angélica María, Verónica Castro, and Lucía Méndez, became cultural icons who influenced the fashion, behavior, and aspirations of millions of viewers.

The book *Telenovelas in Pan-Latino Context*, written by Harvard professor June Carolyn Erlick, chronicles the impact of Hispanic telenovelas on countries throughout Latin America and beyond. Erlick explains how these stories resonated with audiences who found in them a mirror of their own realities and dreams.

Exerting influence through its telenovelas was a calculated strategy by Televisa, leveraging the power of entertainment to consolidate its dominant position in the Spanish-speaking media market. The internationalization of Televisa's telenovelas began with the acquisition of the copyright to everything written by Delia Fiallo for adaptation and broadcast in Mexico and the United States. For the reasons mentioned above, the great Cuban telenovela scriptwriter, based in Miami, was more famous in South America than in Mexico or the United States.

The Spanish-language celebrity press, including magazines like *Vanidades*, *Cosmopolitan*, and *TV Guía*, enticed readers with behind-the-scenes love stories involving El Tigre and other network executives and their preferred actresses, particularly the telenovela leads. Having grown accustomed to blocking and censoring content that might harm his companies' interests, El Tigre never bothered wielding his power against the gossip magazines that portrayed him as the most dashing leading man among the many telenovela heartthrobs who appeared on his network.

Internally, his image was that of a patriarch who protected his talent based on fame and loyalty. There was no need for one-sided contracts that exploit the artists; El Tigre's attitude toward his closest talents was parental. His leadership was based on trust, but any hint of disloyalty or leaking information about remuneration, travels, or private evenings meant being cut off professionally; it was like a curse that everyone feared.

For El Tigre, it wasn't just about protecting his public image; it was about maintaining a solid and trustworthy internal ecosystem. Artists knew that, by following the unwritten rules of discretion and loyalty, they enjoyed unwavering support. But crossing that line was met with severe consequences, such as being exiled from the world of telenovelas.

In conversations I've had with those telenovela producers who dared to broach the topic, they claim that several of the actresses—as well as a few actors—had direct access to the station owners, and that their relationships could easily be considered quite close.

El Tigre paid a great deal of attention to the content his station was broadcasting. It was a means of promoting a sort of social control, and it was a key strategy for exercising the power of communication in a country as large and complex as Mexico. This social control exercised by Televisa was evident in the content it broadcast. The network ensured that telenovelas and other programming reflected a positive image of high society and its leaders, and that topics that might reflect the injustices experienced by ordinary Mexicans were avoided. Unlike other countries, such as Brazil, where telenovelas were starting to address issues of class discrimination, skin color, and corruption, Televisa maintained a narrative that supported the status quo and projected a favorable image of the rich and powerful. Mexican telenovelas, as entertaining as they were, rarely trained a critical eye on the country's political or social reality. Instead, they focused on stories that distracted audiences with dramatic, romantic themes that captivated their attention.

A clear example of this strategy was 1979's *Los Ricos También Lloran,* starring Verónica Castro. This was the first telenovela to show that the rich were not immune to suffering, therefore humanizing the upper classes and diverting attention from real-world social problems. While Brazilian telenovelas like *Roque Santeiro* openly criticized corruption and social hypocrisy, in Mexico the stories centered on personal and romantic conflicts, treading cautiously around any political or social implications that might upset the government or mobilize the masses against them.

On February 11, 1993, in an interview with journalist Alejandro Salazar Hernández published by the newspaper *El Nacional*, Emilio Azcárraga Milmo said that "Mexico is a country whose working class is completely screwed... It'll never get out of this mess. Television has an obligation to bring entertainment to these people and take them away from their sad reality and difficult future."

This statement sparked considerable controversy and has since been widely cited as an example of how Azcárraga viewed television in Mexico and his perceptions of its audience. The comment is a starkly provocative take on social stratification in Mexico and the role of mass media when it comes to the less-fortunate socioeconomic classes. There are, however, those who understand El Tigre's words as a brutally honest portrayal of his television audience and the role his company should take with regards to them. In either case, with this controversial statement, Azcárraga exposed his content strategy, which would later carry over to SIN and, eventually, to Univision.

Meanwhile, from 1980 to the 1990s, telenovelas in Brazil, Colombia, and Venezuela not only tackled moral issues rarely confronted in public, but they denounced economic and racial discrimination and even lobbed direct criticism at their own governments. Without naming names or locations, the storylines were easy to associate with real-life events, and many business and political leaders recognized themselves as the protagonists. Scripts of this kind were fully edited by Televisa in Mexico, and any denunciation of the government or racial discrimination was redacted and replaced.

The telenovela business became a powerful industry not only for its entertainment value but also for its ability to influence public opinion and dramatically reflect the social realities of Spanish-speaking countries. Televisa, under the direction of Azcárraga, understood that melodrama was both a means for capturing mass audiences and also a tool for shaping perceptions and behaviors. This understanding led to the creation of a formula for success based on the repetition of certain tropes and archetypes that guaranteed high ratings.

Mexican and Venezuelan telenovelas became highly valuable as export products and represented an extremely important alternate source of income for Televisa. This phenomenon began in the 1980s and 1990s, when demand for telenovelas grew significantly in a number of international markets. Exporting telenovelas not only drove up Televisa's revenue, it also strengthened its global presence and prestige.

The period between 1986 and 1991 was the only time during which no member of the Azcárraga family held any shares of Univision. El Tigre tried to maintain a relationship through the newscast, but Joaquín Blaya wouldn't allow it. But there was one business that had to maintain a relationship with Televisa: the telenovela business.

Die Hard

El Tigre began making frequent visits to Los Angeles to explore new business ventures. While he was there, he would keep an eye on the sale of content, especially telenovelas, to Univision. To that end, he maintained the Univisa company. In July 1988, the blockbuster hit *Die Hard,* starring Bruce Willis, was released in theaters. El Tigre instructed Jaime Escandón, Univisa's CFO, to purchase the penthouse in the Fox Plaza tower, the very same tower where the movie was filmed and which has since become known throughout the world as the Nakatomi Tower from the film. Perhaps El Tigre was trying to send a message from that penthouse that he was a "die hard" feline. What he never imagined was that the recently retired U.S. president Ronald Reagan would also become enamored with that very same penthouse. According to El Tigre, his friend and now adviser former ambassador John Gavin called him to ask him to let Reagan have it. And so he did: El Tigre gave it up to the Ronald Reagan Presidential Foundation and ended up moving one floor down.

Univision continued purchasing telenovelas produced by Televisa, considering the network's dependence on Mexican productions in order to maintain a popular lineup and cater to the demanding Mexican American audience. A prime example of this is 1982's family-oriented telenovela *Chispita*. Televisa sold the rights to this two-hundred-episode show to Univision for a little more than $12,000 per episode—significant revenue, obviously. For Televisa, the deal was doubly lucrative, because the production costs for *Chispita* and many other telenovelas had already been covered during their original broadcast in Mexico, meaning that all export sales monies were pure profit because there was no need for additional production expenses.

What few people know is that *Chispita* was a remake of a work originally written by the Argentine Abel Santa Cruz and titled *Andrea Celeste*. The work was acquired for Televisa by Pimstein, who changed the name of the show and made a few minor changes to the script. The final credits simply read "Produced and adapted by Valentín Pimstein."

Telenovela Finances

Another example of Televisa's great financial success was its exporting of the hit telenovela *Rosa salvaje*, which we discussed previously. The 198 episodes were seen in fifteen countries, with each episode selling for an average of $16,000. A simple calculation suggests that *Rosa salvaje* generated nearly $50 million in revenue for Televisa during El Tigre's tenure. This also might explain the unique, almost queenlike treatment that El Tigre conferred upon Verónica Castro, the star of the show.

Blaya tried to free himself from his dependence on Televisa's telenovelas, but this proved all but impossible. The only alternative at the time was to turn to Venezuelan productions, but the giant there, Venevisión, couldn't realistically compete with Televisa, largely because of the close-knit relationship between El Tigre and Gustavo Cisneros, who some in Miami even referred to as El Tigrito: (The Little Tiger). The other option was Coral Pictures, which marketed the telenovelas broadcast by Venevisión's rival, RCTV. These productions, however, were extremely expensive, costing more than $80,000 per episode. Brazilian telenovelas were only just beginning to be translated into Spanish, and Telemundo was already in negotiations for the first few. Brazil's Rede Globo was starting to gain international recognition with telenovelas like 1988's *Vale tudo* (*Anything Goes*), which addressed topics like corruption and social inequality.

In the 1980s, economic crises in Argentina, Colombia, and Peru hindered any serious attempts at producing content that could compete with Mexican or Venezuelan telenovelas. In Chile, production of telenovelas had ground to a halt during one of the most turbulent periods of Augusto Pinochet's dictatorship, which was then in its final stages. Blaya was one of the first Hispanic television executives to explore the idea of producing telenovelas in the United States, but he didn't have the time to fully pursue it. El Tigre took advantage of this dependence on Mexican shows produced by Televisa to preserve his financial and strategic control over Univision, ensuring that telenovelas would remain a cornerstone of Hispanic prime-time TV in the United States.

In addition to this astute approach to dominating the television market in both Mexico and the United States, El Tigre, along with his soldier/producer Valentín Pimstein, implemented strategies that prevented many telenovelas from other countries from taking advantage of the booming export market. Televisa acquired the copyrights to telenovelas from various South American scriptwriters, Chileans and Argentines in particular, and then adapted their works, often changing the titles and removing the original writers from the credits altogether. In some cases, the rights were bought with the simple intention of keeping the content out of anyone else's hands, meaning that those telenovelas were never even broadcast in either Mexico or the United States. This practice not only ensured that Televisa could present itself as the creator of original content but also monopolize the telenovela export market and prevent other producers from even having a chance at competing. Under this strategy, Televisa became the leading exporter of telenovelas to a variety of countries, including Israel, Russia, the Philippines, Indonesia, Greece, Turkey, Italy, and Spain, among others. This international expansion further solidified Televisa's power and El Tigre's stature, allowing them to influence audiences' tastes and preferences on a global scale.

During Joaquín Blaya's tenure at Univision, between 1986 and 1991, eighteen of Televisa's telenovelas were aired. Together with Rosita Perú, the two were able to negotiate the rights to three others from Venevisión International. And, in 1990, they also acquired the telenovela *Emperatriz*, independently produced and released that same year by Marte Televisión, owned by Venezuelan businessman Hernán Pérez Belisario. After 1991, Univision would exclusively acquire telenovelas from just two sources: Televisa and Venevisión.

Telemundo produced a few telenovelas in Puerto Rico without much success, but in 1988, it shocked the market by daring to film *Angélica, mi vida* (*Angélica, My Life*) in Miami, starring Mexican actress Laura Fabián and Puerto Rican actor Carlos Montalvo. Then, two years later, Telemundo made an innovative move of its own, partnering with Peruvian businessman José Enrique Crousillat, founder of a new Miami-based production company called Capitalvision International Corporation, which was backed by a wealthy Armenian Venezuelan investor. That same year, this partnership adapted and produced *El magnate* (*The Magnate*), starring Venezuelan actress Ruddy Rodríguez and Dominican-born, naturalized Mexican heartthrob Andrés

García. *El magnate* was an adaptation of the Brazilian telenovela *Novo amor* (*New Love*), written by Manoel Carlos.

This production, broadcast on Telemundo, caught the attention of El Tigre so much so that he agreed to meet with Crousillat and talk business. Televisa would end up buying Capitalvision International, and in the midst of Telemundo's financial crisis and looming bankruptcy, rumors swirled that El Tigre might reenter the U.S. Hispanic television market by purchasing the struggling network. Crousillat, for his part, continued working as a producer, though he began dividing his time between Miami and Peru, having become one of the key communications advisers to the newly elected president Alberto Fujimori: one of the factors that led him to sell his company to El Tigre.

CHAPTER 11

El Tigre Returns

By 1990, Univision was also facing financial and political pressures. CEO J. William Grimes had taken on the challenge of increasing the company's valuation in hopes of selling or refinancing it, but the plan wasn't working. The burden of debt, along with the financial obligations Hallmark had taken on to acquire SIN in 1986, had become truly oppressive. Keep in mind that the $300 million Univision owed was almost entirely issued in bonds, most of which had been purchased by Continental Illinois Bank, which had been deemed "too big to fail" and was bailed out by the FDIC. The first signs of a financial crisis at Univision became public when the company called in creditors to try to negotiate a debt reduction.

It was a difficult negotiation that required the support of a friendly government administration: that of George H. W. Bush. By that time, however, Bush's approval ratings had plummeted, and it seemed increasingly likely that he wouldn't have a second term in office. Hockaday and Grimes knew they had to negotiate the bonds and sell the company before the 1992 presidential election. Once again, Univision was headed toward a forced sale, a scenario that had nothing to do with the positive reception of its content or even its commercial success. It was a necessary liquidation by owners who had overhauled their 1986 investment and overleveraged the company in a now-hostile political climate. Bill Clinton's candidacy was starting to take hold, and 1992 ended with a defeat for the Republican Party at the national level.

Blaya's tireless efforts to meet the goals set by Hockaday and Hallmark, who had bet heavily on a Bush reelection, were paying off—just not enough to carry Bush to victory. A closer look at the results in Florida and Arizona, two states where Univision had significant influence, reveals a different outcome: the Republican Party had narrowly hung on to both critical states. Political analysts suggest that the Hispanic vote in Florida and Arizona had played a central role in tipping the balance in Bush's favor in those states. This was Blaya's final act at Univision. His limited knowledge—or, perhaps, his limited interest—in Univision's financial intricacies kept him from recognizing opportunities to position himself with potential new buyers. The writing was on the wall: the network would be sold by Hockaday, and Blaya's reign would come to an end.

Meanwhile, a separate crisis was erupting at Telemundo, and at the center of it was El Tigre, who was leaning toward what seemed like a very tempting opportunity. Carlos Barba, Telemundo's vice president of programming, won him over, convincing him to produce the 1992 telenovela *Marielena,* starring Lucía Méndez for Telemundo. The telenovela was sure to be a hit, so Méndez had El Tigre's blessing to work with Univision's competition without jeopardizing her relationship with him. At the time, Lucía Méndez was treated like royalty at Televisa. The shows she starred in generated tens of millions of dollars for El Tigre.

During the production of *Marielena*, Barba was contacted by his former boss at NetSpan WNJU, Jerry Perenchio, who was still intent on playing a leading role in this saga. Perenchio informed Barba that he intended to acquire Univision and wanted to bring him onboard as an adviser. Barba then reached out to El Tigre to let him know what was going on at Univision. Barba also told his former boss at Venevisión Internacional, Gustavo Cisneros, about what was going on. He suggested that Perenchio meet with Cisneros before making any decisions.

Grimes accelerated the bond negotiations and the sale of Univision. It was a shrewd and intricate financial maneuver that allowed Hallmark to emerge with its reputation intact. For them, the deal paid off. The biggest loser in this equation was the U.S. government, represented by Continental Illinois Bank. As the largest bondholder and creditor, the bank was forced to accept a 50 percent cut on the bond principal.

Someone who also came out with the short end of the stick was Lucía Méndez. Although the actress had El Tigre's permission to star in the hit show *Marielena*, broadcast on Telemundo, El Tigre abandoned his intentions to buy that station and focused instead on joining Jerry Perenchio and Gustavo Cisneros in buying Univision from Hallmark. In the telenovela, Marielena, played by Méndez, a beautiful young woman of humble origins, falls in love with her wealthy married boss, Luis Felipe, played by Eduardo Yáñez. Many years later, Méndez would explain how El Tigre, by then back with Univision, refused to hire her because doing so would have violated his golden rule for talent in the corporate game: never work for the competition. That act of "infidelity," which El Tigre had once accepted yet never publicly acknowledged, was no longer tolerated.

In April 1992, Hallmark announced the sale of Univision to a group of investors led by Jerry Perenchio, Gustavo Cisneros, and Emilio Azcárraga Milmo for $550 million. The ownership structure established during the transaction gave Perenchio a 75 percent majority stake in the Univision station group and a 50 percent stake in the network's ad-sales company. El Tigre, along with brothers Gustavo and Ricardo Cisneros, each retained a 12.5 percent stake in the station group and a 25 percent stake in the ad-sales company.

The assets included in the sale were nine full-power television stations located in major cities across the United States, as well as four low-power stations, all of which were carrying Univision programming. Financially, Perenchio agreed to contribute up to $50 million of the purchase price, and Hallmark accepted a promissory note payable of up to $100 million. The remainder was structured through a combination of debt and content contributions in exchange for equity from the Azcárraga and Cisneros families. Thus began a new era in the history of the country's most influential Hispanic network.

Telemundo's Bankruptcy

It was around that same time that Telemundo had defaulted on its debts and was sliding into a financial crisis made even worse by the landfall in the United States of Hurricane Andrew. The tropical cyclone, which hit South Florida on August 24, 1992, caused severe damage to the region, including to Telemundo's facilities. The storm, a category 5 hurricane, destroyed more than 63,500 homes and damaged more than124,000 others, delivering a devastating economic blow to the area. Telemundo's headquarters, located in Hialeah, took a direct hit. The network's entire infrastructure was affected, forcing the company to make significant repairs and other adjustments to its operations.

Carlos Barba's star was fading almost in time with Telemundo's financial collapse. In early 1990, Barba's mentor, the magnate Henry Silverman, announced he was leaving Reliance Capital to become a general partner of the Blackstone Group in New York, though he would remain a member of Telemundo's board of directors for four more years. In mid-1991, shortly after *Marielena* wrapped production, Barba resigned. Months after his departure, Telemundo stopped making payments both on interest and principal on its debt. Toward the end of the year, the company was facing bankruptcy, having defaulted on more than $300 million worth of obligations. Creditors started banding together to take action against Telemundo and its principal owner, Reliance Capital. The clash between creditors and owners lasted two years. On June 8, 1993, the creditors filed an involuntary chapter 11 petition in U.S. Bankruptcy Court in New York, and on July 30 of that same year, Telemundo consented to the petition. By then, Blaya was already preparing for his exit from Univision and entering talks with Telemundo. During those negotiations, he offered to bring Don Francisco and *Sábado Gigante* onboard with him.

Mario Kreutzberger, for his part, confirmed that, yes, at the time, Blaya was trying to lure him, his production team, and his show to Telemundo. He requested a meeting with El Tigre. Until that moment, the two had never met in person. El Tigre agreed to the meeting and invited Mario to meet on his yacht, the *ECO*, off the coast of Fort Lauderdale.

Kreutzberger, who owned a yacht of his own, gave instructions to set sail for the *ECO*. When they arrived at the marina, there weren't any large ships in sight, which is when the captain told Mario that the *ECO* was so massive it couldn't even dock there. As he later recounted in one of his two autobiographies, Kreutzberger wrote that his own yacht looked more like a lifeboat next to the imposing *ECO*.

The meeting with El Tigre proved crucial for *Sábado Gigante*'s future. It was there that Kreutzberger and El Tigre reached an agreement to continue broadcasting the show nationally via Univision.

No one knows exactly who made the call for Blaya to leave Univision. Those close to El Tigre say he was fired, while others in Blaya's circle claim he resigned, already having an offer in hand to become CEO of Telemundo.

Then, like a gust of wind vanishing in the night, Blaya's reign at Univision came to an end. In the twilight of his era, this leader found himself stripped of his stronghold. The very company that had once embraced him, in which he had forged what seemed to be an ironclad shield, let all that power slip through his fingers like grains of sand. At Telemundo, he was never able to replicate the success he had achieved at Univision, and one of the key reasons for this was that he was never able to carry over the crown jewel: Don Francisco and *Sábado Gigante*. Fate, as marked by what may have been feline wounds, denied him that final wish. While Joaquín Blaya would continue to find success in the field, I daresay that his symphony of glory ended with Univision.

As Blaya was on his way out, Carlos Barba entered as an adviser to the purchasing group led by Jerry Perenchio.

That year, 1992, also marked El Tigre's return to Univision, now under Perenchio's control. Perenchio moved Univision's headquarters to the thirtieth floor of 1999 Avenue of the Stars, a newly constructed skyscraper in Los Angeles: the beginning of a new and revitalized chapter for the Mexican magnate who, just two years earlier, had publicly announced his romantic relationship with former Miss Mexico and model Adriana Abascal, forty years his junior. That was also the same year he received the delivery of his superyacht, the *ECO*, in English waters.

But 1993 would tell a different story. El Tigre received a diagnosis from MD Anderson in Houston, the same cancer center where his father had been treated decades earlier and to which he had just sent some test results for unusual spots on his skin: melanoma.

The news devastated El Tigre. He underwent immediate treatment and followed with ongoing checkups. His young partner, Adriana Abascal, dedicated herself to caring for him.

Battling this illness wasn't easy. The treatments were withering, involving frequent hospital visits, radiation therapy, and a strict regimen of medications. When his health began to worsen, Azcárraga decided to move to Miami, where he would be far removed from his business world. Very few in the organization knew what was happening, and many were surprised by his move to the city he so often criticized. Adriana, once radiant in the spotlight as a beauty queen and model, now faced her most challenging and vital role: being El Tigre's pillar of support.

On the professional front, Gustavo Cisneros, Azcárraga's close friend and ally, took a more active role in Univision's operations. Recognized for his business acumen and ability to navigate international markets, Cisneros ensured that the company didn't lose momentum during these turbulent times.

The year 1993 was also a year of significant transformations in the media landscape. Under Perenchio's leadership, Univision began to explore new opportunities and expand its programming to attract a more diverse and demanding audience. Amid those changes, news of Azcárraga's cancer diagnosis remained largely out of the public eye. Only an intimate circle of family and friends were aware of his condition. This allowed El Tigre to maintain an image of strength and control while privately dealing with his rigorous treatments. For those who knew, El Tigre's fight against cancer became a testament to his indomitable spirit and ability to face adversity with equal parts courage and dignity, even though his public appearances grew increasingly rare.

There were two people in El Tigre's past with whom he decided to reconnect in order to share his diagnosis and treatment plans. One of them was René Anselmo. But what neither of these two old friends could have possibly imagined was that Anselmo would be the first of them to go.

The other important person in Azcárraga's life was his ex-wife, Paula Cusi. Despite their separation, the two met a number of times to reminisce and discuss the Mexican magnate's health. These meetings, for obvious reasons, took place without Adriana Abascal's presence.

While all of this was going on, Jerry Perenchio took advantage of El Tigre's estrangement from operations, making it unmistakably clear who held the majority stake in Univision now.

CHAPTER 12

Soccer Fever Hits the United States

It was El Tigre Azcárraga who brought soccer fever to the United States. He played a leading role in the exponential growth of FIFA's (the French acronym for Fédération Internationale de Football Association) financial and political power between 1982 and 1998. But before we get to FIFA, we have to go back to the late 1950s through the early 1970s.

The year was 1959, and at the age of twenty-nine, El Tigre made the personal decision to acquire the Mexican professional soccer team Club América from businessman Isaac Bessudo, owner of the Mexican soft drink company Jarritos, for MX$ 425,000, equivalent to US$23,120, according to the exchange rate at the time. El León celebrated his son's decision, seeing it as a demonstration of his vision, determination, and independence.

El Tigre hired Guillermo Cañedo de la Bárcena, who was then the president of the Mexican Football Federation (FMF). The federation was the governing body that regulated and made decisions about everything related to the country's professional league and the Mexican national soccer team. As a result, Club América was now at the forefront of Mexican soccer, as it also had the backing and broadcasting power of Telesistema Mexicano. In other words, El Tigre quickly became the primary promoter and perhaps even the czar of what was then the budding soccer craze in Mexico.

The 1962 World Cup was being played in Chile, a nation whose fan base was already as massive and passionate as any in Europe. Uruguay, Brazil, Argentina, and Chile were countries where the sport was a religion. Chile built the monumental Estadio Nacional in Santiago to host the final. It was at that event that Cañedo suggested El Tigre elevate the status of soccer in both Mexico and the world by building the largest stadium in all of the Americas in Mexico City.

With the help of the Mexican government, Telesistema Mexicano broke ground on the construction of the Estadio Azteca in 1962. It opened four years later with a match between Club América and the Italian Torino Football Club, a very popular franchise in European soccer at the time. FIFA officials were present at the match, which ended in a 2–2 draw, and were already scouting for the next host for the 1970 World Cup. The 1966 tournament was played in England, and it was there in London that Mexico was announced as host for the following World Cup in 1970. It was a tremendous achievement for the Emilio Azcárraga Milmo–Guillermo Cañedo de la Bárcena duo.

The 1970 World Cup was not only a sporting triumph for Mexico but also a milestone in the history of global television. The push to broadcast the matches across the globe via satellite was a masterstroke orchestrated from the heart of Telesistema Mexicano. The young Emilio Azcárraga Milmo saw satellite technology as a golden opportunity to position Mexican television at the forefront of global media innovation. But he knew that, in order to achieve this, he would need to convince two key figures: his father, Emilio Azcárraga Vidaurreta, El León, and, more important, the man who could truly open the doors to this revolution: the president of Mexico, Gustavo Díaz Ordaz.

El Tigre recognized that the World Cup represented the perfect platform for Mexico to demonstrate its technological prowess. However, successfully broadcasting an event of this magnitude live via satellite would require government intervention, because Intelsat, the consortium that governed telecommunications in space, operated under the control of its member countries' governments. Achieving this successful broadcast would require major political maneuvering.

Azcárraga Vidaurreta, leveraging his influence within Mexico's power structure, did what his son asked. Through Interior Secretary Luis Echeverría, El León conveyed the proposal directly to Díaz Ordaz: it wasn't enough to simply host the World Cup. Mexico had to be the first country in history to broadcast the event live, in color, via satellite. It was an ambitious idea, but it aligned perfectly with the image of modernity that the government wanted to project. In the end, it was agreed that Mexico would not only host the world's greatest sporting event but would also become the epicenter of an unprecedented media and technological revolution.

It was in this context that René Anselmo saw his first great opportunity, and thanks to his closeness to the Azcárragas, he was able to gain access to the heart of this televised experiment. He observed, firsthand, the negotiations with Intelsat, how Mexico was integrating itself with the global broadcast network, but more than anything, he saw how the power of television could transcend borders. That moment was a revelation for Anselmo. As we've seen, years later, he would become one of the key players in the private satellite television revolution, but back then, in the late 1960s, his first lesson in the immense power of global broadcasting came courtesy of the Azcárragas' vision.

On Sunday, May 31, 1970, President Gustavo Díaz Ordaz inaugurated the FIFA World Cup with a match that resulted in a 0–0 draw between Mexico and the Soviet Union. Millions of viewers around the world were able to watch the opening match in full color, but one of the most anticipated matches for the global audience was when soccer superstar Pelé's Brazilian squad faced Czechoslovakia. The Czechoslovakian team shocked everyone by scoring first, but the magic of the Brazilian team soon took control of the match. With goals from Rivellino and Pelé, and a brace from Jairzinho, Brazil, sealed a resounding 4–1 victory. But beyond the score, it was the iconic canary yellow jersey of Brazil that shone with a clarity never before seen on TV screens, highlighting every move of Pelé, whose dazzling skills captivated the global audience. For the first time, people were able to experience the excitement of soccer at its finest from the comfort of their own homes. It was an innovation for which El Tigre is rarely, if ever, given credit.

The Estadio Azteca was the venue for the final match in which Brazil, led by the great Pelé, was crowned champion. The government of Mexico, as the host country, also negotiated agreements with the other nations who competed in the tournament. As a result of this massive event, not only was Pelé catapulted into global stardom as the first true soccer celebrity, having captured his third World Cup, but fans around the world also began to identify and admire the colors that defined the national teams.

THE NEW YORK TIMES JUNE 21, 1970

PELE!

BRAZIL BEATS ITALY 4-1 FOR WORLD CUP

Brazil struck first, with Pelé heading in a cross by Rivelino at the 18th minute, Roberto Boninsegna equalized for Italy after a blunder in the Brazilian defence. In the second half, Brazil's firepower and creativity was too much for an Italian side that clung to their cautious defensive system. Gérson fired in a powerful shot for the second goal, and then helped provide the third, with a long free kick to Pelé who headed down into the path of the onrushing Jairzinho. Pelé capped his superb performance by drawing the Italian defence in the centre and feeding captain Carlos Alberto on the right flank for the final score. Carlos Alberto's goal, after a series of moves by the Brazilian team from the left to the centre, is considered one of the greatest goals ever scored in the history of the tournament.

King Pelé lifts his third trophy at the Mexico 1970 World Cup. (Image: Clipping from the June 21, 1970, edition of *The New York Times.*)

However, the financial benefits weren't immediately evident, as the scale of the investment in the stadium by the Azcárragas and the Mexican government, along with the technology used for the live broadcasts, weren't quite met by the business that staging the World Cup would later generate.

At the time, the World Cup was a great gift to the Mexican people and a powerful platform for the country's propaganda on a global stage. Two years prior, in 1968, Mexico had also hosted the Olympic Games with tremendous success, and the role of the Azcárraga-owned television station was crucial then as well. SIN used Telesistema Mexicano's signal to broadcast first the Olympics and then the World Cup. To give an idea of the limited awareness the Anglo-American television networks in the United States had when it came to the significance of soccer for a significant portion of the population, ABC, which had acquired broadcasting rights for the World Cup for pennies on the dollar, waited until Christmas to air the final match, which originally took place on June 21. To put it another way, ABC made its audience wait six months to see a historic match that all of Latin America and Europe had eagerly watched live. That was one of the few times that El León and El Tigre were seen together in the Azteca's presidential box, celebrating the successful organization of a world-class sporting event, and a powerful image of Mexico on the world stage.

El Tigre wasn't just a key figure on the national soccer scene. He also played a key role in the sport's international expansion. Cañedo saw a great opportunity: only sixteen countries were competing in the World Cup, but that number could grow. Plus, the global appeal of O Rei "the King" Pelé, and the Brazilian team made it increasingly feasible to envision FIFA's leadership shifting from being led predominantly by Europeans to Latin

American leaders. El Tigre began moving the pieces on his chessboard to implement a strategy for gaining control of FIFA. At the 1968 Olympic Games, Azcárraga Milmo met the president of the Brazilian Olympic Committee, Jean-Marie Faustin Godefroid "João" Havelange. From that moment on, João Havelange and El Tigre built a lifelong friendship that lasted until the latter's death in 1997.

El Tigre's plan for soccer and television also extended to his relationship with Havelange and FIFA. Since 1974, his influence helped transform the organization and elevate the sport's profile worldwide. By the end of the 1970 World Cup, El Tigre had already identified a significant source of revenue through advertising sales during the broadcast of World Cup matches and understood the growing importance of the World Cup's brand image to the governments of both the host and the participating countries. El Tigre and Cañedo decided to convince Havelange to run for president of FIFA, given Brazil's status as the world leader in soccer. Cañedo was then tasked with working with the president of the South American Football Confederation, known as CONMEBOL— a Peruvian named Teófilo Nicolás Salinas Fuller—to develop a campaign aimed at taking control of FIFA through the election of João Havelange and Guillermo Cañedo de la Bárcena as president and vice president, respectively. On May 8, 1974, one month before the start of the World Cup in what was then West Germany, elections for the new FIFA Council were held behind closed doors in Frankfurt. Havelange, a Brazilian, was voted president, and Cañedo, a Mexican, became his vice president.

Starting that same year, FIFA changed its business model, significantly increasing its revenue through the sale of radio and television broadcasting rights and official sponsorships of global corporate brands. FIFA's new business branch (as it were) was established by Cañedo and Havelange. They also implemented an expansion plan that increased the number of participating nations from sixteen to twenty-four, with the tournament still being a quadrennial event. For the next several years, El Tigre acquired World Cup broadcasting rights throughout the Americas, from Canada to Argentina, on behalf of Televisa. Salinas Fuller was in charge of coordinating the South American federations, while El Tigre managed the broadcasting in Mexico and the United States. Brazil was easy to negotiate with thanks to Havelange's relationship with Roberto Marinho, a media magnate with Brazil's media monopoly Grupo Globo.

In June 1974, just before the World Cup kicked off in West Germany, the host nations for the two upcoming tournaments—Spain for 1982 and Colombia for 1986—were announced. But just a few months after the conclusion of España '82, Colombian President Belisario Betancur announced that his country would not be able to meet the requirements for hosting the event. Immediately, Mexico, Canada, and the United States submitted bids to serve as a replacement. The FIFA Council decided on Mexico, causing great controversy and anger among the American and Canadian governments. The United States even requested a meeting with Havelange, which included Henry Kissinger as head of the delegation in order to prove that they would be the ideal host for the 1986 World Cup. But FIFA, led by Havelange, Cañedo, and Salinas Fuller, was steadfast in its choice of a Spanish-speaking country that had a much deeper fervor and passion for soccer than the American public. Snubbing Kissinger resulted in a wave of rumors of corruption and collusion between Havelange and Cañedo that even extended to Azcárraga Milmo himself.

As a result of this commercial strategy implemented by El Tigre and FIFA, the Spanish-language broadcast rights for every World Cup from 1970 through 2014 were owned by Televisa and Univision in both Mexico and the United States. World Cup television rights began to represent FIFA's primary source of income. The success of this marketing strategy is reflected in the rising value of those rights, from the $20 million paid by ESPN for the USA '94 and France '98 World Cups to the $428 million paid by Fox in 2018 and 2022.

El Tigre and Cañedo developed an extraordinary ability to negotiate through their deep understanding of the global market, allowing FIFA to both expand its reach and increase its revenue, which benefited the sport and the countries that supported it. On January 20, 1997, Guillermo Cañedo de la Bárcena suffered a fatal heart attack. This was a devastating blow to El Tigre, whose own health was also in rapid decline. Shattered, Azcárraga Milmo would die just three months later.

The Havelange and Cañedo dynasty at FIFA ended abruptly with the deaths of these two Mexican visionaries. Havelange would step down as president of FIFA a year later. El Tigre asked that the Estadio Azteca be renamed after Guillermo Cañedo, and his wish was granted. Shortly after El Tigre's death, though, the stadium reverted to its original name, the Azteca.

CHAPTER 13

Latina USA and Latin Music

To understand the evolution of the image of Latinas in the United States, it's essential to look at the career of Cristina María Saralegui Santamarina, a Cuban woman who came from a family in the paper industry on the island before the arrival of Fidel Castro and his revolution in 1959. Like many Cuban families after Castro's rise to power, the Saraleguis decided to move to Miami, where Cristina grew up bilingual. She went on to study communications and began her career working for the magazine *Vanidades*.

In the 1950s, Venezuelan businessmen Armando de Armas and Miguel Ángel Capriles acquired the Spanish-language rights to the Hearst magazines *Mecánica Popular* (*Popular Mechanics*), *Buenhogar* (*Good Housekeeping*), and *Cosmopolitan*, in addition to creating Editorial América. This publishing group also took over ownership of *Vanidades*, which had belonged to Editorial Carteles in Cuba, where Cristina Saralegui's father worked. Capriles left the group in 1970 and Editorial América was taken over by the newly created Venezuelan publishing group Bloque De Armas.

In her book *Cristina! My Life as a Blonde*, Saralegui confesses that her career was shaped by everything she learned while working for Armando de Armas, whom she describes as a "formidable man who started working at the age of nine, selling newspapers to support his family. Don Armando, as everyone affectionately calls him, grew up to become the most important Spanish-language publisher in all of Latin America and owned the largest magazine conglomerate in the region."

It was through working with the De Armas family since 1970 that Cristina learned to write in a style she describes as "Pan-American Spanish," because *Vanidades* was distributed in twenty-three countries where different terms were used. Saralegui supported the inclusion of many Spanish words and expressions from the Hispanic readership in the United States.

With the editorial freedom granted to her by De Armas at *Vanidades*, Saralegui learned to communicate in a Spanish that, although different from that of the various Latin American countries, could be understood by all, including U.S. Hispanics. She also imposed a rule of not using any word that could be perceived as obscene in any Spanish-speaking nation. For example, as Cristina says, "María Conchita Alonso, a Cuban-Venezuelan singer and actress, was referred to simply as María when she toured in Argentina," where "concha" is a slang term for vagina.

Saralegui was later transferred from *Vanidades* to work on a magazine project called *Intimidades*, situating herself closer to the lives of Latina women. In 1979, she was appointed editor in chief of *Cosmopolitan en español*, which was the first magazine to talk openly about sex with Latinas in their own language. But it was Saralegui herself who imposed her editorial stamp, "Cristina Style," which journalists would later refer to as "Latina Style." "Our most important organ is located between our ears, not between our legs," she said when defining the editorial style she intended to establish at the magazine, one that derived from the Anglo-American editorial tradition of focusing heavily on the exploitation of sexual content. The difference, according to Cristina, was that Hispanic women didn't need liberation; they needed empowerment. *Cosmopolitan en español* became a powerful source of information for Latinas.

There wasn't a single singer or actress who would skip a visit to the magazine's editorial offices. In 1992, Editorial América was acquired by El Tigre, who transformed it into Editorial Televisa and moved its headquarters from Miami to Mexico City.

In the early 1980s, Saralegui was contacted by Joaquín Blaya, who was just starting out as the director of SIN in Miami, inviting her to speak on camera with Don Francisco on *Sábado Gigante.*

When Blaya became president of Univision in 1986, he invited Saralegui to write and appear in a show called *TVMujer*, which focused on reviews of telenovelas with the occasional topic she covered for *Cosmopolitan* mixed in for good measure. In 1989, Saralegui quit her job at *Cosmopolitan*, said goodbye to Don Armando de Armas, and took a full-time job at Univision as the host of a daily variety program called *El Show de Cristina.* Although the show's owners at Hallmark had instructed her to imitate the style of Oprah Winfrey's famous show, during the twenty-one years *El Show de Cristina* was on the air, Saralegui imposed her own style, shifting away from Hallmark's Anglo-American editorial philosophy. She ran her show the same way she had run her magazine. She always helped promote and empower Latina women in the United States and often used her time to educate Hispanic families on topics that were sometimes difficult to discuss at home, such as AIDS, family planning, homosexuality, political activism, sex, abortion, and the professional and economic advancement of Hispanic immigrants. Cristina always insisted that the only thing she and Oprah had in common was a birthday—January 29—though Cristina is six years older. Still, the show's successful marketing campaign focused on pitching her as the "Latina Oprah." In one episode, Winfrey herself joked that she was actually the "Black Cristina Saralegui."

El Tigre was once overheard saying, "That Cuban girl has balls."

The Latin Music Crossover

Talking about the progress Latin music has made on the international stage requires a different book, one that chronicles and describes the many factors in the global music industry that successfully managed and distributed the most popular songs composed and performed by established artists in Latin America and Spain.

Before MTV, streaming platforms, and iPods even existed, a song's success depended on television, radio, print media, and record labels. In Mexico, the Televisa empire controlled most radio stations and the primary record distributor, Fonovisa, as well as the leading entertainment magazine publishing group. In other Spanish-speaking countries, major international record labels like CBS and EMI, among others, had a strong presence, dominating music production and distribution.

In the United States, SIN (and, later, Univision) was hindered by many restrictions in its efforts to expand into radio due to FCC restrictions and the aforementioned Fouce lawsuit. These limitations prevented both Univision and the Azcárragas from acquiring radio stations until the early 2000s.

In the 1980s, Hispanic radio stations in the United States were local initiatives focused primarily on the East and West Coasts. Univision, though, played a vital role in promoting Latin artists through televised musical segments on shows like *Siempre en Domingo* and *Sábado Gigante*.

Two outstanding Latin American phenomena emerged during this era. On the East Coast, the Miami Sound Machine, led by Gloria and Emilio Estefan, became iconic, thanks to their blend of Latin rhythms with pop music. From its early days in the late 1970s through the mid 1980s, the Miami Sound Machine was a sensation both in the United States and Latin America. On the West Coast, Selena Quintanilla, a Mexican American from Texas who rose to prominence in the 1980s, set a precedent with her Spanish-language music before posthumously achieving international success.

The term "crossover" refers to the moment when a song successfully bridges cultural and linguistic barriers, breaking into new music markets. While many consider the guitarist Carlos Santana or the Christmas classic song recorded by the Puerto Rican singer José Feliciano as the first major examples of crossover success, it's fair to point to the Spaniard Julio Iglesias as the first true ambassador of Hispanic culture in the United States. His impact on English-speaking radio was significant, particularly with his hit "To All the Girls I've Loved Before," an oddly unique duet with Willie Nelson that reached number one on Billboard's Adult Contemporary chart. To manage his career in the United States, Iglesias hired Cuban executive Ray Rodríguez as his artistic manager, as well as Frank Sinatra's manager, Eliot Weisman, to handle his U.S. promotional tour, thus cementing his position in the American market. Interestingly enough, Rodríguez would later be hired by Joaquín Blaya as director of programming and business at SIN's Miami station, closing a circle that connected music, television, and business.

The case of Gloria and Emilio Estefan deserves special attention. In 1985, they signed with CBS to produce their first English-language albums, resulting in megahits like "Conga" and "Rhythm Is Gonna Get You," both of which topped the Billboard charts. Cristina Saralegui's support was also significant, first as editor of *Cosmopolitan en español*, where she provided constant coverage of the band and their achievements, and later at Univision, where she used her television platform to boost the Estefans' visibility. And on one of her show's first episodes in 1989, Cristina interviewed the entire Estefan family, further solidifying her role as a key ally.

Another important element in the rise of Latin music was Univision's morning programming. Producing competitive content for the morning segment had been a challenge for years. Univision executives had tried to replicate shows like NBC's *Today* show or ABC's *Good Morning America*, though without success. Grappling with these challenges, music videos helped fill that morning gap until April 14, 1997, when Univision launched *Despierta América*. This program not only became a hit; it served as a platform for new and established Latin artists alike. Incidentally, that same week Televisa news anchor Jacobo Zabludovsky solemnly announced the death of El Tigre Azcárraga, which happened April 16.

On September 21, 1998, Univision premiered another locally produced show, *El Gordo y la Flaca*, an entertainment program that quickly became a hit with Hispanic audiences in the United States. Hosted by Raúl de Molina, "el Gordo," and the already well-known Lili Estefan, “la Flaca,” the show offers a unique blend of entertainment and pop-culture news with a lively and accessible tone. Since its debut, the show has remained popular for more than twenty-five years.

The internet era, which ushered in the age of streaming, exploded onto the scene in 2000, with the rise of the MP3 digital format and platforms like Napster, and then again in 2001, with Apple’s release of its first iPod.

Plenty of artists, including Ricky Martin, Shakira, Daddy Yankee, and Luis Fonsi, have benefited greatly from the digitalization of music distribution, conquering charts not only in Latin America but also in the United States and other international markets, both Spanish- and English-speaking. Univision has always served as a channel of distribution and influence when it comes to this expanding market, and has been a definitive factor in the success of artists such as these.

In 2000, Univision was finally authorized to begin acquiring Spanish-language radio stations, and two years later, the FCC approved its acquisition of the Hispanic Broadcasting Corporation, which was not affiliated with the company of the same name owned by Gustavo Godoy. This allowed Univision to extend its reach beyond television by incorporating key radio stations essential for promoting Latin artists and musical genres. By becoming the largest Spanish-language media conglomerate, Univision not only reaffirmed its status as the industry leader but also strengthened its ability to connect with U.S.-based Hispanic artists. Eventually, the company would come to own seventy Spanish-language radio stations in fourteen regions across the country.

Puerto Rican–born Ricky Martin was another one of the first Latin artists to achieve true crossover success in the English-speaking market. His career began with Menudo, an iconic Puerto Rican band formed in 1977 that was known as one of the first boy bands in Latin music. The band rose to prominence in the 1980s with hits like "Súbete a mi moto" ("Hop on My Bike") and "Quiero ser" ("I Want to Be"). Ricky Martin achieved international stardom with the smash hit "La copa de la vida" ("The Cup of Life"), which was the official theme song for the 1998 World Cup held in France. This was followed by the release of his single "Livin' la Vida Loca" the following year. That song, which blended Latin rhythms with pop rock, became an instant hit, topping the Billboard charts in multiple countries.

Univision played a key role in promoting Ricky Martin, featuring him on popular shows like *Sábado Gigante* and *El Show de Cristina*. These appearances not only increased his visibility among Hispanic audiences but also helped capture the attention of Anglo-American audiences. Martin's performance at the 1999 Grammy Awards, where he performed "La copa de la vida," marked a turning point in his career and solidified his status as a crossover star.

Figures such as Shakira, Enrique Iglesias, Marc Anthony, Jennifer Lopez, and Daddy Yankee also benefited from the expansive reach of the network, which promoted their music videos, concerts, and interviews while also increasing their visibility through events like the Premios Lo Nuestro and the Premios Juventud. Although they were already well-known within the Hispanic community, their international fame was bolstered by Univision. Shakira, for example, was a superstar in Latin America before releasing *Laundry Service* in 2001, but it was 2006's "Hips

Don't Lie" that garnered her global fame, with Univision boosting her image among Hispanic audiences in the United States. Similarly, Enrique Iglesias reached number one on the Billboard Hot 100 with "Bailamos" in 1999. Marc Anthony solidified his success with "I Need to Know" that same year, and Jennifer Lopez positioned herself in both the English and Spanish markets with *On the 6*. Later on, reggaeton experienced its own crossover movement with artists like Daddy Yankee, whose 2004 hit "Gasolina" marked a turning point in the genre's global expansion, thanks in large part to exposure on platforms like Univision.

CHAPTER 14

Jerry Perenchio, Univision's Man with the Midas Touch

The Beverly Hillbillies was an American sitcom that aired on CBS from 1962 to 1971. The show chronicled the lives of the Clampetts, a poor rural family from the hills of Tennessee who moves into luxurious Beverly Hills, California, after oil is discovered on their land.

The mansion where the series was filmed, built in 1933, is a French neoclassical house located in Bel Air; it served as their fictional home. In 1986, Jerry Perenchio, who was by then a fifty-six-year-old millionaire, acquired the mansion and named it Chartwell, the same as his Hollywood talent management firm and the legendary estate where Winston and Clementina Churchill spent their best years on the outskirts of a tumultuous London. That year, Perenchio proposed to his third wife, Margaret Rose, and he married her on June 6, 1987.

Jerry lived in Chartwell until his death in May 2017. The mansion was then sold for slightly less than the asking price of $245 million to Lachlan Murdoch, son of the media mogul Rupert Murdoch, in 2019.

Renovating and remodeling Chartwell took five years. When it was finished, Perenchio blew out fifty-nine candles at a birthday party held there on December 20, 1989. At the same time, at Hallmark's headquarters back in Kansas City, a closed-door meeting was being held between CEO Irvine O. Hockaday and several of his advisers to discuss Univision Holdings. It was essential for Hallmark to capitalize on it so it could make a $10 million interest payment due on February 1, 1990, and keep current on the bonds issued to finance the purchase of the Spanish-language network. Much to the surprise of everyone in the room, Hockaday announced that Hallmark would not be contributing a single penny more in capital to Univision Holdings.

Hockaday had ordered the team to seek more debt to cover the interest payments. The funds never came through, and Univision Holdings announced it would default on the outstanding interest payments on the bonds. "A bankruptcy foretold," as one experienced investment banker said. One of the bondholders was Jerry Perenchio, who had purchased a small amount of the bonds in order to stay informed at all times: a truly opportunistic hunter.

From a young age, Andrew Jerrold "Jerry" Perenchio was known in his native Fresno as an enigmatic individual. At fifteen, he attended the Black-Foxe Military Institute in Los Angeles, California: the entertainment capital of the world. In 1949, Perenchio graduated from the military academy and immediately enrolled at UCLA. Shortly after that, to help finance his studies, he founded Party Management. Always impeccably dressed, Jerry began organizing the university's most elaborate parties, famously filled with music and charm.

He later joined the Air Force ROTC, where he trained as a pilot and which paid for his entire college tuition. In 1954, Perenchio married Robin Gardner Green, with whom he had his only biological son, John Perenchio. In 1958, he joined the Music Corporation of America, known as MCA, one of the most renowned agencies representing Hollywood artists in the 1950s.

In the long shadow of the big Hollywood agencies, he founded Perenchio Artists, where his clientele were a kaleidoscope of rising stars and established legends, such as Ronald Reagan, Andy Williams, Johnny Mathis, Henry Mancini, José Feliciano, Glen Campbell, and Sergio Mendes. It was at a jazz club in London that Jerry Perenchio discovered Elton John. He moved Elton to the United States permanently and booked the Troubadour club in LA for two weeks straight to showcase him on a daily basis. Thanks to Perenchio's bet, Elton John became a household name on this side of the pond. Eventually, Perenchio Artists merged with the Hugh French Agency to form Chartwell Artists, representing actors, directors, writers, musicians, and singers, including stars as bright as Marlon Brando and Elizabeth Taylor. Perenchio maintained his focus on musicians and artists who could present their talents live onstage in front of an audience.

Jerry Perenchio was more than an entrepreneur. He was a visionary who understood the value of exclusive ceremonies in a world hungry for spectacle. In March 1971, he orchestrated "The Fight of the Century" at New York's Madison Square Garden, bringing together two undefeated heavyweight boxing champions: Muhammad Ali and Joe Frazier. "This wasn't just a prize fight," reflects Mike Silver, a historian and author of several books on boxing. "This had other dimensions to it: the dimensions of race, politics, the Vietnam War."

In 1966, the American forces had entered their fifth year in Vietnam, and the government expanded the draft. Ali requested an exemption as a conscientious objector, which the government formally denied him. For staying true to his beliefs, Ali was ar-

Muhammad Ali (center) with Jerry Perenchio (right), in 1971. (Photo: AP.)

rested and stripped of his world championship title. When Ali's boxing license was reinstated in 1970, Joe Frazier was the reigning heavyweight champion of the world, and Perenchio came up with the brilliant idea of organizing and promoting the so-called Fight of the Century between two world champions.

Perenchio stunned everyone when he offered each boxer $2.5 million guaranteed for the fight—an astronomical sum at a time when athletic talent was undervalued. The event fused sport and spectacle, bringing glamour to the sweet yet often brutal science of boxing. Part of the allure was the Garden's crowd, which included such celebrities as Frank Sinatra, Sammy Davis Jr., Barbra Streisand, Diana Ross, Dustin Hoffman, and the owner of the *Playboy* empire, Hugh Hefner.

For this event, Perenchio pulled off an unprecedented feat: he sold 1.5 million tickets to watch the fight exclusively in venues where it was shown via closed-circuit television. It was the first time a boxing event was broadcast exclusively to paying audiences in locations that had already paid Perenchio for broadcasting rights. This marked the beginning of cable TV's pay-per-view era. On top of that, Perenchio sold broadcasting rights outside the United States to more than one hundred countries.

He was also the mastermind behind the Battle of the Sexes: the September 1973 tennis match between Billie Jean King and Bobby Riggs that took place at the Houston Astrodome. With 30,472 spectators in attendance, it was the largest live audience for any tennis match ever held and was the highest-rated telecast of the year when it aired in prime time on ABC, the network to which Perenchio had sold the exclusive broadcasting rights. It was that same year that Perenchio divorced his second wife, Jacquelyn C. Matthews, whom he had married in 1969.

Perenchio operated from the shadows, always shrouded in mystery. He never appeared onstage or in front of cameras. He was often credited with grand gestures and philanthropic donations, yet his name remained elusive, as if he were shrouded in mist. Jerry Perenchio was like a ghost who changed lives and wove together dreams without ever seeking either credit or glory. After casual, chance encounters with him, people often described a mystical aura surrounding him. Those who truly knew him, like his wives, his last partner, and his collaborators, often felt enveloped in a kind of spell. Those fortunate enough to have been touched by his generosity spoke of a level of abundance and splendor in his attentions that was almost unimaginable.

Since the 1970s, Perenchio had believed in the potential of the U.S. Hispanic market. He was one of the few white businessmen who was intent on targeting this Spanish-speaking audience. His own Spanish was quite broken—or at least that's what he let on—but he was born in Fresno and had lived for decades in the Los Angeles area, so he would have known from a very young age that Spanish was a widely spoken language, not only in California but in many other parts of the country as well. Some Hispanic executives who worked with him tell me they always suspected that Perenchio understood Spanish, though he never actually showed it.

In 1984, Jerry Perenchio, along with Norman Lear, Alan D. "Bud" Yorkin, Frances Lear, and Peg Yorkin, invested just under $5 million to purchase the New Jersey television station WNJU, which was already experimenting with Hispanic content brought in by Carlos Barba from Venezuela. Barba had relocated from Caracas, where he'd been working with Gustavo Cisneros at Venevisión, and now he was partnering with Perenchio, who consulted him during his attempt to buy SIN. The two of them, along with the aforementioned partners, registered and used the legal entity Spanish American Communications Corporation (SACC) for both its investment in WNJU and the failed attempt to purchase SIN.

After losing his bid to Hallmark, Perenchio abandoned the idea and put WNJU up for sale. On June 1, 1987, he and his partners sold SACC to Reliance Group. A document I obtained from the SEC details this transaction: the purchase price consisted of a promissory obligation to pay $60 million in cash with an initial payment of $10 million. The remainder would be covered by another $30 million from Reliance's working capital and approximately $20 million through bank loans secured by pledged shares of SACC stock.

Carlos Barba stayed onboard as vice president of programming for Reliance, which, as we've learned, would continue acquiring other stations, including Telemundo in Puerto Rico. Barba suggested rebranding NetSpan, which Perenchio had created and used for WNJU, with the newly acquired Telemundo brand.

This series of events underscores the significant effect Perenchio had on the expansion and evolution of Hispanic television in the United States. His ability to identify opportunities, and the advice he received from Carlos Barba, allowed stations like WNJU and, later, entire networks like Telemundo, to grow and establish themselves in the market. Selling WNJU to Reliance was not only a significant financial transaction but also a crucial step in the development and furthering of Hispanic programming in this country.

While Perenchio failed in his attempt to acquire SIN, the transformation of NetSpan into Telemundo under Reliance, with Barba's continued involvement, is a testament to the lasting impact these strategic decisions had—decisions that led Perenchio to maintain his relationship with Barba, and wisely so. It's entirely possible that some of the proceeds from the sale of WNJU were later invested in the junk bonds issued by Univision Holdings, which Hallmark used to acquire SIN.

February 1990 came, and Perenchio's political and business acumen led him to immediately request a meeting with the prestigious investment bank Rothschild, which represented the Univision bondholders. He offered to buy the bonds, though at a discount, while at the same time meeting with Hockaday to discuss a possible buyout of Univision Holdings. Hockaday accepted the offer to meet with Perenchio, willing enough to listen to what he had to say. Hallmark was clear about its position: financially, it didn't want to face the consequences of a possible Univision bankruptcy, nor did it want to be remembered as the company responsible for the collapse of the leading Spanish-language television network in the United States. That being the case, Hallmark saw Perenchio as a potential "white knight," a slang term used in the financial industry when a friendly buyer is given favorable terms in order to fend off a hostile takeover or prevent bankruptcy. He was a Republican with friends in the highest political circles, including then-president George H. W. Bush. These political affinities facilitated smooth communication between Perenchio and Hockaday. Thus, Hockaday granted Perenchio permission to begin the due diligence process and take the necessary steps to set up a purchase proposal, provided that any negotiations would be concluded before the November 1992 elections. Perenchio began his work immediately, and one of the first people he reached out to was the Cuban Carlos Barba, who was already looking to leave ill-fated Telemundo.

Barba orchestrated the first meeting with Venezuelan businessman Gustavo Cisneros, another Republican with close ties to President Bush. A partnership between Perenchio and Cisneros had the White House's blessing, and the message was sent to Hallmark's headquarters in Kansas City. Barba had also informed El Tigre, who had already learned of Univision's defaulting on its bond payment and potential bankruptcy.

Jerry Perenchio first focused on discussing the technical and financial aspects. For this, he relied on his longtime CFO, Andrew Hobson, who ran Chartwell Partners, LLC, Perenchio's private equity investment firm. The professional relationship between the two men was forged during Perenchio's time working with Bankers Trust, one of the largest banks in the United States at the time. That financial organization was acquired by Deutsche Bank in 1998, and it was there that Hobson, with his perpetually crooked tie and passion for mergers and acquisitions, had been vice president for six years. Bankers Trust was one of the Bush administration's favorite investment banks, and was Perenchio's primary banking partner as well. And so the Perenchio-Hobson duo walked into Hallmark's headquarters to conduct the financial due diligence that would lead to the purchase of Univision Holdings. When it came to programming, content, and talent, Perenchio began consulting with Barba and Cisneros before facing El Tigre, who, meanwhile, was trying to draw up an alternative plan using his political connections in both Mexico and the United States. Barba had already told El Tigre that he was advising Perenchio and that one of his goals was to consolidate the relationship with Televisa as a content provider, but that wasn't enough for El Tigre. He wanted to buy Univision himself and be the one leading that charge. Returning to Univision in grand fashion through the front doors was one of his dreams, and while he wasn't yet facing a terminal diagnosis, his health in general was making him wonder whether this might be his last chance to fulfill that dream.

Barba, Cisneros, and Perenchio decided to approach El Tigre together, but not before laying the groundwork for what a partnership among the three capitalists—Perenchio, Cisneros, and Azcárraga—might look like. They designed a structure that was sound and long-lasting enough to ensure that no one could attempt to increase his own power, ensuring the rules governing Univision's shareholder structure were crystal clear. Perenchio was adamant about maintaining control, leveraging U.S. legal restrictions of foreign ownership (the infamous 20 percent rule). Well aware of the lengthy litigation that had led to El Tigre's departure, Perenchio had to prevent any chance of such a conflict rising again. He knew that Cisneros and El Tigre were two shrewd titans of the business world who would seize any opportunity to gain more power.

Unlike on other occasions, this time the priorities were financial health, business viability, and blocking the slightest possibility of shareholder distraction from anything other than Univision's development and growth as the undisputed leader of Hispanic television. It was Cisneros who came up with the idea of splitting the share distribution, giving Perenchio majority control while dividing the remaining 25 percent equally between Cisneros (Venevisión) and Azcárraga (Televisa). And so it was. Perenchio demanded exclusivity from both Cisneros and El Tigre. Neither of the two Hispanic businessmen could sell any content in the United States without Perenchio's permission. Perenchio required this exclusivity for twenty-five years. Cisneros agreed and promised to convince El Tigre to get Televisa to accept the terms, which is exactly what happened.

Cisneros became Perenchio's spokesperson when it came to dealing with El Tigre, who ultimately accepted the terms of the contract, which they referred to as the PLA, or program license agreement. The PLA kept Televisa tied to Univision for twenty-five years as its exclusive content provider in exchange for royalty payments that could be adjusted every five years.

In addition to the royalties, Perenchio agreed that Cisneros and Televisa would be paid for the rights to the content they sold for U.S. distribution at market value. In other words, both Cisneros and Televisa received cash payments for the content they supplied exclusively to Univision.

Both Cisneros and Azcárraga demanded that these payments be convertible into Univision shares until they reached the full percentages agreed to in the PLA. In short, neither El Tigre nor

Cisneros had to pay cash in order to enter into the Univision equation. This structure ensured that all the interests of all partners were aligned with Univision's long-term success, solidifying its position as the undisputed leader of Hispanic television in the United States. Perenchio's strategic vision, combined with key alliances with Cisneros and Televisa, marked a turning point in Univision's value and trajectory.

In order to move forward, Perenchio asked Hockaday to come to a swift agreement with the creditors: those bondholders controlled by the Bush administration. The path had been cleared for the announcement of the sale of Univision to the Perenchio, Cisneros, and Azcárraga group. There was no turning back. El Tigre, the Mexican mogul, asked Perenchio and Cisneros for an honorary condition that—at the time of this book's publication—I have not been able to confirm: he never wanted to see Joaquín Blaya at Univision's helm.

In an article published by *The New York Times* on April 9, 1992, written by Richard W. Stevenson, Hallmark announced the sale of Univision Holdings, the largest Spanish-language television network and station group in the United States, for $550 million. The paper confirmed that the buyer was a consortium led by "A. Jerrold Perenchio, a Hollywood producer [whose] group includes Venevision, Venezuela's largest broadcaster, and Grupo Televisa, Mexico's largest broadcaster."

The paper went on to provide further details about the transaction, which included the Univision network, distributed through local affiliates and cable systems as well as thirteen Spanish-language broadcast stations, including WXTV Channel 41 in New York and KMEX Channel 34 in Los Angeles. This deal marked the end of Hallmark's five-year involvement in Spanish-language broadcasting, a period of time during which the company invested more than $550 million in acquisitions, infrastructure, and programming improvements.

The Hispanic market in the United States, described in the article as rapidly growing, was highlighted by Perenchio as an opportunity to offer high-quality content in entertainment, news, cultural, and children's programming. The article also noted that, while the acquiring group did not announce any specific programming changes, the alliance with Venevisión and Televisa suggested a possible increase in the acquisition of content produced by these companies for the U.S. market, thereby moving away from the trend of producing content locally.

The article also mentioned how federal regulations prohibited foreign companies from having controlling interest in U.S. television stations. In order to comply with this rule, the deal was structured such that Perenchio would retain 75 percent control with Venevisión and Televisa sharing the remaining stake.

As mentioned in previous chapters, Perenchio wouldn't rest until he acquired Univision, and El Tigre wouldn't give up on his goal of returning to the company his father had once dreamed of owning in the United States. It's all part of a fascinating media story forged alongside the exponential growth of the Hispanic population during the 1970s, '80s, and '90s.

The FCC hadn't approved the purchase by Perenchio, El Tigre, and Cisneros, and yet the story was already beginning to spread through the corridors of pro-Hispanic organizations in the United States. Several Hispanic leaders opposed Univision's content being dependent on non-U.S. entrepreneurs, fearing that the new owners would cancel local production in favor of content from Televisa and Venevisión, while others responded to political interests that wanted to prevent the sale from taking place before the presidential elections.

Even Univision's own CEO, Joaquín Blaya, dared to challenge the future under new ownership, declaring to the media that local production was at risk of being replaced by content from Mexico (Televisa) and Venezuela (Venevisión).

On May 27, 1992, a headline in the *Los Angeles Times* shocked the media industry by announcing "Univision President Bolts to Rival Telemundo." That day, Joaquín Blaya, the man who had helped shape Univision for twenty-two years, charting a course that had enriched its cultural identity, announced he was leaving his position in order to join the company's fiercest rival: Telemundo. The reasons behind this seismic shift were clear, though no less surprising. According to Blaya himself, he'd found himself in a conflict with the new investment team led by Perenchio, in a deal that was still pending FCC approval. Plans had emerged to alter Univision's heart—its programming—in ways that Blaya found irreconcilable with his vision.

"The document states that, with the exception of local news and public affairs, everything would be [sourced] from Venevisión and Televisa," Blaya said, referring to Perenchio's application for FCC approval.

A Perenchio spokesperson responded to Blaya's statement, rejecting the idea that existing programming would undergo such a radical change. "The commitment will remain to program at the station level in order to reflect the needs of the community, local and national viewing habits, and advertising markets," the spokesperson said.

It was at this very juncture that the Univision buyers group received authorization from the FCC in a time frame that can only be described as impeccable: just before the elections. In the annals of American politics, it is customary that, when the winds of electoral change displace one party from power, the machinery of regulatory agencies—those under the judiciary notwithstanding—tends to enter something of a dormant state.

As soon as Perenchio took over the reins, he announced the exclusive contract for purchasing content from Mexico and Venevisión of Venezuela. Gustavo Cisneros's role was extremely important in the Perenchio-Azcárraga-Cisneros trifecta. In 1992, the year after the acquisition, Cisneros was forty-seven years old and in good health, while Azcárraga and Perenchio were both sixty-two at the time and El Tigre was already battling cancer. Perenchio had a reputation as a bold investor in the entertainment and television world; El Tigre was known as an eccentric, almost feudal Mexican millionaire who was always surrounded by celebrities; Cisneros, a graduate of the prestigious Babson College in Massachusetts, had a reputation as a success-driven executive who wielded a lot of power in Venezuela, a wealthy if politically vulnerable country at the time. Cisneros saw this as his chance to make his mark as a global leader.

Cisneros is credited with the brilliant idea of dividing the programming schedule: one for the East Coast and one for the West Coast. While the programs would be the same, Mexican content would appear primarily during Pacific prime-time hours while Caribbean and South American content was broadcast during Eastern prime-time hours. This same content was played in other regions of the country, just not during prime time.

Univision continued broadcasting the national newscast hosted by María Elena Salinas and Jorge Ramos as well as the programs *Primer Impacto*, *El Show de Cristina*, and *Sábado Gigante* with Don Francisco, shows that audiences eagerly awaited every week.

It couldn't have been easy for El Tigre to accept the fact that this successful programming had nothing to do with Televisa and was instead part of the lasting legacy of Joaquín Blaya, who had been a champion of U.S.-based programming and a fervent defender of local voices on the Spanish-language network. "For the last four years, I have emphasized the need for product made in the United States that was in tune with the needs and concerns of Hispanics in this country," Blaya said in that same *Los Angeles Times* article.

Telenovelas were key to Cisneros's new programming schedule. There needed to be two prime-time slots for telenovelas: one on the East Coast, when telenovelas ran from 7 p.m. to 11 p.m., when the second edition of the national news began, and another on the West Coast, where telenovelas aired from 4 p.m. to 8 p.m. Two time zones, four shows, and a perfect business model for Televisa and Venevisión, ensuring a loyal audience and substantial revenue from the sales of their content.

Perenchio promoted Cuban Ray Rodríguez to be president of Univision, as well as a managerial team. He imposed a set of twenty rules that were to be strictly followed at all times. They were known as The Perenchio Rules of the Road, and breaking them could very well mean losing your job.

The Perenchio Rules of the Road

1. Stay clear of the press. No interviews, no panels, no speeches, no comments. Stay out of the spotlight—it fades your suit.
2. No nepotism, no hiring of friends.

3. Never rehire anyone.
4. Hire people smarter and better than you. Delegate responsibilities to them. Doing so will make your job easier.
5. You've got to know your territory. Cold!
6. Do your homework. Be prepared.
7. Teamwork.
8. Take options, never give them.
9. Rely on your instincts and common sense. If you go against them, you generally regret it.
10. No surprises. We don't give them. We don't want to get them.
11. Never lose sight of what business you're in. Stick to your "last."
12. When you suit up each day, it's to play in Yankee Stadium or Dodger Stadium. Think big.
13. If you have a problem, don't delay. Face up to it immediately and solve it.
14. Loose lips sink ships!
15. Supreme self-confidence, never arrogance.
16. A true leader is accessible—no job too big, no job too small.
17. Communication is our business. You can reach any of your associates anytime, anywhere, anyplace.
18. If you make a mistake, admit it. Just don't make too many.
19. Don't be a "customer's person" (man or woman).
20. Always, always take the high road. Be tough but fair and never lose your sense of humor.

These commandments are like a set of sacred principles that many at Univision today still follow religiously. I encountered a peculiar situation while speaking with a number of people during the process of writing this book, many of whom implored me not to reveal their names as a gesture of respect to Perenchio's rules. When I reminded them that he had passed away, the response was a silence filled with equal parts fear and respect.

Jerry Perenchio, with Ray Rodríguez by his side, successfully led Univision until 2007. In 1992, the Hispanic population of the United States was already at thirty million. Perenchio was something of a legend, operating in a world of neon lights and golden dreams, though always from the shadows. Those who knew him remember him as an "enigmatic American with a heart of gold that didn't shine because he wasn't interested in polishing it." The man who had it all but never cared about typical recognition. Someone who remained, to the end, "a mysterious figure who enjoyed knowing that everyone knew, though no one would ever say."

When Ray Rodríguez became Univision's president, he realized he'd been put in charge of a circus whose owner imposed his unique autocratic style and tone. One of the many Univision executives I spoke with said working with Perenchio was like being in a jungle. "Perenchio was the hunter and Ray was the head gorilla. In the jungle, Ray was the king."

In September 1992, Univision hosted a free concert featuring Gloria Estefan's Miami Sound Machine, along with salsa legend Celia Cruz and many other artists, in a fourteen-hour live broadcast called the Votatón. All you needed to get into the concert was a valid U.S. voter registration card. If you didn't have one, there were tables set up all around the entrance of the venue where you could register to vote. This political operation was a huge success, and many credit Joaquín Blaya with the idea.

But a rift was growing between El Tigre Azcárraga and Cisneros. In 1994, the latter announced his investment, along with that of the Hughes Electronics Corporation, in Galaxy Latin America, which exclusively distributed DirecTV in the region. DirecTV was already the undisputed leader in direct-to-home television transmission services through the use of small satellite dishes installed on the roofs of houses. The announcement caught media moguls by surprise, including El Tigre, who felt that he was being treated unfairly by his longtime friend and protégé. The announcement was quite aggressive in tone: Cisneros and Hughes laid out their immediate expansion plan, which included Chile, Mexico, Argentina, Brazil—virtually every Latin American country. El Tigre never forgave Cisneros for not inviting him into this partnership and politely asked the Venezuelan businessman to resign from Televisa's board of directors because he was planning on entering the DTH business himself, and Cisneros's investment in a competitor had created a conflict of interest.

In 1995, Rupert Murdoch, Emilio Azcárraga Milmo (representing Televisa), and Roberto Marinho (representing Globo) announced the creation and launch of Sky TV to compete head-to-head with DirecTV, meaning El Tigre would be squaring off with Cisneros.

This fallout was strategically exploited by Perenchio, who used the division between the two minority partners to further consolidate his control over Univision.

CHAPTER 15

Opulence, Extravagance, and Power

Like the Roman emperor Nero himself, in his days of unbridled opulence, El Tigre Azcárraga seemed to rise even higher than the sacred Santa Monica Mountains and the iconic Hollywood sign by acquiring a mythical property that had earned the distinction of being a Los Angeles Historic-Cultural Monument. What was once the Sunset Plaza Apartments, a gilded haven for classic movie stars, including Columbia Pictures CEO Harry Cohn, character actress Mary Boland, and musician Tommy Dorsey, a symbol of old Hollywood glamour and elegance, had given way to a sprawling mansion. Adorned with Renaissance details, carved wood frames, and arched windows, it stood like a fortress amid the modern city.

This imposing estate, the largest residence in a neighborhood where luxury is the norm, is notable not only for its sheer scale—12,000 square feet of living space on 2.3 acres of land—but also for its location along the edge of the bustling Sunset Strip. There, in defiance of the city's maelstrom of chaos and fury, El Tigre erected his bastion of grandeur and peace: La Hacienda. With five bedrooms, each with its own bath, two swimming pools, a party room, and a tennis court, this fortress was the setting for gatherings and celebrations where El Tigre put his power and opulence on full display.

On the bustling streets of Mexico City, he mingled with ordinary folks, enjoying the warmth of the people. He was known to eat at street food stands and carts and ride around the city on his motorcycle, feeling himself in tune with the vibrant urban pulse. But in Hollywood, El Tigre's personality transformed into that of a distant, mysterious magnate, an almost untouchable figure.

In a diary belonging to Elia Zavarce, El Tigre's personal assistant at the Los Angeles offices, there are a number of anecdotes that revolve around La Hacienda, particularly the presence of "El Chispa," the person in charge of spiritual protection. In El Tigre's LA corporate offices, everyone knew about this man. Unremarkable and insignificant in appearance, El Chispa supposedly served a vital role. In exchange for a generous salary, he spent his days meticulously reviewing hours of videotape, making sure that everything bore copyright marks and the corresponding disclaimers. The assistant never quite understood the importance or the pay behind such a seemingly simple task. Later, though, she would learn that this individual had a second identity, cloaked in mysticism and secrecy: he practiced Santería as a babalawo, a Yoruba high priest. Whispers in the hallways spoke of El Chispa performing ceremonies, and many believed his true role in the company was to protect the family from bad energy and wandering spirits. With his babalawo at his side, El Tigre, driven by his hunger for control and conquest, was intent on leaving absolutely nothing—not even luck—to chance. He wanted to bargain for success with cosmic energies, currying favor with both the living and the dead through these West African–rooted rituals.

On one particular night, those whispers took shape and became disturbingly real. In her diary, Zavarce recounts how one of the butlers and one of the cooks, a devout Christian couple who worked and lived in the mansion, called her in the early hours of the morning. They were leaving La Hacienda immediately, claiming El Chispa was practicing witchcraft. In her bosses' absence, Zavarce decided to go and see what she could do to calm things down and restore order.

There, the couple led her to a hidden corner beneath the garage where they swore El Chispa was performing his Santería rituals. The space seemed quite clean, though it did smell of blood, herbs, liquor, and flowers. Nothing particularly macabre was present, but the atmosphere exuded a troubling air of solemnity. Zavarce describes dark candelabras with unknown emblems, mysterious objects, and strange symbols. Lacking any better option, she called a cab for the complainants, who vanished into the night like a pair of frightened shadows. Only later would she discover why the so-called "copyright verifier" slept on site and earned such a high salary.

In her diary, Zavarce writes:

> Working with El Tigre during that time (1988–1991) exposed me to a world I only knew about through movies or television. The hit TV series *Dynasty* was the closest I'd ever come to this kind of monumental wealth. I credit that job with so many personal improvements: I learned how to throw an unforgettable party! I had my own personal "buyer," a lovely woman by the name of Margarita. It wasn't uncommon for me to accompany the wives of Mexican dignitaries or VIPs to boutiques like Cartier or Harry Winston where they selected

> the pieces they liked while the salespeople would suggest gifts for their husbands. The finest, most dazzling diamonds, pearls, rubies, emeralds, and other precious stones I'd never even heard of before. Most of this jewelry rarely left La Hacienda's vault.

For Azcárraga Milmo and Perenchio, power and opulence weren't mere accessories. They were the air they breathed, the ground on which they walked.

With a captivating eye, Jerry Perenchio meticulously planned his own destiny, assembling each piece of his life with the precision of a master watchmaker. For one lavish celebration, he demanded the creation of a French mirage: an exact replica of the Versailles ballroom conceived for just one single night of revelry. His fascination with that palace, a colossus of opulence and power, was so palpable that he ended up building his own. But this grand palace bore Perenchio's unmistakable mark: only those welcomed into his fold could enjoy its private splendor. In Beverly Hills, the tour busses still stop in front of the Perenchio estate, now owned by one of the Murdochs, and the guide describes it as the famous mansion where the Beverly Hillbillies once "lived."

Perenchio meticulously immersed himself in the reconstruction of Chartwell, the namesake of his talent management and entertainment business. The backstory to this majestic property reads like a ballet of triumph and tragedy from the moment it was built in 1930. Its first owner was never able to live in it.

Lynn Atkinson, a renowned engineer known for his work on the Hoover Dam, commissioned a miniature replica of the dam itself to be built in the entry hall to show guests the source of his fortune. His wife rejected the glitzy reflection of grandeur, which bordered on the absurd. In a time of financial desperation, Atkinson used the mansion as collateral for a loan guaranteed by his friend hotel magnate Arnold Kirkeby. Kirkeby would eventually take possession of the mansion, and Atkinson, drowning in hopelessness, surrendered to his demons and ended his life by jumping from his twelfth-floor apartment.

Arnold Kirkeby owned some twenty hotels, including the Drake hotel in Chicago and the Hotel Nacional de Cuba in Havana. He died in March 1, 1962 in a tragic American Airlines crash just after takeoff from JFK en route to Los Angeles. Carlotta, his widow, lived in the mansion until her own death in 1985.

Six months after Carlotta's passing, the Kirkeby heirs decided to sell the iconic property, which is how Jerry Perenchio became its owner, purchasing it for $13.5 million. Like a hunter stalking grandeur, he became the new guardian of the estate's long and layered history and then embarked on a five-year renovation, before renaming it Chartwell.

Perenchio wanted the interior to evoke the French ambiance of Versailles, so he turned to the most celebrated French garden and interior designer of the time, Henri Samuel.

During those prosperous times, Perenchio began his third marriage, this time to Margaret Rose Perenchio. At Samuel's suggestion, the newlywed couple added three adjoining lots to the property, expanding the estate across a full ten acres. To find limestone that most closely resembled the original used in the construction of Versailles, Samuel and Perenchio embarked on an aerial odyssey, flying from quarry to quarry across a region of France. When they finally found the right shade of stone, they hired a local couple to live at the quarry, overseeing and ensuring proper cutting. The roof, also crafted in France in one single piece, proved too large to fit through a 747's cargo door, so it had to be cut into pieces for transport and then, like a puzzle, reassembled at Chartwell.

In November 1991, the Perenchios moved into their newly renovated residence. "It was a wonderful adventure and one of the most important learning experiences of our lives," Perenchio would later confess.

Today, the house boasts some glamorously excessive features that pushed the value from Perenchio's original purchasing price up to the $150 million mark, paid by Rupert Murdoch's son Lachlan in 2018, a year after Perenchio's death.

Some of those lavish features include a seventy-five-foot resort-style pool with an adjoining pool house, a ballroom, a tennis court with lights, a helipad, a guest house spanning 5,700 square feet, an underground garage for up to forty vehicles, and a world-class wine cellar that holds up to twelve thousand bottles and has a formal tasting room for private events and celebrations.

El Tigre's Boat

But residential mansions weren't the only luxuries that media tycoons and other executives enjoyed at the time.

Stories of J. P. Morgan's yachts fascinated El Tigre Azcárraga, who loved to talk about the behind-the-scenes power the American financier once wielded. When people wanted to flatter El Tigre, they referred to him as the J. P. Morgan of Mexico. In 1990, El Tigre commissioned renowned engineer and designer Martin Francis to create for him his own vessel. Francis owned the engineering firm used by famed architect I. M. Pei to build the glass pyramid installed in the entrance courtyard of the Louvre in Paris.

This was the first time Francis would design a boat, and it would be no less than a 245-foot superyacht powered by turbines capable of speeds in excess of 36 knots, making it the fastest superyacht in the world. Azcárraga Milmo was drawn to Francis's expertise in glasswork and named the project *ECO*, after his efforts to emulate Ted Turner with a twenty-four-hour Spanish-language news channel.

El Tigre wanted to wake up to the best possible view and insisted that his master bedroom be located at the top of the vessel: an unorthodox decision, as that space is normally reserved for the navigation crew. Inside, he ordered a replica of the lobby of Morocco's Mamounia hotel and insisted on the installation of both a small seaplane and a Harley-Davidson motorcycle on the deck, both of which could be lifted on and off by crane. All of this had to be completed before Televisa's planned IPO on Wall Street in the summer of 1991. Upon arriving at the Solent docks in England to accept the *ECO*, El Tigre was heard proudly proclaiming, "I'll park my *ECO* right in the marina near Manhattan so those bastards on Wall Street know I'm here."

This vessel was worlds apart from the sportfishing yachts typically seen in U.S. waters. The *ECO*, with the capacity for fourteen passengers along with nineteen crew members, marked the American arrival of the superyacht: a concept already well established in Europe, where monarchs and moguls like the queen of England or Aristotle Onassis already boasted luxurious vessels on such a scale. Not since the heady days of J. P. Morgan and the first industrialists had the United States seen anything quite like it.

Eco was designed to carry a seaplane · Credit: Martin Francis

The *ECO* was designed to carry a seaplane. (Photo: Martin Francis.)

Every time the *ECO* docked at a marina, its imposing presence and unparalleled luxury captured attention, projecting a sense of exclusivity that had, until then, been foreign to American shores. Names like Larry Ellison, Steve Jobs, and Jeff Bezos would later follow this precedent, kicking off the trend of commissioning their own superyachts in hopes of emulating that sense of prestige and exclusivity that the *ECO* had pioneered in the United States.

As fate would have it, that was the same year that El Tigre's health began to decline. Just as he returned as a shareholder of Univision in 1991, his Mexican media empire, Televisa, went public on Wall Street, signaling his willingness to be scrutinized by U.S. financial regulators. It was also that same year that *Forbes* listed Emilio "El Tigre" Azcárraga Milmo among the world's billionaires, crowning him as the wealthiest Latin American on the planet. *Forbes* based its valuation on the financial data disclosed in Televisa's IPO (initial public offering) prospectus.

Adriana Abascal was his faithful companion during his voyages aboard the *ECO* and throughout his battle with cancer. Together, El Tigre and Abascal set out to explore the world by sea, making repeated trips throughout the Caribbean islands, along the eastern coast of the United States from Florida to New York, and eventually crossing the Atlantic to Saint-Tropez on the French Riviera.

The futuristic yacht still sails the world's oceans today. Its arrival in port cities was so impressive that Larry Ellison, founder and CEO of the tech consulting giant Oracle, spotted it one day near Tiburon, outside San Francisco, and was instantly captivated. In 1998, El Tigre's heirs agreed to sell the yacht to Ellison. The *ECO*, later renamed *Katana*, then *Enigma*, and now *Zeus*, is currently docked in Switzerland, owned by a European businessman well aware of his megayacht's storied past.

Recently, Martin Francis donated a 1:50 scale replica of the *ECO* to the International Maritime Museum in Hamburg, Germany.

Perenchio's DC-9

Perenchio never forgot a tour given by Hugh Hefner aboard the *Big Bunny*, the DC-9 jet proudly owned by the founder of the *Playboy* adult-media empire. That trip must have left an indelible mark on Perenchio's memory, because in 1976, he tried to buy that exact plane for himself, though his efforts were ultimately thwarted by an irrefutable offer from the Venezuelan government, operating through the national airline Aeropostal, which ultimately acquired the iconic private jet. The *Big Bunny*'s tail number, a trace of its glamorous past, changed from N950PB to YV-19C.

However, in 1980, Perenchio, driven by his unwavering desire, tried again to purchase the plane from the Venezuelan government, only to find that it had already been transferred to the Mexican government and assigned to the Aeroméxico fleet. The remains of that famous plane now rest, like a forgotten skeleton, at an airport in the city of Querétaro, Mexico.

Perenchio remained stubbornly fixated on his goal, refusing to give up on his quest to own a DC-9 of his own. When he finally got his hands on one, he meticulously remodeled it, equipping it with a master bedroom, a working office, a meeting room, and a kitchenette. Not much is known about this airborne toy. Perenchio occasionally loaned it out to ferry celebrities from place to place, but eventually he lost interest and sold it to a Texas oil magnate. In his memoir, Don Francisco recalls how Perenchio flew him in that DC-9 to his appearance at Jay Leno's Burbank studios in 1992.

Art and Society in Emilio Azcárraga Milmo and Paula Cusi's Mexico

Paula Cusi, wife of the richest and most powerful man in Mexico in the 1980s, became a patron and collector of contemporary art. El Tigre always admired and appreciated the way in which Paula managed to open doors to the upper echelons of New York society. Her education in the field began under the tutelage of Patricia Phelps de Cisneros, a sophisticated Venezuelan socialite with a degree in philosophy from Wheaton College in Massachusetts and the wife of media mogul Gustavo Cisneros. Patricia, younger than her husband, left a lasting impression on Paula Cusi, whose birth name was Encarnación Presa Matute.

Fueled by this newfound love of art, Paula Cusi convinced El Tigre to found the Centro Cultural Arte Contemporáneo in México in 1986. She also persuaded her husband to hire Robert R. Littman, director of the Grey Art Gallery and Study Center at New York University. This decision catapulted Paula, as co-director of this new Mexican museum, to the heights of the American art world and positioned her as a major figure among Mexico's high society.

After El Tigre's death, relations between Cusi and her late husband's family cooled. Although the couple had been separated, El Tigre ensured that Cusi continued to hold and exercise power in various circles within the Televisa ecosystem, which included the Centro Cultural Arte Contemporáneo. After his death, though, everything seemed to change.

In a dramatic turn of events, just four months after El Tigre passed away, Paula Cusi made a bold move that rocked Televisa to its core. In August 1997, with an astonishing swiftness, she severed all ties with the iconic company, selling off all the shares El Tigre had bequeathed to her in his will. Cusi's decision wasn't just quick, it was also harmonious, having opted to sell her stake to El Tigre's designated successor, his son Emilio Azcárraga Jean. The $45 million transaction was merely a prelude of a more profound change yet to come. Shortly after this historic sale, the new administration made a decision that ignited a new cycle in Cusi's relationship with the Azcárragas. Televisa decided to close the Centro Cultural Arte Contemporáneo, and in doing so, it erased any traces of Cusi's influence on El Tigre's vast legacy.

Without any fanfare, the Centro Cultural Arte Contemporáneo, once praised by critics as Mexico's finest forum for modern art, closed its doors on Sunday, September 18, 1998, just over a year after Azcárraga Milmo's death. With that, the museum, located in a facility that during the previous twelve years had hosted 172 exhibitions that included retrospectives of both Mexican and international artists, ceased to exist.

But Paula Cusi's journey didn't end there. She continued to be a highly regarded collector of contemporary art, which led her to join the board of directors of the Metropolitan Museum of Art in New York. Despite the quick and amicable sale of her shares of Televisa, Cusi's relationship with the Azcárraga family's heirs turned harsh and scandalous in the wake of the museum's arbitrary closure. There isn't enough space in a work of this scale to fully explore that stage of the game, though there is certainly enough material to write an entire telenovela about El Tigre's women, with several episodes being devoted to Paula Cusi.

The Art and Wines of Jerry Perenchio

A. Jerrold "Jerry" Perenchio was born in the rugged town of Fresno, California. He was a wide-eyed child who grew up in a family far removed from aristocracy and museums. At one of the auctions of his personal collection, following his death in 2017, the auctioneer recounted something Perenchio once said about having grown up so far removed from art and culture: "I was born in Fresno. We didn't have any artwork. I was taken to night-clubs and boxing matches! I had no appreciation or knowledge of art or any other kind of culture."

Never having been privy to such things as a child, Perenchio grew up to be one of the great art collectors of his day. But getting there required a long journey of learning, discovery, and a great deal of money.

During the final years of his life, he shared both his presence and his love of art with his last love, the actress Anjelica Huston, known for 1985's *Prizzi's Honor*, for which she won the Oscar for Best Supporting Actress, as well as her role as Morticia in the 1991 film *The Addams Family*, alongside Puerto Rican actor Raul Julia.

Perenchio was a man who believed in the boldest of dreams. He invested in Ridley Scott's *Blade Runner*, a project few were willing to bet on yet one that would become a cult classic in cinema history. He also financed the multiaward-winning *Driving Miss Daisy*, starring Morgan Freeman and Jessica Tandy. "It was very foolhardy of Perenchio to gamble on a film starring an elderly woman and her Black chauffeur," as one film critic put it. Yet in 1989, *Driving Miss Daisy* was a resounding critical and box office success, winning four Oscars. Perenchio's money also flowed into the 2002 film *Frida*, further solidifying the fame of Mexican actress Salma Hayek.

"A big part of the heart and soul of any city is its dedication and commitment to the arts," Perenchio declared at a press conference at the Los Angeles County Museum of Art. It was 2014, and at the age of eighty-three, he pledged to donate at least forty-seven masterpieces to the museum, including works by Monet, Picasso, and Degas. This gift, valued at just under half a billion dollars, was made after his death from lung cancer in 2017. Perenchio enjoyed his art until the very end. The rest of his personal collection was auctioned off by Christie's in 2018 and 2020.

Perenchio was also quite generous with his wives. He acquired a beachside mansion on several acres of land in Malibu on which he built a golf course for his wife Margaret, herself an avid golfer. This gift led to a lawsuit against the city of Malibu, which prohibited the construction of golf courses solely for the enjoyment of a single family. According to city regulations, all golf courses had to belong to a membership-based club or be open to the public.

Perenchio also owned a California vineyard valued at more than $20 million. His private wine cellar was located in the basement of Chartwell and was accessible to only a select few. James Ritchie, global head of wine and spirits at Sotheby's, wrote the following preface to the auctioning of Perenchio's wine collection a few months after his death:

> The Jerry Perenchio Cellar is without doubt one of the greatest collections of mature wines ever to be offered for sale at auction. It includes previously unthinkable quantities of legendary vintages from Domaine de la Romanée-Conti, Leroy and de Vogüé, as well as Petrus, Mouton Rothschild, Lafite, Latour, Margaux and Haut Brion. While Mr. Perenchio was perhaps best-known as the former chairman and CEO of Univision and for championing some of the entertainment world's greatest talents, he also applied his instincts for excellence and his unbridled passion to assembling his cellar.

Cisneros's Passion

Gustavo Cisneros was obsessed with being recognized as a global leader. His palatial estates in Aspen, the Dominican Republic, and Venezuela were meeting places for world business leaders and politicians alike, including George H. W. Bush, Gianni Agnelli, King Juan Carlos of Spain, the Dalai Lama, Ted Turner, Henry Kissinger, and Michael Eisner, among many others. Bush even made a number of unofficial visits to Venezuela just to go fishing with Cisneros.

Cisneros also had residences in New York, Miami, and Madrid, which he used on business trips. The Venezuelan businessman also organized and participated in high-level meetings aimed at fostering geopolitical progress between Latin America and more developed countries. For example, thanks to his friendship with the elder Bush, Cisneros was a key factor in the organization and signing of NAFTA, the North American Free Trade Agreement among the United States, Canada, and Mexico. He acted as an intermediary between parties, particularly Bush and the Mexican president, during the early planning stages.

The Colección Patricia Phelps de Cisneros is one of the most important and internationally recognized collections of Latin American art. It was founded in the 1970s by Patricia Phelps de Cisneros and her husband, Gustavo. Its focus is promoting the visibility and recognition of Latin American art on the international stage and includes works by Lygia Clark, Lygia Pape, Jesús Rafael Soto, Alejandro Otero, Tomás Maldonado, Willys de Castro, Hélio Oiticica, Juan Mele, Mira Schendel, and Gego.

In addition to having served for a number of years on Televisa's board of directors, Cisneros also held board positions at Barrick Gold, the International Advisory Council of Chase Manhattan Bank, and he served as chairman of the board of the All-American Bottling Company, which bottled and distributed such beverages as Dr Pepper, Snapple, 7Up, and Crush.

When Cisneros called someone directly, he never announced himself and would become quite irritated when the person on the other end of the line didn't recognize his voice on the phone. And if the call was to someone in his organization and that happened, it could be cause for dismissal. Cisneros liked to assert his control and leadership through sudden, uncomfortable instructions—calling one of his executives from Asia or Europe in the middle of the night just for a restaurant recommendation, for example. On more than one occasion, he ordered an executive to disembark a plane right before taking off for a vacation in order to handle some emergency, or instructed a subordinate to prepare him a whiskey just the way he liked it in front of others. He would often take family and friends on extravagant outings: like flying a helicopter over the tepui mesas in the Venezuelan Amazon. When the helicopter landed, waiters would serve a unique culinary experience, and once back home, the guests would receive a visual summary of the experience titled *The Jungle Book*. He gave younger members of the family Rolex watches engraved with the date of the gift and his initials, GCR (Gustavo Cisneros Rendiles).

There's a particularly noteworthy story that's been confirmed by the famous Spanish singer Julio Iglesias, a personal friend of Cisneros's and a neighbor of his in the Dominican Republic. Iglesias recounted how, on that occasion, the Venezuelan businessman called him to fly immediately to Caracas in order to perform a private concert for the president of China, who was meeting with Venezuelan President Hugo Chávez. Cisneros provided his private jet, and Iglesias agreed. As incredulous as that may seem, you can see it all on YouTube by searching "Julio Iglesias canta con el presidente chino Jiang Zemin y el presidente Venezolano Chávez," which includes a shot of Cisneros witnessing the very event he, himself, orchestrated.

Anselmo Versus the Status Quo

Unlike El Tigre Azcárraga, Jerry Perenchio, or Gustavo Cisneros, René Anselmo never aspired to be known as a mogul. Although he built himself a mansion in Greenwich, Connecticut, inspired by the Petit Trianon at Versailles and valued at $39 million, his true passion wasn't about accumulating wealth but changing the status quo and improving his surroundings. In his later years, activism led him to confront municipal regulations, promoting changes that had a lasting impact on the community. He wasn't content with simply living in the lap of luxury; he was looking to transform his city according to his vision of beauty and order.

Anselmo became a passionate advocate for Greenwich's urban aesthetics. Frustrated with the proliferation of real estate signs, he began removing them himself and piling them up at his own home, daring the agencies to come and remove them from his property. This crusade earned him a pair of arrests and vandalism charges, but it also prompted a change in municipal policy in 1993, two years before his death.

Beyond the controversy, Anselmo also left a legacy of generosity. He funded improvements to a number of public schools, from wooden fences to recreational areas and jogging trails. His love of nature led him to plant tens of thousands of flowers in Greenwich, including tulips and daffodils that to this day bloom every spring. Until his final days, René Anselmo defied established norms, being guided more by idealism than the pursuit of recognition.

These television moguls not only established Univision and PanAmSat as unstoppable forces in the communications industry, they also left a lasting impression through their mansions, yachts, aircraft, and eccentricities: the embodiment of power and opulence at its finest.

CHAPTER 16

The Never-Ending Sale

Perenchio's skill at navigating the complex world of business was undeniable, but his understanding of Univision's content consumers remained cryptically distant. He was the architect of a media empire, a true mogul, and yet his interest seemed more focused on the machinations of global success than on the voices and lives of his audience.

For many at Univision, Perenchio didn't show a particular interest in Hispanic culture. He did, however, have an almost innate ability to benefit from this audience without harboring any malicious intent. His approach was pragmatic, perhaps even standoffish, but in business terms it was effective. He never accepted invitations from El Tigre and Gustavo Cisneros to visit Mexico, the Dominican Republic, or Venezuela. Meetings with him took place only at Univision headquarters, Chartwell, and occasionally at La Hacienda.

Univision's executives were in a constant struggle to exceed the big boss's demands. Whether from Chartwell or his office in Los Angeles, Perenchio directed this ecosystem with a clear vision in place. While El Tigre and Cisneros were partners in Univision, Perenchio managed to establish a framework that placed him at the forefront of the most important decisions. Aspects ranging from finance, corporate governance, and procedures fell under his firm control. Cisneros accepted the power's being concentrated in Perenchio's hands, but El Tigre always believed he deserved greater participation.

During his first year as CEO and top boss of the network in 1991, Perenchio decided to entrust his strategy to two executives he had placed within the organization: Carlos Barba, whom he had known since his time at NetSpan in the 1980s, was appointed vice president of programming, and Andrew Hobson, one of Perenchio's closest confidants, became the chief financial officer. In his search for managers and executives who wouldn't simply cast their loyalty at the feet of either El Tigre or Cisneros, Hobson found Ray Rodríguez, the coordinator of Channel 23 in Miami.

Ray Rodríguez was passionate about programming and already had an impressive track record at Univision. And he was no stranger to the entertainment industry: before his time at the network, he had earned his keep as a manager and key figure in establishing Julio Iglesias's success in the United States. When Perenchio learned of Rodríguez's previous exploits, which reflected his own past as an agent representing famous Hollywood actors, the chemistry was instantaneous. All he had to do was make sure Rodríguez wasn't beholden in any way to El Tigre or Cisneros, let alone Joaquín Blaya. Acting on Perenchio's orders, Hobson sent out an internal memo asking for suggestions for a chief operating officer. When that memo reached the desks of El Tigre and Cisneros, they fell into the trap. Each sent in a list of candidates, and Rodríguez's name wasn't on either of them.

Cisneros suggested Carlos Barba as COO. El Tigre was inclined to mention Rosita Perú, but she already had one foot out the door. Rosita then recommended Jaime Dávila, a key player in content management between Televisa and Univision and a close associate of the Azcárragas.

The alchemy between Perenchio and Rodríguez worked like magic. Rodríguez quickly rose to become COO; by 1992, he was already president of Univision reporting directly to Perenchio. He became Perenchio's most trusted right-hand man. Barba and Dávila were assigned two important positions in programming and content production. Barba was seen as Cisneros's man, as Dávila was for El Tigre.

Ray Rodríguez's role wasn't only about execution; he was also a mediator and strategist. He understood the delicate balance that had to be maintained in this corporate jungle. On the one hand, he had to be faithful to Perenchio's vision and objectives, while on the other, he had to ensure that the Univision team, comprised of diverse talents and personalities, functioned harmoniously and efficiently. His ability to navigate this complex environment made him a key player in Univision's success.

Rodríguez served as Perenchio's eyes and ears, giving him a crucial role as his most trusted confidant and adviser. Naturally, Perenchio compensated him quite generously. Rodríguez's loyalty was especially significant considering the presence of two other powerful magnates on the scene: El Tigre Azcárraga and Gustavo Cisneros.

Univision thrived, hitting important milestones and consolidating its position as a giant in the Spanish-speaking market by the mid 1990s. However, this dynamic also revealed a clear hierarchy and power structure where crucial decisions came from Perenchio.

Beginning in 1993, Hobson, the new CFO, took over the financial reins, having accepted the resignation of most of the company's administrative and accounting staff, who had come from Hallmark or SIN. Perenchio's goal was to ensure the financial health of the company, which was still struggling with its massive debt.

In 1994, under Ray Rodríguez's leadership, the company gradually began cutting local programming and reducing local staff. Programming began to consist primarily of Mexican content from Televisa, along with some from Venevisión. The only surviving local productions were *El Show de Cristina*, *Primer Impacto*, *Sábado Gigante*, the morning show called *Mundo Latino*, and the nightly news.

When El Tigre died in 1997, foreign programming on Univision accounted for more than two-thirds of its lineup, the company's revenue surpassed $400 million, and its finances were looking better by the day. Perenchio's commercial pragmatism had won again. Hispanic community organizations were right—their criticisms about mass layoffs and the lack of locally produced programming were valid—but for the new owners, financial health was the top priority. That same year, Reliance Capital announced the sale of Telemundo to Sony Pictures Entertainment and Liberty Media for $539 million.

The Hispanic community continued to grow, and it was in the interests of the authorities to have just two major networks to rely on in case they needed to deliver a unified message. With great business acumen, Univision and Telemundo both capitalized on the strength of the Hispanic market in the United States, bringing together a variety of cultures under a single commercial vision. As a result, national corporations and regional governments began trusting them with their advertising.

If we delve deeper into Perenchio's life and mind, we can better understand the strategy that led him to consolidate Univision as one of the largest and most successful corporations on the American media landscape. In 1991, already in his sixties and with a fortune estimated at $500 million, Perenchio had a clear plan in mind: build a media empire that would validate his bet on the emerging Hispanic market in the United States. At that time, the Spanish-speaking population was around twenty-two million, and Perenchio, ever the visionary, projected that this number would reach thirty million within the next decade and a half. Reality exceeded even his own expectations: by 2007, the nation's Hispanic population numbered more than forty-five million.

To transform this new acquisition of his into a North American corporation so colossal that no competitor, regardless of how powerful it might be, could ever hope to challenge it, Perenchio needed to convince the capital markets and sophisticated American financial ecosystem that Univision was a diamond in the rough.

Latin Envy

One of the burning aspirations in Perenchio's heart was to see his company listed on the New York Stock Exchange (NYSE). Some of those closest to the CEO saw this wish as mere indulgence by the boss. But Perenchio knew that, if he succeeded, it would spark envy among industry giants who might be eager to take over Univision. Perenchio never expressed any interest in selling, though. Instead, as he hinted, his intention was always to buy.

There was a lot of buzz on Wall Street in 1996, with IPOs from companies such as Cox, Ralph Lauren, Children's Place, and TD Ameritrade. Amid this wave of stock market debuts, on Friday, September 27, months before Jeff Bezos's Amazon went public, Univision joined the club.

The company announced it was making 19 percent of the company's capital available to the public at an initial share price of $23, giving Univision a valuation close to a billion dollars. This figure was nearly double what Hallmark had been paid just five years earlier.

Perenchio decided to launch the IPO on the same day that fourteen other companies were issuing their own initial offerings. Even so, the event didn't go unnoticed on Wall Street, as Univision's stock price rose to $31 that very same day. Perenchio and his CFO, Hobson, selected a triumvirate of leading investment banks—Goldman Sachs, Morgan Stanley, and Deutsche Bank—to coordinate the offering's strategy and marketing. These banks structured a setup with different classes of shares, and even though Perenchio's ownership was diluted to just 26.5 percent of the company's total shares, his "Class A" shares still controlled 78.5 percent of the voting power for the company's operational decisions. The IPO was a resounding success, with an immediate secondary market appreciation of around 30 percent and a public validation of the recognition that Univision had built and Perenchio had meticulously sought. As part of the pre-IPO marketing, in the summer of 1996, a survey emerged suggesting that U.S. Hispanics knew Univision better than the Bible. This led to comments among advertising agencies suggesting Hispanics trusted Univision more than the church itself.

Like a script taken from a hit TV series, the world of Spanish-language television was about to experience a multibillion-dollar burst of corporate stardom. There was something in the air, some irresistible allure that industry insiders began calling "Latin envy." The architect of this new era was the newest American media mogul: Jerry Perenchio. The absence of El Tigre Azcárraga and Gustavo Cisneros from the various press statements about Univision's debut on the New York Stock Exchange was all part of Perenchio's strategy.

El Tigre Announces His Retirement and Hands Over the Reins to His Son, Emilio Azcárraga Jean

The surging euphoria of Latin envy coincided with Emilio Azcárraga Milmo's rapidly deteriorating health. El Tigre began distancing himself from the decision-makers at Univision. At the time of the company's IPO in September 1996, between treatments, surgeries, and Televisa-related meetings, he was busy preparing his son, Emilio Azcárraga Jean—who at twenty-eight years of age was aware of what was coming, if not yet ready to accept it.

Before his father's death, Emilio Azcárraga Jean knew little about Univision. Just months after El Tigre's departure, the young executive inherited an avalanche of challenges, ranging from internal strife at Televisa to family conflicts and mounting debts. By contrast, Univision didn't seem to pose any significant problems.

In a private meeting with Jaime Escandón, his CFO for Televisa's U.S. operations, El Tigre delivered two unexpected instructions: to find a good office space in Miami, because he would be relocating there soon, and to transfer 1,786,977 shares of Univision to his most trusted executive at the company, Jaime Dávila. That transfer was formalized on February 14, 1997, and from that day on, Dávila became Univision's richest executive.

It was then that El Tigre's inner circle came to grasp the seriousness of his health problems. While he'd never felt a particular affinity for Miami, El Tigre chose to face his terminal illness far from the media spotlights of Mexico and Los Angeles. The last time Televisa's executive team saw him in person was in LA, when he decided to grant an interview that would mark the end of his era at the company's helm. Early in 1997, during his final public appearance as president of Televisa, he sat next to his son for a special broadcast with Jacobo Zabludovsky. Without mentioning his health in any way, he explained that he was handing over control of the company to his son, stating that his new task was to dedicate himself to "developing images through satellites." The news was an unexpected and shocking blow to everyone at the Mexican organization. The Miami offices that Escandón had secured would never be occupied by El Tigre.

Euphoria

Between 1997 and the arrival of the new millennium, Univision's sales skyrocketed, as did its stock price. The U.S. Hispanic population was then in excess of thirty million. Despite the shuddering impact felt by global financial markets from the September 11, 2001, terrorist attacks that brought down the World Trade Center twin towers in New York, Univision was generating more than $1 billion in advertising revenue by the very next year, and its stock had doubled from its 1997 IPO price to more than $50 per share. The 19 percent of Univision listed on the New York Stock Exchange now reflected a market valuation of more than $2 billion. Wall Street analysts estimated the value of Univision's controlling stake at more than $5 billion in 2002. The wealth of brothers Gustavo and Ricardo Cisneros, as well as that of the heir, Emilio Azcárraga Jean, had multiplied not only from their equity stake in the company but also from additional income generated by content sales. The Cisneros name started appearing on *Forbes*'s list of billionaires: for Cisneros, Univision was, without a doubt, the best financial decision of his career. But it wasn't just Univision's owners who benefited from this surge in value—Jaime Dávila was now one of American society's new millionaires. By 2002, neither Ray Rodríguez nor Andrew Hobson was a shareholder. But in December 2003, both received a bonus in the form of stock options: each had been granted the right to purchase a hundred thousand shares of Univision at $35.85 apiece, an offer that would expire in 2013. This sort of incentive was becoming more common for top executives at publicly traded corporations in the United States. Rodríguez and Hobson would go on to receive more such options in the years that followed.

Univision's rival, Telemundo, wasn't impervious to the temptations of Latin envy and didn't wait long to act. In 2002, Sony Pictures Entertainment and Liberty Media announced that the company was up for sale. General Electric, through its NBC network, moved quickly to cut its competitors off at the pass with a bold offer of nearly $2 billion.

Viacom, a true entertainment giant that, at the time, owned both CBS and MTV, wasn't going to sit idly by. Within days, it came knocking on Univision's door with a takeover proposal. The dance was in full swing, with each competitor trying to outdo the last with more extravagant and audacious moves. Perenchio was king, and the king had his general, Ray Rodríguez, commanding the party.

AOL Time Warner Inc., the Walt Disney Company, and other major players were on the prowl, all curious to see what Univision had to offer. Michael Eisner, Disney's well-known CEO, didn't mince words when he expressed interest in entering the Hispanic market, though it would all come down to one key question: "How much does it cost?"

"Anyone who is going to acquire Univision is going to pay a premium over the current equity value," noted David Joyce, an astute analyst at Coral Gables–based investment firm Guzman & Company. "They are strong financial players and they have no reason to sell." Furthermore, it was clear that a merger or acquisition with one of the country's major media companies could unlock valuable synergies like cost savings and potential additional profits through cross-promotion. Once again, the idea of a merger or buyout presented itself as a major growth opportunity, and the sellers—Perenchio, Cisneros, and Emilio Azcárraga Jean, who was thirty-two by then and an active member of Univision's board of directors—would have to be enticed with a share in those projected gains.

Amid the frenzy, some truly staggering figures began to circulate. Analysts speculated that Univision's price could reach as high as $12 billion. It was like being in the midst of a gold rush, with Univision as the mother lode.

During NBC's celebrations for having acquired Telemundo on October 11, 2001, Perenchio sent a playful note to NBC's chairman, Andrew Lack: "I was looking for a white flag to wave, but I couldn't find one." Perenchio was indicating that, despite NBC's big acquisition, Univision would neither surrender nor give up its status as the market leader. Many analysts interpreted the message as Perenchio's way of saying Univision was not for sale.

The fever was spreading. Everyone wanted their share of this pie, which served a population that was not only growing faster than other demographic group in the United States but also watching more television. In fact, a study by the Strategy Research Corp. of Miami revealed that Latinos watched more television than the general population: an average of 4.4 hours per day for Latinos versus 2.9 for non-Latinos. Latin envy was in full swing, and the stage was set for battle. But what Perenchio didn't know was that Emilio Azcárraga Jean was lurking in the shadows, waiting to strike.

For the past year, Perenchio, oblivious to the beating of the drums of war, had ignored the messages being sent by Emilio Azcárraga Jean, who wanted to renegotiate the terms of the twenty-five-year programming agreement his father had signed back in 1992. Azcárraga Jean's goal was to increase his stake in Univision, the network his grandfather had helped bring to life in 1961, under the name SIN, which now loomed like a giant over the American media landscape. But El Tigre's signature still graced that deal, granting Univision total control over all of Televisa's programming in the United States through the year 2017. It felt like a curse.

Perenchio was maneuvering the pieces on this chessboard with masterful precision. Financial analysts sat nervously in their seats, murmuring that Televisa held veto rights over certain types of transactions within Univision. Everything was in motion, in flux, and no one knew how the game would end.

Meanwhile, Emilio Azcárraga Jean was contemplating his next move. In 2003, at the age of thirty-five, he announced that he was considering applying for U.S. citizenship, dreaming of expanding his Spanish-language empire. "If it's in Televisa's best interests to apply for dual citizenship, then that's what I would do," he said, making it clear that his loyalty lay with his company.

With a U.S. passport, Azcárraga Jean could follow the path blazed by Rupert Murdoch, who, despite having been born in Australia, obtained his U.S. citizenship in order to circumvent legal restrictions on foreign ownership of media. If Azcárraga Jean were to become a citizen, he could acquire or increase stakes in American media companies.

By this time, his relationship with Perenchio was beginning to sour. Even so, Azcárraga Jean still claimed he was hoping for an amicable agreement.

Univision continued to feed primarily on content from Televisa and Venevisión, which ranged from melodramatic telenovelas to comedy shows like *El Chavo del Ocho*, *El Chapulín Colorado*, and *Bienvenidos* to soccer matches passionately narrated by fervent, vociferous announcers and colorful commentators.

Emilio Azcárraga Jean pressed the issue of renegotiating the programming agreement, even attempting to separate the rights to television broadcasting content from internet streaming rights: something that was just beginning to emerge at the time. But Perenchio remained unswayed. He would rather pay more than change the terms of the original agreement. He believed he could calm the storm with gold, but through Emilio Azcárraga Jean the ghosts of El León and El Tigre seemed to haunt the dream they had begun even from the great beyond. In 2005, the tension between Perenchio and Azcárraga Jean reached its breaking point. The pieces were out of place, and the chessboard awaited a decisive move.

The air was charged with electricity in the boardroom of Univision Communications Inc. when, in May 2005, the long-simmering turmoil finally boiled over. The bombshell: Emilio Azcárraga Jean, Univision's second-largest shareholder, had resigned as vice chairman of the board of directors. Whispers among analysts that his abrupt departure, which coincided with the eve of Univision's annual shareholders' meeting, was a provocative gesture of defiance, a signal foreshadowing a hostile push to wrest control of the company from Perenchio's grip. "He has thrown down the gauntlet," said Leland Westerfield, a media analyst with Harris Nesbitt Gerard. Words that made headlines and set off a wave of speculation.

At the time, the president of Televisa had already established himself as a media magnate in Mexico, and had been engaged for months in a power struggle with the president of Univision, the veteran Jerry Perenchio, who was old enough to be his grandfather. Perenchio was too rigid, too private, and no one knew what his succession plan was. Negotiations could be conducted only directly through him, and attempts to understand his intentions regarding future control of Univision had proved fruitless. But the drama didn't end with Azcárraga Jean's resignation. Adding fuel to that fire, Televisa filed a lawsuit in U.S. District Court in Los Angeles alleging that Univision had shorted it roughly $1.5 million in programming royalties. Univision flatly denied the allegations and declared itself ready for legal battle.

Azcárraga Jean's desire to control Univision was an open secret. The young heir could circumvent the 25 percent stake by partnering with local investors, particularly private equity firms that had no interest in running the network, just in being financial partners. Wall Street experts considered such a move to be premature. "At some point, Televisa should buy Univision, but right now it doesn't make sense to go up against Perenchio," they said,

Emilio Azcárraga Jean, Jerry Perenchio y Gustavo Cisneros, 1992. (Fotografía: HBusiness.)

suggesting that it might be wiser to simply wait him out, considering his advanced age.

Emilio Azcárraga Jean's persistence and pressure ultimately prevailed. Months after Azcárraga Jean's resignation from Univision's board, Perenchio leaked to the press his willingness to sell. It now seemed that Azcárraga Jean was the one pushing the endgame in this chess match, and investors, the American press, and employees at both Televisa and Univision wanted front-row seats to the final outcome.

As soon as it became known that Perenchio, the legendary industry captain, was ready to sell, a polished group of investors teamed, through Televisa, with Emilio Azcárraga Jean in a crusade to purchase Univision. The reality of the numbers, though, quickly cast a shadow over the negotiations, and the three giants originally expected to join Televisa—Kohlberg Kravis Roberts & Co., the Carlyle Group, and the Blackstone Group—walked away from the negotiating table, having decided the asking price was too high. Undeterred, Azcárraga Jean and Televisa played their next card, adding (among others) Providence Equity Partners, Bain Capital, and Cascade Investment, the investment vehicle of none other than Bill Gates. (In reviewing Univision's shareholder books, I was able to determine that Gates personally held a small number of Univision shares in 2006: proof that he was genuinely interested in delving into the Hispanic market.)

Meanwhile, on the other side of the chessboard, Haim Saban, an LA billionaire who had earned his fortune thanks to the *Power Rangers* television series, was assembling his own army, having recruited Texas Pacific Group, Madison Dearborn Partners, and Thomas H. Lee Partners. Then, in an eleventh-hour twist worthy of a TV drama, which stunned the Mexican side with its brazenness, Providence Equity Partners switched sides, abandoning the consortium organized by Emilio Azcárraga Jean to join Saban's ranks.

The Bostonian Thomas Lee was key in this last-minute betrayal. On top of that, rumors and analyst speculation suggested that Perenchio didn't want Azcárraga Jean to win the bid, considering him a spoiled, arrogant rich kid—at least according to the whisperings. In this game of power chess, Cisneros's role became crucial, because he could act as a mediator between Televisa and Univision's new owner in the event that Televisa lost the bid. So despite everything to the contrary, Televisa still held the high ground, because even if it lost the bidding war, the new owner would still have to work with them in order to obtain content.

The final battle was waged between two groups of titans. On one side of the chessboard was the Televisa group, whose victory would present federal regulators with the challenge of unraveling a business structure that could potentially violate both the letter and spirit of the 25 percent rule. On the other, the Saban group, whose main appeal to Perenchio was that all members of the team were U.S.-based entities and didn't include Azcárraga Jean.

In a coup de grâce, Haim Saban emerged as the undisputed victor, signing the winning bid at a price of $12.3 billion, while taking on Univision's $1.4 billion debt, in a deal valued at $13.7 billion all told. For many analysts, this move, while it represented a substantial increase in Perenchio's coffers, was a blow to the hopes of his mortal rival, Emilio Azcárraga Jean.

Amid the conflicts and controversies, Gustavo Cisneros had positioned himself as a clear beneficiary of the transaction. The increased price meant a larger payout for him. Cisneros handled the situation shrewdly, portraying himself as a seller to the highest bidder, remaining neutral and showing no particular preference for any of the candidates looking to acquire Univision. He was receptive to both Saban's group and that of Televisa, always accepting their requests for meetings and responding to their inquiries. This behavior did not sit well with Televisa.

Cisneros received a significant sum—in excess of $1.5 billion—in addition to establishing key relationships, like the one he developed with Thomas H. Lee, with whom he would go on to engage in other content and TV broadcasting ventures throughout the subsequent decade. This alliance was also frowned upon by Televisa.

Thus we had the winning group, comprised of expert investors, including Thomas H. Lee Partners, Texas Pacific Group,

Madison Dearborn Partners, Providence Equity Partners, and businessman Haim Saban. Televisa did not sell all of its shares and remained a minority shareholder with a seat on the board of directors.

Haim Saban was born in Alexandria, Egypt, in 1944 to a Jewish Egyptian family. In 1956, the Saban family immigrated to Israel, along with most of their community. Eventually, Haim moved to the United States, where he became a naturalized citizen.

It's worth noting that after several years as Univision's primary owner, a number of company employees considered him a contender to achieve Perenchio-esque levels of success. Perenchio's shadow was long, and his legacy at Univision is undisputable. Upon taking the reins, Saban seemed to be constantly trying to replicate his predecessor's style and success. He even kept Ray Rodríguez, Perenchio's most trusted man, as CEO and COO for a time.

Meanwhile, the television industry was beginning to experience a major revolution with the arrival of digital platforms like Google, Facebook, Twitter, and YouTube. The latter's emergence in 2005, and the launch of on-demand movie and TV show services led by Netflix in 2007, signaled a profound transformation in the way audiences consume content. This sea change represented a monumental challenge for traditional television networks that were beginning to feel the impact of declining household viewership and the resulting drop in traditional advertising revenue.

The evolution of YouTube, which was acquired by Google in 2006, played a crucial role in redesigning advertising models in the media and entertainment world. The platform became an essential tool for content creators, significantly disrupting the industry and challenging the hegemony of traditional media. At the same time, Facebook and Twitter began to integrate with the experience of television, changing the way viewers interacted with one another.

The world of on-demand digital streaming has continued to grow to this day, with platforms like Hulu, Amazon, and Apple TV joining Netflix, increasing the number of competitors while further expanding content options for consumers. This transitional era saw not only a shift in viewer consumption patterns but also a redefinition of the entire media landscape.

In this rapidly evolving context, Univision's role and its leadership found itself at a critical juncture, facing the challenge of adapting to a constantly changing media environment and the expectations of an increasingly diverse and digitally connected audience.

Perenchio Retires

On March 29, 2007, Jerry Perenchio left Univision.

As planned, the sale of the company for $13.7 billion closed two business days after March 25, when the transaction was approved by the FCC. That day, in a written statement, Perenchio said, "I am enormously proud of all that Univision has accomplished since 1992 and look forward to following the next phase of its growth."

This historic 2007 transaction was a milestone in the history of Hispanic-focused companies. To this day, in 2025, it is still considered the largest sale ever made in the sector by a private company dedicated to this audience. This achievement reflected the exceptional vision, leadership, and savvy of Perenchio, Azcárraga Jean, and Cisneros.

Perenchio was never able to shake the ghost of El Tigre. In 2009, Televisa and its U.S. licensee, Univision, by then already under Saban's control, found themselves once again in federal court, arguing about who held the rights to distribute Televisa-produced programs online and via streaming platforms in the United States. The first witness in the trial was former Univision CEO Jerry Perenchio, who, at the age of seventy-eight and in poor health, appeared via videoconference. In his statement, he brought up an old story from his days battling El Tigre:

> The signatures were barely dry before the fireworks started. He [El Tigre] told me himself he was going to launch a satellite television channel without taking into account the contract we had signed. It was unacceptable. They never liked it... they never thought it was fair to Televisa. They took the position that they had rights for their programming for the internet. He never understood that this agreement is vital to Univision. One of our greatest fears is if we loose the noose, Televisa will enter the U.S. market with some or all of its programming and destroy or severely wound Univision.

For the first and only time in history, Jerry Perenchio had revealed his fear of El Tigre Azcárraga, both before and after his death.

CHAPTER 17

The Story Comes to an End

A new era began in 2007 with Haim Saban as Univision's principal owner. Joseph "Joe" Uva, a successful advertising agency executive, was appointed CEO, while Perenchio associates Ray Rodríguez and Andrew Hobson continued on as president and CFO, respectively, though the former would leave the company in August 2009. Hobson's and Perenchio's accountant, Peter Lori, would remain with the organization for many more years.

Before joining Univision as CEO, Joe Uva already had a solid, extensive track record in media and advertising. He headed the renowned communications agency OMD Worldwide as president and CEO from 2002 to 2007. Prior to that, he worked in the commercial division at Turner Broadcasting, leading sales and marketing for cable channels like TBS, TNT, and the Cartoon Network.

Univision's board of directors, appointed in 2007 by new shareholders, made history by including, for the first time, a woman among its members: the iconic singer Gloria Estefan. Along with her, the board included Haim Saban, CEO and principal shareholder of Saban Capital Group; David Bonderman, founding partner of Texas Pacific Group; Jonathan M. Nelson,

CEO and founder of Providence Equity Partners; and Henry Cisneros, former mayor of San Antonio, among seven others.

Having assumed the position, Uva faced a significant financial challenge, as Univision was, yet again, heavily in debt. During Uva's tenure, Univision achieved steady growth in ratings numbers, even surpassing one of the major English-language networks in numbers among prime-time adult viewers. The Univision.com website saw a significant increase in traffic, maintaining its status as the top Spanish-language digital destination for the Hispanic community. In the fourth quarter of 2010, Univision reported a 11.8 percent increase in sales, reaching $576.7 million.

Saban needed the company to justify the more than $13 billion that was invested in it, and the aforementioned accomplishments weren't enough. In January 2011, Univision's majority shareholder, Haim Saban, announced the hiring of executive Randy Falco as COO. Falco had previously served as COO of NBCUniversal, owner of Telemundo. This decision was deeply upsetting to Uva, who, offended by the hiring of such a high-caliber officer without having been consulted, saw it as unfair punishment and decided to resign. His departure took many by surprise. Saban acknowledged his valuable contributions to the company, stating that "Univision is a better company today due to Joe's efforts in building a strong leadership team and positioning Univision for long-term success." In 2013, Joe Uva was hired by NBCUniversal to lead Telemundo.

In 2011, television veteran Randy Falco took over as Univision's CEO, replacing Uva at a time when the company was still facing significant financial challenges. His arrival came with an ambitious mission assigned by Haim Saban and Thomas Lee: take Univision public through an IPO in the next few years, a step aimed at recouping the multibillion-dollar investment that had been made in the company. But the path to the stock market would not be easy, and Falco acknowledged that a substantial capital influx would be needed to achieve the growth in value expected by the owners.

To accomplish this, Falco drove significant growth at Univision, thanks to the guidance of Cesar Conde, who held the programming reins in his hands and was the longest-serving executive at Univision since the days of Jerry Perenchio and Ray Rodríguez. In order to achieve his objectives, Falco requested more resources and approved more debt, adding to the company's already considerable liabilities. Isaac Lee, a Colombian journalist and president of Univision News, had just kicked off his role in December 2010, having been hired by Conde, who had given him full support to invest in a newsroom at the Newsport production facilities in Doral, Florida, aiming to rival CNN's newsroom in Atlanta when it came to technology, size, and reach. Conde left Univision in 2013 to become executive vice president of Telemundo, having himself been hired by Joe Uva.

Telemundo: An American Television Station in Spanish

The arc of Telemundo's trajectory was distinctly different from that of Univision. The price paid by NBCUniversal, six and a half times less than what Haim Saban paid for Univision, allowed the network's finances to stabilize. After the financial crisis that led Telemundo to bankruptcy in the 1990s, it found refuge within one of the three major U.S. networks while Univision had been sold to the highest bidder.

NBCUniversal executives understood that the key to success in the Hispanic market wasn't improvisation. Instead of betting on leaders unfamiliar with the idiosyncrasies of the Latino audience, they chose to recruit the top talent that had trained at Univision. With this strategy in mind, when Joe Uva left Univision to take the helm at Telemundo, one of Uva's first decisions was to hire Cesar Conde, one of the former company's rising stars.

Cesar Conde had an impeccable track record. A Harvard graduate with an MBA from the University of Pennsylvania's Wharton School, his career had been enriched by the unique experience of having served as special assistant to Secretary of State Colin Powell during the George W. Bush administration. Conde, the son of a Peruvian cardiologist and a Cuban mother, was born in New York but raised in Miami, which gave him firsthand insight into the cultural diversity of Hispanics in the United States.

Under the leadership of Ray Rodríguez and the strategic vision of Jerry Perenchio, Conde signed on with Univision in 2003 at the age of twenty-nine. He rose rapidly through the company's ranks, serving in various roles until reaching the position of executive vice president. His career continued to ascend after the 2011 arrival of Randy Falco, who kept him in that position until Joe Uva recruited him over to NBCUniversal as EVP in charge of Telemundo and NBC's international business. In 2020, he became the first Hispanic to lead one of the big three English-language news networks in the United States, having been named chairman of NBCUniversal News Group, overseeing NBC News, Telemundo, MSNBC, and CNBC.

Conde had been a key figure when it came to transforming Hispanic television, and his influence also extended beyond the broadcast media's scope. As of 2024, he served on the boards of Walmart and PepsiCo, and was also involved in the Aspen Institute and the Paley Center for Media.

Cesar Conde's story reflects the power of a Univision training combined with an education at the world's top academic institutions. His rise to leadership at NBCUniversal represents the height of recognition for a Hispanic American in all of media. For many, Telemundo represents the truest realization of the dream once envisioned by Joaquín Blaya: an American television station in Spanish.

Falco's Univision

In 2012, Randy Falco successfully launched Univision Deportes, a cable channel dedicated to broadcasting sports content twenty-four hours a day. It quickly became a cornerstone of the company, running neck and neck with ESPN Deportes. To spearhead this ambitious project, Falco brought in Juan Carlos Rodríguez, known as La Bomba ("the Bomb," but in a positive way), a prominent Mexican sports media executive. Under his leadership, Univision Deportes secured broadcasting rights to most matches in Liga MX, the Mexican professional soccer league, along with other international leagues, while also gaining exclusive coverage rights to the 2014 FIFA World Cup in Brazil.

But not all of Falco's decisions were without scrutiny. The executive was looking to draw in English-speaking audiences, and in 2013, he launched Fusion, a joint venture between Univision Communications and the Disney-ABC Television Group, aimed at producing and broadcasting content for both Hispanic and

Anglo-American young adults, particularly millennials. Fusion, offering a mix of news, lifestyle, pop culture, satire, and entertainment programming, represented Univision's first significant foray into English-language content creation. However, the ambitious initiative began to show cracks when Disney pulled out of the partnership in 2016, leaving Univision in full control of both Fusion and its mounting losses. While no official figures are available, industry executives estimated that Fusion's failure resulted in losses exceeding $120 million.

Univision also saw a major shakeup in its programming with the farewell episode of one of its most iconic shows: *Sábado Gigante*. On September 19, 2015, the final episode aired under the title "Sábado Gigante: ¡Hasta Siempre!," led by Don Francisco and his co-stars, Javier Romero and Lili Estefan. After fifty-three years on the air (including the first decade broadcast only in Chile), the final show was a deeply emotional event that featured appearances by Luis Fonsi, Paulina Rubio, Enrique Iglesias, Juanes, and Shakira.

In 2015, rumors that Univision was preparing for an initial public offering gained even more momentum when Falco announced the hiring of Goldman Sachs, Morgan Stanley, and Deutsche Bank for structuring the company's registration on the NYSE. The anticipation at Univision's offices was tangible, and many of the executives there—who had received stock options as bonuses—began picturing themselves as soon-to-be millionaires. But economic challenges and increasing losses from failed investments were complicating the negotiations.

In 2015, Telemundo acquired the broadcast rights to the 2018 and 2022 FIFA World Cups, for which it paid $600 million. For the first time in U.S. history, the massive global sporting event wouldn't be presented by Univision. It was a serious body blow to the company's image.

Televisa, for its part, secured the broadcast rights to those World Cups for Mexico. Internally, executives remarked that while the price Telemundo paid seemed absurd, Univision, in the context of a pre-IPO environment, should not have allowed itself to miss out on such an important deal.

In July 2015, Univision and Televisa took a decisive step in their partnership by announcing significant changes to their program license agreement. With this renewal, Univision extended its exclusive rights to Televisa's programming through 2030. Televisa ultimately negotiated compensation that was more in tune with the value of their content. This agreement replaced the historic and controversial contract signed between El Tigre Azcárraga and Jerry Perenchio, which had originally been slated to expire in 2017.

As part of this new agreement, Televisa also documented the conversion of $1.125 billion in obligations into Univision stock subscription rights known as warrants, thus strengthening its stake in and long-term commitment to the company. This financial engineering was led by Alfonso de Angoitia Noriega, Televisa's executive vice president and a close confidant of the Azcárraga family, who stated, "With these agreements, we further solidify our relationship and reaffirm our commitment to Univision and its future. On a personal note, I want to thank Haim Saban for his leadership at the company and his dedication to making these agreements possible." Randy Falco, Univision's president and CEO at the time, emphasized that the agreement put Univision "in a stronger competitive position going forward."

With this extension, Univision and Televisa not only closed a chapter rife with controversies but also secured collaboration for at least another fifteen years, consolidating a strategic relationship that reinforced the future of both companies.

In November 2015, Isaac Lee assumed the newly created role of chief news and digital officer: a position that expanded his influence within Univision. The following year, Juan Carlos Rodríguez announced the Copa América Centenario, a soccer initiative designed to celebrate the tournament's one-hundredth anniversary. Unlike the regular Copa América cycle, which takes place every four years, this edition was a one-time commemorative edition designed to bring the tournament to the United States. With exclusive broadcasting and commercial rights granted to Univision, the event was a resounding success.

That same year, in a risky yet strategic move, Falco approved the acquisition of Gawker Media, an entertainment news and gossip website, for $135 million. This purchase, however, wasn't without controversy, as Gawker came saddled with a tarnished reputation following a high-profile lawsuit filed by the professional wrestler Hulk Hogan, whose real name was Terry Bollea. In 2012, Gawker had published a ten-second clip of an intimate encounter with Hogan, who sued them for invasion of privacy, as he had been recorded without his consent. The case gained particular notoriety when it was revealed that Peter Thiel, co-founder of PayPal, had secretly funded the lawsuit with approximately $10 million. Thiel, the recipient of critical Gawker reporting in the past, called his action "one of my greater philanthropic things that I've done."

The trial concluded in March 2016 with a Florida jury awarding Hogan $140 million in damages. Despite the risk, Falco defended the acquisition of Gawker as part of a strategy to strengthen Fusion and diversify Univision, aiming to attract an English-speaking audience and improve on the corporation's image ahead of a potential IPO. Furthermore, Falco made the decision to acquire a stake in *The Onion*, the satirical digital media outlet, in hopes of capturing a greater slice of that broadening English-language market. But when the results were in, the decision not to invest in the World Cup and instead attempt to increase the corporation's value by competing for English-speaking viewers turned out to be quite a costly failure for Univision.

On May 23, 2017, another unfortunate piece of news hit the company: Andrew Jerrold "Jerry" Perenchio, a key figure in Univision's history, passed away, five months after having been diagnosed with lung cancer.

That same year, the abounding rumors that Univision would never be going public became a virtual certainty. The debt-ridden company's situation, further burdened by the additional weight of failed investments in Gawker, *The Onion*, and Fusion, was becoming increasingly unsustainable, and the early enthusiasm for the long-awaited IPO was crumbling. In the end, Randy Falco confirmed the inevitable: an initial public offering wouldn't be possible, and his time at Univision was coming to an end. This announcement triggered an exodus of executives, as well as massive layoffs across various departments. Those executives who, at one time, had felt like millionaires in waiting, thanks to their stock options, saw that promise of wealth fade away, leaving them unemployed and searching for new opportunities.

Unexpectedly, Discovery, Inc., one of the global giants in content and entertainment, approached with an offer to acquire Univision. The proposal was valued at around $12 billion: a considerable sum. Surprisingly, Univision rejected Discovery's offer. According to various reports, shareholders and executives were convinced that Univision's value could reach nearly double that figure: $20 billion.

Falco's leadership was a combination of audacity and controversy. His vision drove innovation and ambitious expansion but left behind a trail of risky decisions that failed to deliver the expected results.

In June 2018, Haim Saban and Thomas Lee appointed Vincent Sadusky, a financial executive and former CFO of Telemundo, as the new CEO, assigning him a single objective: get Univision ready for sale. With this decision, Emilio Azcárraga Jean began to envision a new opening within the company: not to acquire it but to expand his traditional role beyond that of a content provider, exploring initiatives to deepen the relationship between Televisa and Univision. El Tigre's heir had always been critical of Univision's unchecked growth.

In May 2019, Televisa Deportes from Mexico and Univision Deportes from the United States surprised everyone with an announcement: the two were merging under a single brand—the Televisa Univision Deportes Network, or TUDN. This move hinted at El Tigre's dream possibly coming true: integrating the two giants.

While the new name didn't formerly signify a merger per se, the growing collaboration in sports broadcasting, marketing, and joint acquisition of international event rights was evident. The idea, driven by Juan Carlos Rodríguez, CEO of Univision Deportes, undoubtably had Azcárraga Jean's approval and transformed the "crown jewels," Televisa Deportes and Univision Deportes, into a symbol of strategic union. TUDN not only consolidated the strength of both brands but also paved the way for an innovative and attractive commercial structure, boosting the potential for a future sale to investors. Immediately following that announcement, the maneuverings for selling the two companies began, with Sadusky representing Univision and Alfonso de Angoitia Noriega representing Azcárragas and their Televisa.

Closing the Circle

In February 2020, just before the official declaration of the COVID-19 pandemic in the United States, Televisa announced its merger with Univision. Through a combination of debt conversion into equity and the consolidation of assets in Mexico, the Mexican company acquired a 36 percent stake in the new entity, which would be called Televisa Univision. Private equity firms Searchlight Capital Partners and ForgeLight took majority control of Univision, acquiring 64 percent of the company from investors led by the Saban Capital Group and Thomas H. Lee Partners. This merger was valued at $7.5 billion.

To fully grasp the scale of the losses sustained by shareholders who had invested in 2007, when they bought Univision for $13.7 billion, consider that, at the time of the merger, they held just 64 percent of the new entity, a stake worth approximately $4.8 billion, or 64 percent of $7.5 billion. To put it bluntly, the group led by Haim Saban and Thomas Lee lost roughly $8.9 billion on the venture.

At the request of Emilio Azcárraga Jean's lawyers, on December 23, 2020, the FCC approved allowing foreign investors to own more than 25 percent of Univision. In 2021, Wade Davis was appointed CEO of Televisa Univision, which was in the process of merging. The Televisa-Univision merger was authorized by the FCC on January 24, 2022, and completed a week later. Emilio Azcarraga's name had returned to Univision with a gale's force.

In March 2022, Davis announced the launch of a new streaming platform called ViX. This high-priced project was part of a bold mission to compete with Netflix, Amazon, Disney, Hulu, and other video-on-demand giants. The idea among the new American shareholders was to build out three distinct brands—three assets with three separate values—with the option to sell them off individually. One would be the free-to-air TV channels in Mexico and the United States, another would be TUDN, and the third would be ViX.

Between 2022 and 2024, Televisa Univision's executive leadership was in the hands of three key figures, all with seats on the board of directors: two Mexicans and one American. Alfonso de Angoitia Noriega, with more than two decades of experience at Televisa, assumed the role of executive chairman; Wade Davis, born in Vermont, became CEO of Televisa Univision, bringing with him twenty years of experience in media that included time at Viacom, where he played a crucial role in the merger with CBS that gave rise to what is now Paramount Global; and, finally, Emilio Azcárraga Jean, who also served as executive chairman of Televisa Univision.

On February 23, 2023, there was breaking news in the new company's headquarters: Thomas H. Lee, a former owner of Univision, had been found dead in the bathroom of his Manhattan office. The renowned investor had suffered a bullet wound to the head, and next to his body was a Smith & Wesson revolver registered in his name. He was seventy-eight years old.

In November 2023, Televisa Univision stirred controversy by interviewing Donald Trump in a tone that contrasted sharply with its previous, much more critical stance. This interview, conducted at Mar-a-Lago, Trump's exclusive residence and private club in West Palm Beach, generated significant media attention. Mexican journalist Enrique Acevedo hosted the conversation, surprising many with the placid manner in which he addressed issues that had previously caused friction between Trump and Univision. Alfonso de Angoitia Noriega was also present, though behind the scenes. During this interview, Trump made a general reference to Televisa Univision's new owners, calling them "unbelievable entrepreneurial people."

Jorge Ramos publicly voiced his disagreement with the interview's tone, casting doubt on the independence of Televisa Univision's news division. For many, this divergent approach felt like a step backward, as it inevitably recalled the incident that had occurred between Ramos and Trump on August 25, 2015, during a press conference in Dubuque, Iowa. Ramos had attempted to take the floor and question Trump about his stance on immigration. Trump, with a dismissive gesture that resonated throughout the Latino community, told Ramos to sit down, that it wasn't his turn to speak. When Ramos persisted, Trump replied with a curt "Go back to Univision," and when Ramos refused to leave, Trump's security team escorted him out of the room. That widely reported and circulated clash became a symbol of the tense, confrontational relationship that Univision and its journalists had maintained with the presidential candidate.

The 2023 conversation between Acevedo and Trump took on an even more complex dimension, so much so that Televisa Univision hired a public relations firm to urgently implement a communication strategy to help contain the fallout triggered by that interview. Months later, in April 2024, Acevedo would once again take center stage when he sat down with President Joe Biden. This time, the interview took place in the Oval Office and was part of Biden's reelection campaign.

On December 29, 2023, sad news hit Televisa Univision's Miami offices: Gustavo Cisneros Rendiles had died unexpectedly after contracting pneumonia following spinal surgery at a New York hospital. He was seventy-eight years old.

Jorge Ramos announced his departure from Televisa Univision on September 9, 2024, surprising his audience and marking the end of an era at the network after a distinguished forty-year career—thirty-eight of those as co-anchor of *Noticiero Univision.* The veteran journalist would remain in his position until December 2024, just after the presidential election in which Donald Trump secured his return to office. In his live farewell address, Ramos described his decision as "difficult and sad."

Ten days after Ramos's departure from the company was announced, Wade Davis stepped down as CEO of Televisa Univision and was replaced by Mexican executive Daniel Alegre.

Alegre brought with him more than thirty years of global experience in media, entertainment, and technology. He rose through the ranks at Google during his sixteen-year tenure there. He held various key executive roles, including president of Global and Strategic Alliances and president of Asia-Pacific, and Latin America. In 2020, Alegre became president and COO of Activision Blizzard, one of the world's leading video game companies. During his time there, he was involved in the early stages of Microsoft's acquisition of the gaming giant: a $68.7 billion deal, considered to have been one of the most significant ever in the tech industry. After leaving Activision Blizzard, he spent slightly more than a year at Yuga Labs, the company behind Bored Ape Yacht Club, or BAYC for short, one of the biggest players in the world of digital collectibles, also known as nonfungible tokens (NFTs). Alegre graduated from Princeton before going on to complete his MBA at Harvard Business School and a juris doctor from Harvard's law school.

On October 24, 2024, shocking news was reported by several U.S. media outlets: Emilio Azcárraga Jean had requested a leave of absence from his role on the Televisa Univision board of directors while the Justice Department investigates alleged bribes paid to FIFA officials in connection with the broadcast rights for the 2018, 2022, 2026, and 2030 World Cups.

At the time of this writing, the Televisa Univision board of directors included Alfonso de Angoitia Noriega of Televisa; Bernardo Gómez Martínez of Televisa; Wade Davis of ForgeLight; Eric Zinterhofer of Searchlight Capital Partners; Jeff Sine of Raine Group; Enrique Senior of Allen & Company, also a member of the Televisa board of directors; Gisel Ruiz, former COO of Sam's Club (Walmart); María Cristina "MC" González Noguera of Popular, Inc.; and Oscar Munoz, retired executive chairman of United Airlines Holdings.

Mexicanization

The media landscape in 2025 presented significant challenges for Televisa Univision. Ongoing technological transformation, shifting audience preferences, and rising competition required a profound reflection on its future.

Televisa Univision operates in two very different territories but is united by the power of its audience, who speaks the same language. In both Mexico and the United States, the company and its two main brands have decades of cultural resonance, giving them an insurmountable advantage over competitors like Telemundo, which lacks clout in the Mexican market. For example, although Amazon has a media presence in Mexico through its Prime Video platform, it faces challenges in growing and consolidating its offerings to address local, cultural, economic, social, and operational nuances.

In terms of distribution in the United States, direct-to-home satellite TV services (DTH), like DirecTV and Dish Network, have seen a sharp decline and are now relegated largely to rural areas. This stands in stark contrast with Mexico, where DTH remains a key distribution channel for television signals. This divergence is due in part to DTH's being more practical for Mexican consumers compared with bundled cable and internet packages, especially in areas with limited broadband infrastructure. Furthermore, the transition to streaming has been slower in Mexico than in the United States. In Mexico, Televisa consolidated its position in this DTH market by completing the acquisition of 100 percent of Sky México, thus securing a privileged position in that signal distribution segment.

The audience for telenovelas continues. Juan Antonio Fernández, an expert in international television content marketing, explained that Turkish telenovelas have now successfully infiltrated audiences across both Latin America and the United States. The reason? Their themes and plot lines are centered on romance without all the additives. "Just like Televisa's telenovelas were before. No narcos, no politics, no social complications.

Turkish telenovelas maintain a style that's 100 percent pink," Fernández says, referring to the simple, conservative content. For Televisa, getting back to its roots by producing rosy telenovelas wouldn't be all that difficult.

International sales of Televisa's historic content library continue to generate steady revenue. Televisa is recognized globally in the business of television content distribution: a reputation it has been building since the 1960s. In 2025, Televisa Univision decided to consolidate both the buying and selling of content in Mexico.

Acquiring rights to sporting events has become fiercely competitive, with no clearly dominant player. In 2024, Televisa Univision obtained the rights to broadcast the Super Bowl in both Mexico and the United States. Companies like Amazon and Netflix have ventured into the production and distribution of sports content, investing heavily in rights to professional leagues, pay-per-view events, and festivals. Amazon recently acquired the rights to broadcast matches played by Chivas Guadalajara, the second most popular team in Mexico's professional Liga MX. However, in Mexico, no entity can surpass Televisa Univision in sports, thanks to its affiliation with Club América, the country's top sports franchise. Club América is the equivalent of Manchester United in England, Real Madrid or Barcelona in Spain, or Paris Saint-Germain (PSG) in France. It is the most popular team on social media, with more than twenty-eight million followers. Its matches draw the highest viewership in North America, regardless of language. It's estimated that Club América has more than forty-four million fans across both Mexico and the United States.

Emilio Azcárraga Jean established a company called Grupo Ollamani to transfer ownership of Club América and Estadio

Azteca into that entity. The term "ollamani" comes from the Nahuatl language and means "ball game" or "ballplayer." This word reflects the historical and cultural importance of the ball game in Mesoamerican civilizations, where it was more than just a sport, having significant ritualistic and social connotations as well. On February 20, 2024, Emilio Azcárraga Jean took Grupo Ollamani public. The IPO was a resounding success, and the total value of the group—including the brand, players, facilities (the Estadio Azteca), and commercial rights—is estimated at $750 million.

In the television industry, for Netflix, Amazon, and Disney to achieve in Mexico and Latin America the kind of market position they enjoy in the United States, they need a partner like Televisa Univision. And for Televisa Univision to survive the whirlwind of competition in the United States, it needs to renew its technological infrastructure and partner with Netflix, Amazon, Disney, Apple, Oracle, Microsoft, Alphabet (YouTube), or Meta (Instagram, Facebook, and WhatsApp).

Today, the industry is facing a new, technology-driven period of transition—an imminent shift whose outcome is impossible to predict. This new era of Televisa Univision, under predominantly Mexican leadership, has a future that's uncertain, for sure, though not quite as dire as some executives and artists—victims of the recent waves of layoffs in both Mexico and the United States—might suggest. According to one of those executives currently leading the company, the idea isn't just to cut staff for the sake of reducing costs in the face of uncertainty: "It's a decision to adapt to new technologies and new horizons, to be profitable, and to take advantage of the fact that we are, now, truly, a single, unified media company."

El Tigre's vision of forging a Mexican empire for the U.S. Hispanic market remains a motivating factor for his son, Emilio Azcárraga Jean. It is a vision that still permeates the executive ranks of Televisa Univision. El Tigre always knew how to roar the loudest when everyone else thought he was finished.

In 2024, on the sixty-fifth anniversary of his father's acquisition of Club América, Azcárraga Jean told everyone in attendance: "My father was a visionary... and he's probably up there right now, throwing back a tequila and shouting, 'It's about damn time, cabrón!'"

EPILOGUE

The story I've told in these pages comes to a pause here, not a definitive conclusion. Throughout this journey, I've worn two hats: that of a meticulous researcher and that of being a witness to the very history I'm recounting. Many may ask whether I was the right person to do it . . . and the answer lies in my background, in my roots.

From a young age, I've been drawn to two very powerful, very enduring institutions: religion and the media. As a child, I drew close to religion, though I would later gradually distance myself from it. And much like the enduring power of religion, iconic media outlets like *The New York Times*, founded by the journalist Henry Jarvis Raymond and banker George Jones in 1851, or the *Financial Times*, founded by journalist James Sheridan and his brother in 1888, have transcended their creators, establishing powerful legacies that continue to shape and reflect the global narrative, generation after generation. So, in 1999, I decided to embark on my own journey through the world of media, with a clear focus on garnering a deep understanding of the business behind the industry. I realized it was easy to educate myself about renowned reporters, famous writers, and other key figures in the world of news, entertainment, and content creation, but little has been written about the founders and owners of media companies—even less so if you're looking for information that hasn't already been approved and authorized by these ambitious individuals referred to, in English, as media moguls.

For example, I've always been struck by the fact that one of the most respected media outlets for editorial integrity is the London-based *The Economist*, founded by British entrepreneur and banker James Wilson in 1843. What few people know is that Wilson's ambitions were centered on his personal agenda and financial interest in advocating for the repeal of import tariffs on corn. To this day, *The Economist*'s editorial mission reflects that original stance: "Take part in a severe contest between intelligence, which presses forward, and an unworthy, timid ignorance obstructing our progress."

I've always been fascinated by the way most journalists relate to the business side of the industry. Marty Baron, former executive editor of the *Miami Herald*, *The Boston Globe*, and *The Washington Post*, once shared his experience with me: "In difficult times, I don't remember a single journalist who came to my desk with ideas on how to save—or how to make—more money."

I admire the courage and resilience many media owners show in taking risks and sharing information that can calm people with hope or impact leaders, governments, and human beings in transformative ways.

In 2000, I emigrated from Venezuela to the United States. No matter how much research I did, I found scant information on the history of the largest Hispanic media outlet in the country: Univision. Every time I had the opportunity to dig in to how it all began and who its driving forces were, I was amazed by what I uncovered.

On March 16, 2006, I published in a Venezuelan newspaper an article titled "Llegó el momento de Cisneros" ("Cisneros's Moment Has Arrived") in which I offered both a diagnosis and forecast of what was likely to happen to Univision in the coming months, including its possible sale for an estimated $10 billion. Days after the publication, Venezuelan magnate Gustavo Cisneros contacted me privately to share his impression of what I had written. "You almost nailed it," he said.

For nearly twenty-five years, I've spoken with executives, managers, producers, executive assistants, security guards, pilots, financiers, presidents, lawyers, journalists, broadcasters, entertainers, and even a few artists who were and are part of the Spanish International Network, which would later become Univision and also give rise to Telemundo.

In 2009, I realized the vast majority of this story still remained unwritten, so I started thinking about taking it upon myself to publish it. At the time, though, I was dedicating myself to being a father and businessman. Later, in 2015, I was convinced to tell part of this story at Tufts University. I prepared a syllabus for an elective course called The History of Latin American Media, which was approved for the university's Experimental College. To my surprise, registrations for the class were full, and it turned out to be a great success... though I quickly realized that teaching wasn't for me. I got bored the second time I had to teach it, and that was the end of my career as a professor.

With time, I came to realize that this book isn't just the chronicle of a business. It's a fundamental chapter in an entire community's experience. That's why I took on the responsibility of telling it rigorously and passionately. I knew that recounting the rise of Spanish-language television meant unraveling the history of millions of Latinos whose lives had been woven into those broadcasts.

Two common threads that run throughout this book from beginning to end are the Spanish language and the Latino identity in the United States. Decades ago, Spanish was barely even whispered in certain corners of this country, often relegated to the home or to intimate, confidential circles. Today, the language echoes resoundingly in television studios, packed sports stadiums, and on digital platforms that reach across the entire world. This is no coincidence: as of 2024, the United States is now home to 57.4 million Spanish speakers, making it the second-largest Spanish-speaking nation in the world, second only to Mexico.

Older generations remember the thrill of hearing news in their native language for the first time on their local stations. The younger generations, born here, have Spanish in their blood, though they sometimes blend it with English in their own unique rhythms. This bicultural identity is being built every day in music that fuses urban rhythms with bilingual lyrics, in family conversations where Spanish-speaking grandparents and bilingual grandchildren coexist, and in the shared pride of family, community, and even national celebrations.

Will Spanish continue to flourish in the United States? The answer is revealing itself before our eyes: every time it seems to be weakening with one generation, a new wave of migration or a renewed cultural interest brings it back to life. No language, of course, survives in a foreign land without overcoming a few challenges.

Demographic growth in the United States means that Latino cultural influence will continue expanding and, with it, the prominence of Spanish in the public sphere. Latino identity in this country is never static: it is redefined by every child of immigrants who learns to appreciate where their grandparents came from, by every content creator who blends languages on YouTube, by every writer who tells stories in English but with a heart rooted in Spanish.

The Spanish-speaking community in the United States is an economic engine. A Central American president who surprised everyone with his electoral victory started his campaign with funding from the U.S. diaspora. A Colombian bank offers mortgages to U.S.- based clients so they can invest in real estate in Colombia. As of 2024, nearly a quarter of all Major League Baseball players, almost all of them millionaires, are Spanish speakers. And with a limited command of English, world soccer superstar Lionel Messi now lives and plays in Miami, Florida.

Unlike in many Arab or European countries, where immigrants often form communities that aren't actively involved in politics or strong economic engines and where their languages aren't always respected, the Hispanic community has earned its socioeconomic place in the United States.

This book is an account that demonstrates just how difficult the journey has been when it comes to defending the use of Spanish and Hispanic cultural pride in the United States. If it hadn't been for the ambition and resilience of the owners and executives at Univision and Telemundo from the earliest entrepreneurial stages, perhaps the Spanish language wouldn't be used as effectively as it is today in this nation. Perhaps Latino power would be something else entirely—just another immigrant enclave inside a developed country.

It's clear that this story is far from over. If we've learned anything from this historical journey, it's that Spanish-language television in the United States has always found ways to reinvent itself. The pioneers founded the first networks against all odds, and their successors competed, innovated, and consolidated a media empire. Now, new challenges and opportunities loom on the horizon. The digital age has reshaped consumer habits: audiences no longer feel tied to the TV in the living room—they now carry Spanish-language content on the phones in their pockets. The major networks appearing in this book are currently exploring platforms and formats that would have been unimaginable just two decades ago.

In closing, I'd like to leave you with one lasting image: a grandmother sitting in front of the television, smiling as she listens to some news being reported in the language she's known all her life, with a grandson by her side, scrolling through viral videos created by Latino influencers on his mobile device. Two distinct generations connected by an invisible thread of language and culture. That's the true power of what has been built.

ACKNOWLEDGMENTS

To Carola, my wife, who has been with me throughout this journey—thirty-five years and counting. ¡Te amo, y más!

To my children, Andrés, Alejandro, and Caylin, who have inspired me to love the United States even more, and—without realizing it—to push myself to make them proud of their dad.

To my nephew Marcos Marin Quintero, for taking care of the family business and allowing me the time to fully enjoy the conception and birth of this book.

To Patricia Padauy, Guac's mom, who, along with Carola, gave me great support and encouragement from the very beginning. San Luis Obispo was the spark!

To Manuel Oliver, Guac's dad, for being my buddy, my brother, and for always being a powerful example of survival and strength.

To Ana Julia Jatar, for her friendship and for being a constant source of motivation.

To Marty Baron, for his friendship and insights.

To Arturo Marcano, for his friendship and for encouraging me to write this book on my own. He was the only person to have read the entire first draft.

To Winston Peraza, for always inspiring me to lend importance to music, art, and design in everything that encompasses both this story and my life.

To Gilberto Lopez, for offering me a year-long residency at Arizona State University to develop the book.

To Víctor Melillo, for his friendship, knowledge, and for recommending that I watch *The Offer*.

To Antonina Melillo, for her friendship and for introducing me to her Italy.

To Cristóbal Pera. Besides being my publisher and editor, you were essential in the quest for the perfect final product. And we're not done yet! You believed in this project from day one.

To Jon Urruzuno, for his friendship and for reading another one of the drafts and reviewing the story with me chapter by chapter.

To Rufi Guerrero, for his kindness and friendship, and for giving me honest feedback that led me to change my course.

To my attorney, Enrique "Kike" Antequera, for calming my fears and telling me not to worry so much about the legalities because, in the end, the only real protection is the quality of my writing, which makes the final product unique.

To Gustavo Lucardi and his Trusted Translation.

To Pancho, for his friendship and corrections.

To Marianna Branco, for her otherworldly connections.

To Juan Antonio Fernández, for his friendship, connections, and unconditional advice.

To Sheila Benoliel, for helping me with fact-checking and organizing the bibliography.

To my dear friends who were kind and patient enough to have been constantly listening to my stories about this book

With eternal gratitude to attorney Norm Leventhal. In this photo I took a few years ago, he is posing next to his vehicle, whose personalized license plate—RVA, for Reynold Vincent Anselmo, and EAM, for Emilio Azcárraga Milmo—reflects how these two clients left an indelible mark on his personal and professional life.

project: Carlos Martin Rengifo Ducharne, José Gabriel Cabrera, Michael Flaherty, Carlos and Federica Ponce, Rafael Ulloa, Michi and Miguel Divo, Boris Muñoz, Eugenio Enrique Ball Felce, Abbie Peraza, Alessandro Caballera, Sam Leizorek, Ricardo Longoria, Mauricio Espinosa, Doug Fabbricatore, Andres Matetic, Ken Shapiro, and Alfredo Vergara.

To Luis Miguel Mesianu, for his friendship and ideas.

To Gustavo Cisneros, for his feedback in 2006.

To all the current and former employees of Televisa, SIN, Univision, and Telemundo who contributed to this book and whom I promised not to name out of respect for Jerry Perenchio's rules of the road.

To Norm Leventhal, attorney for Televisa, Emilio Azcárraga Milmo, and René Anselmo.

To Isa Traverso, for her friendship, connections, and her vibe.

To Beatrice Rangel, for her friendship and insight.

To June Erlick, for her friendship and insight.

To Mindy Marquez, for her insight.

To all the publishers who rejected my proposals: they encouraged me to persist.

To Vincent Sadusky, for his time at Cannes.

To those my memory has failed me in mentioning: know that my affection and gratitude remain fully intact.

And a special mention to my yoga instructors, who—along with Carola—keep me healthy and happy!

BIBLIOGRAPHY[1]

PREFACE

United Nations. *United Nations Treaties Collection: Convention on the Law of the Sea* (Montego Bay Convention). United Nations, 1982.

Relevant excerpt: International legal framework regulating territorial and extraterritorial waters with regard to the decision to practice euthanasia in international waters.

Treaty of Guadalupe Hidalgo. National Archives and Records Administration (NARA), 1848.

Relevant excerpt: Historical context on the cession of Mexican territory to the United States and the rights promised (including the use of Spanish) to Mexicans who choose to remain on the ceded lands.

Roeder, Mark A. *A History of Culver and the Culver Military Academy*. Self-published, 2016.

Relevant excerpt: History of the military academy to which El Tigre Azcárraga was sent by his father, where he experienced discrimination and extreme discipline.

[1] The works cited are presented thematically, not alphabetically, in each section. [Ed. Note]

National Archives Office of Strategy and Communications: Nixon Hispanic Strategy. National Archives and Records Administration (NARA), 1973.

Relevant excerpt: Study on how the Nixon administration officially defined the term "Hispanic" and its impact on U.S. politics.

Fernández, Claudia, and Andrew Paxman. *El Tigre: Emilio Azcárraga y su imperio Televisa*. Raya en el Agua/Grijalbo, 2000.

Relevant excerpt: Detailed biography of El Tigre and his impact on television and the media industry.

Arana, Marie. *LatinoLand: A Portrait of America's Largest and Least Understood Minority*. Simon & Schuster, 2024.

Relevant excerpt: Statistics, growth, and socioeconomic importance of the Hispanic population in the United States.

CHAPTER 1
The Transition: El León, René Anselmo, and El Tigre

Tello Díaz, Carlos. *Porfirio Díaz: Su vida y su tiempo.* Vol. 1, *La guerra (1830–1867).* Conaculta/Debate, 2017.

Relevant excerpt: Historical context of the Porfiriato, the education of the Mexican elite, and U.S.-Mexico relations.

Garner, Paul, and Porfirio Díaz. *Porfirio Díaz: Profiles in Power.* Routledge, 2001.

Relevant excerpt: Analysis of the Porfiriato's impact on the Mexican business class and the Azcárraga family's ties to power.

Olivares Arriaga, María del Carmen. *Emilio Azcárraga Vidaurreta: Bosquejo biográfico.* Universidad Autónoma de Tamaulipas–IIH, 2002.

Relevant excerpt: Account of the life of the founder of Telesistema Mexicano and his role in the television industry.

Lopez, Nicole. *Raoul A. Cortez: Pioneer of Spanish-Language Broadcasting.* Texas State Historical Association, 2014; text updated 2016.

Relevant excerpt: History of one of the pioneers of Spanish-language television in the United States and his relationship with Emilio Nicolás Sr.

Flynn, Jean. *Henry B. Gonzalez: Rebel with a Cause*. Eakin Press, 2004.

Relevant excerpt: Biography of the first Hispanic congressman in the United States and his connection with SIN.

Lyndon B. Johnson Presidential Library and Museum, Presidential Records. National Archives and Records Administration (NARA).

Relevant excerpt: Documents about President Johnson's political influence on the Hispanic community and his relationship with Cantinflas.

Harding, Art, and Erwin Krasnow. "The Road Map for Potential Foreign Investors." *Radio & Television Business Report*, March 1, 2017. https://www.foster.com/newsroom-publications-The-Road-Map-For-Potential-Foreign-Investors.

Relevant excerpt: Explanation of Section 310(b)(3) of the Communications Act, which limited foreign investment in U.S. media, known as the 20 percent rule.

Flowers, Katherine S. "The Origins of the English-Only Movement." In *Making English Official: Writing and Resisting Local Language Policies*, 29–60. Cambridge University Press, 2024.

Relevant excerpt: Analysis of the impact of the English-only movement on the Hispanic community in the United States.

González, Henry B., 1916–2000. United States House of Representatives History Archive. https://history.house.gov/People/Detail/13906.

Relevant excerpt: Describes how Cantinflas and Lyndon B. Johnson helped Henry González win his first election.

CHAPTER 2
From On the Air to Outer Space: René Anselmo and the Satellite Television Revolution

Leventhal, Norm. *Rene, El Tigre & Me: Up Close & Personal—Spanish Television in America*. Rosedog Books, 2018.

Relevant excerpt: Memoirs of Emilio Azcárraga Milmo's and René Anselmo's attorney, including details about their relationship and the growth of SIN.

Krige, J., A. Russo, and L. Sebesta. *A History of the European Space Agency, 1958–1987*. 2 vols. ESA Publications Division, 2000.

Relevant excerpt: Analysis of the impact of the European Space Agency and the SES company on the private satellite industry.

Besas, Peter. "Televisa Buys into PanAmSat." *Variety*, January 7, 1993. https://variety.com/1993/biz/news/televisa-buys-into-panamsat-102778/.

Relevant excerpt: Explains Televisa's investment in PanAmSat and El Tigre's influence on the satellite industry.

Kuznik, Frank. "A Piece of Outer Space to Call His Very Own." *New York Times*, April 1, 1990. https://www.nytimes.com/1990/04/01/business/a-piece-of-outer-space-to-call-his-very-own.html.

Relevant excerpt: Describes René Anselmo's battle against the Intelsat monopoly and his impact on telecommunications.

Landler, Mark. "A Widow's Pique." *New York Times*, June 16, 1996. https://www.nytimes.com/1996/06/16/business/a-widow-s-pique.html.

Relevant excerpt: Interview with René Anselmo's widow, who reveals a private meeting with Emilio Azcárraga Milmo to discuss the sale of PanAmSat.

CHAPTER 3
The Rise of a Mexican Media Mogul and His Expansion into the United States

Delarbre, Raúl Trejo, ed. *Televisa, el quinto poder*. Claves Latinoamericanas, 1985.

Relevant excerpt: Analysis of Televisa's power and its impact on politics and media in Mexico.

Wilkinson, Kenton T. *Spanish-Language Television in the United States: Fifty Years of Development*. Routledge, 2016.

Relevant excerpt: Examines the growth of Spanish-language television in the United States, including the role of Televisa and Univision.

"History of the Ibero-American Telecommunications Organization (OTI)." OTI Digital Archives.

Relevant excerpt: Documents Televisa's involvement in the OTI and its influence on Ibero-American television.

Ferreira, Leónardo, Alfonso Grados Bertorini, and Gonzalo Peltzer, eds. *Comunicación: desafío del presente y futuro*. Universidad de San Martín de Porres, 1993.

Relevant excerpt: Explains media power concentration in Latin America, including the case of Televisa.

Bachelet, Pablo. *Gustavo Cisneros: Un empresario global*. Planeta, 2004.

Relevant excerpt: Biography of Gustavo Cisneros, his relationship with El Tigre, and his role in the acquisition of Univision.

"Siempre en Domingo: El programa que definió la televisión mexicana". *El Universal* (Mexico), 2005.

Relevant excerpt: Details the show's impact and why it failed in the United States.

"La relación entre televisa y el PRI: Un pacto de poder". *Proceso*, 1997.

Relevant excerpt: Analyzes Televisa's role in consolidating the PRI's power during the 1970s and 1980s.

CHAPTER 4
The Struggle for Control of SIN and the Rise of the Hispanic Audience

Leventhal, Norm. *Rene, El Tigre & Me: Up Close & Personal—Spanish Television in America*. Rosedog Books, 2018.

Relevant excerpt: Firsthand account by René Anselmo's lawyer regarding the legal battles over control of SIN.

González, Juan. *Harvest of Empire: A History of Latinos in America*. Penguin Books, 2001.

Relevant excerpt: Analyzes Hispanic migration to the United States and its impact on politics and the media.

González, Francisco Javier. *El 86: el año en que México cambió al mundo*. Planeta, 2022.

Relevant excerpt: Examines the importance of the 1986 FIFA World Cup in Televisa's media expansion.

Horowitz, Daniel. *Jimmy Carter and the Energy Crisis of the 1970s: The "Crisis of Confidence" Speech of July 15, 1979. A Brief History with Documents*. Bedford/St. Martin's, 2004.

Relevant excerpt: Explains the economic and energy crisis that spurred Latin American migration to the United States.

"Rubén Salazar's Death Scrutinized." *Línea Abierta*, on Radio Bilingüe. American Archive of Public Broadcasting, August 29, 2020.

Relevant excerpt: On the fiftieth anniversary of Rubén Salazar's death, an analysis of the journalist's death and its impact on the Chicano community.

Powers, Charles T., and Jeff Perlman. "One Dead, 40 Hurt in East LA Riot: Times Columnist Rubén Salazar Killed by Bullet." *Los Angeles Times*, August 30, 1970.

Relevant excerpt: News report on the death of Rubén Salazar during the Chicano Moratorium march against the Vietnam War.

Gailey, Phil. "Courting Hispanic Voters Now a Reagan Priority." *New York Times*, May 19, 1983.

Relevant excerpt: Explains the Republican strategy for capturing the Hispanic vote and SIN's role in it.

"Frases Famosas de El Chapulín Colorado". *BBC Mundo*, November 28, 2014.

Relevant excerpt: Explains why El Chapulín Colorado became an icon for immigrants in the United States.

Cannon, Lou. "Reagan Stays Home to Woo the Support of Hispanics, Blacks." *Washington Post*, September 10, 1984. https://www.washingtonpost.com/archive/politics/1984/09/11/reagan-stays-home-to-woo-the-support-of-hispanics-blacks/38506fec-d0d2-40a2-800a-ca97d977d3ff/.

Relevant excerpt: Describes how Ronald Reagan acknowledged the importance of the Hispanic electorate in the United States.

"Tango Argentino!" *Sports Illustrated*, SI Latino issues, July 7, 1986.

Relevant excerpt: Explains, among other things, how the FIFA World Cup boosted the relevance of SIN and Univision in the United States.

CHAPTER 5
The Fouce Lawsuit and the Conflict That Transformed SIN into Univision

Ramos, George. "Owners to Sell KMEX-TV, Four Sister Stations: Sale of Spanish-Language Outlets Comes Amid FCC Ruling to Lift Licenses." *Los Angeles Times*, May 10, 1986.

Relevant excerpt: Investigative report explaining one version of the Fouce lawsuit and mentioning the potential forced sale of SIN.

Stevenson, Richard W. "Hispanic Network Under Fire." *New York Times*, November 14, 1985.

Relevant excerpt: Article that outlines, in some detail, the FCC's stance regarding the possible revocation of SIN's license.

Wilkinson, Kenton T. *Spanish-Language Television in the United States: Fifty Years of Development*. Routledge, 2016.

Relevant excerpt: Details of the Fouces' litigation.

Ono, Kent A., and John M. Sloop. *Shifting Borders: Rhetoric, Immigration, and California's Proposition 187*. Temple University Press, 2002.

Relevant excerpt: Presents one version of Judge Mariana Pfaelzer's role in the litigation between the Fouces and SIN's shareholders.

Krattenmaker, Thomas G. *Media Ownership and Control: A Legal Perspective*. Westview Press, 1998.

Relevant excerpt: Mentions the case of foreign ownership of a media outlet in the United States.

Molina-Guzmán, Isabel. *Latinas & Latinos on TV: Colorblind Comedy in the Post-Racial Network Era.* University of Arizona Press, 2018.

Relevant excerpt: Discusses the evolution of the SIN and Univision brands.

McChesney, Robert W. *Telecommunications, Mass Media, and Democracy: The Battle for the Control of U.S. Broadcasting, 1928–1935.* Oxford University Press, 1993.

Relevant excerpt: Legal explanations regarding the FCC and its regulatory role over television networks.

FCC Records on the SIN License. Library of Congress, FCC Archives, 1985–1986.

Relevant excerpt: Confirms the existence of SIN's broadcast license and its legal characteristics.

Testimonies in the Case *SIN v. FCC.* Legal Documentation of the Case in the U.S. District Court for the Southern District of California, 1980–1986.

Relevant excerpt: Confirms the existence of the legal case filed by the Fouces against SIN's shareholders.

CHAPTER 6
1986: The Year That Revolutionized Televised News

Randolph, Eleanor. "Reporters Walk Out at Hispanic TV Network." *Washington Post*, November 2, 1986. https://www.washingtonpost.com/archive/politics/1986/11/02/reporters-walk-out-at-hispanic-tv-network/9baf79ad-9eb8-4a51-a38c-fd9224e22c89/.

Relevant excerpt: News report on tensions among the news staff at SIN.

Salinas, María Elena. *Yo soy la hija de mi padre: Una vida sin secretos.* (*I Am My Father's Daughter: Living a Life Without Secrets*). Rayo, 2006.

Relevant excerpt: Firsthand account of the journalist's rise through SIN.

Wolff, Michael. *The Man Who Owns the News: Inside the Secret World of Rupert Murdoch*. Broadway Books, 2008.

Relevant excerpt: A take on the development of CNN's competitor, Fox News.

Albarran, Alan B. *The Media Economy*. Routledge, 2016.

Relevant excerpt: Content on the Hispanic audience and its commercialization (in one of the chapters).

González, Juan, and Joseph Torres. *News for All the People: The Epic Story of Race and the American Media*. Verso, 2011.

Relevant excerpt: On diversity in media audiences.

Schonfeld, Reese. *Me and Ted Against the World: The Unauthorized Story of the Founding of CNN*. HarperCollins, 2001.

Relevant excerpt: Another account of CNN's evolution.

Ono, Kent A., and John M. Sloop. *Shifting Borders: Rhetoric, Immigration, and California's Proposition 187*. Temple University Press, 2002.

Relevant excerpt: Report on the California referendum aimed at depriving immigrants of their rights.

Taladrid, Stephania. "Jorge Ramos, the Voice of Latin America." *New Yorker*, August 17, 2024.

Relevant excerpt: Mentions the impasse caused by the mass resignation of journalists at SIN.

"Noticias SIN 1983." YouTube video. Published June 14, 2022. https://www.youtube.com/watch?v=fVcjZ4u0P_c.

Relevant excerpt: Verifies the on-screen participation of SIN's news director Gustavo Godoy.

CHAPTER 7
Telemundo and Univision: Finance, Power, and the Battle for Viewership

Fox, Margalit. "Daniel Villanueva, a Creator of Univision, Dies at 77." *New York Times*, June 22, 2015. https://www.nytimes.com/2015/06/23/business/daniel-villanueva-creator-of-univision-dies-at-77.html.

Relevant excerpt: Obituary and biographical profile of Daniel D. Villanueva.

Cuff, Daniel F. "Univision Names Head of Spanish Network." *New York Times*, August 31, 1988. https://www.nytimes.com/1988/08/31/business/business-people-univision-names-head-of-spanish-network.html.

Relevant excerpt: Biographical profile and appointment of Joaquín Blaya.

"Robert Baker, Steinberg May Have Trouble Making Money in Spanish." *BusinessWeek*, August 10, 1987.

Relevant excerpt: Details on Telemundo's financial crisis in 1987.

George, Lisa. "Media Competition, Information Provision and Political Participation." *Journal of Economics*, 2007.

Relevant excerpt: Research paper on media diversity and its impact on information and political engagement in the United States.

Dávila, Arlene. *Latinos, Inc.: The Marketing and Making of a People.* University of California Press, 2001.

Relevant excerpt: Covers key aspects of how bilingualism is marketed in commercial contexts.

Mullen, Megan Gwynne. *Television in the Multichannel Age: A Brief History of Cable Television*. Wiley-Blackwell, 2008.

Relevant excerpt: History of cable television in the United States.

Negrón-Muntaner, Frances, Chelsea Abbas, Luis Figueroa, and Samuel Robson. *The Latino Media Gap: A Report on the State of Latinos in U.S.*

Media. Columbia University: Center for the Study of Ethnicity and Race, 2014.

Relevant excerpt: Research study done on the prosperity or marginalization of Latinos in the United States.

Testimony by Carlos Barba on the Origins of Telemundo. *Hispanic Business Magazine*, 1989.

Relevant excerpt: Mentions and confirms Barba's involvement in NetSpan and Telemundo.

"Desi Arnaz Ed Sullivan Show Speech." YouTube video. https://youtu.be/qNRRCE-nWmM?si=AhJJH0Z_f_aC_7VZ.

Relevant excerpt: The strong statements made by Desi Arnaz on the most-watched show in the United States.

Bruck, Connie. *The Predators' Ball: The Inside Story of Drexel Burnham and the Rise of the Junk Bond Raiders*. Penguin Books, 1988.

Relevant excerpt: Report on junk bonds and the financial forces behind media acquisitions.

CHAPTER 8
Rosita Perú and Don Francisco with Their *Sábado Gigante*

Naisbitt, John. *Megatrends: Ten New Directions Transforming Our Lives*. Warner Books, 1982.

Relevant excerpt: Prediction that English, Spanish, and computer science would be the three primary languages of the future in the United States.

Kreutzberger, Mario (Don Francisco). *Life, Camera, Action!: Autobiography*. Grijalbo, 2001. (Also published in Spanish as *Entre la espada y la TV: Autobiografía*. Grijalbo, 2001.)

Relevant excerpt: Autobiography detailing Don Francisco's career in Hispanic television.

Kreutzberger, Mario (Don Francisco). *Con ganas de vivir*. Aguilar, 2021.

Relevant excerpt: Reflections on Don Francisco's cultural impact and his experience in the television industry.

"The Evolution of Hispanic Marketing." *Advertising Age* Hispanic Fact Pack, May 1989.

Relevant excerpt: Analysis of brands' awakening to the Hispanic market's potential.

Puig, Claudia. "Univision President Bolts to Rival Telemundo; Communications: Joaquín Blaya Was Concerned About the New Owner Using Fewer U.S.-Produced Shows." *Los Angeles Times*, May 27, 1992.

Relevant excerpt: Insight into the challenges of leading Univision in a competitive market, as well as Blaya's departure as president of the network.

Valle, Víctor. "Ethnic Fight Heats Up at Latino Station." *Los Angeles Times*, May 19, 1989. https://www.latimes.com/archives/la-xpm-1989-05-19-ca-289-story.html.

Relevant excerpt: Mentions Grimes's view on Blaya's and Rosita Perú's roles in Univision's programming decisions.

Dávila, Arlene. *Latinos, Inc.: The Marketing and Making of a People*. University of California Press, 2001.

Relevant excerpt: How the Hispanic marketing industry plays a central role in both public recognition and ongoing marginalization of Latinos.

CHAPTER 9
Hallmark Cards: The Hockaday and Blaya Era at Univision

Regan, Patrick. *Hallmark: A Century of Caring*. Andrews McMeel Publishing, 2010.

Relevant excerpt: History of Hallmark and the role of Irv Hockaday at Univision.

Kreutzberger, Mario (Don Francisco). *Life, Camera, Action!: Autobiography*. Grijalbo, 2001. (Also published in Spanish as *Entre la espada y la TV: Autobiografía*. Grijalbo, 2001.)

Relevant excerpt: Don Francisco's version of his decision to remain at Univision and not leave when Blaya did.

Kreutzberger, Mario (Don Francisco). *Con ganas de vivir.* Aguilar, 2021.

Relevant excerpt: Reflections on the evolution and cultural impact of *Sábado Gigante.*

"Hallmark Adds Univision." Special report for *New York Times*, November 21, 1987.

Relevant excerpt: Explanation of the impact of Hallmark's purchasing of SIN and the arrival of Irv Hockaday.

Puig, Claudia. "Univision President Bolts to Rival Telemundo; Communications: Joaquín Blaya Was Concerned About the New Owner Using Fewer U.S.-Produced Shows." *Los Angeles Times*, May 27, 1992.

Relevant excerpt: Analysis of internal tensions at Univision and the attempt to change the station's identity.

Newman, Maria. "Move to Miami Is Matter of Time, Univision Says." *Los Angeles Times*, September 6, 1990.

Relevant excerpt: Mentions the "Cubanization" of Univision and resistance to it from the Mexican American community.

Lippman, John. "Tortorici Named Telemundo CEO in New Owners' Management Shuffle." *Wall Street Journal*, August 14, 1998.

Relevant excerpt: Mentions Telemundo's "bankruptcy."

Shiver, Jube. "Keeping Univision Alive: Media: Hallmark Has a Plan to Rescue Its Troubled Subsidiary, the Nation's Largest Spanish-Language Television Network." *Los Angeles Times*, February 19, 1990.

Relevant excerpt: Hallmark Cards and Irv Hockaday's plans for Univision.

Netto, David. "The Enduring Legacy of French Interior Designer Henri Samuel." *Town & Country*, March 15, 2018. https://www.townandcountrymag.com/style/home-decor/a19421619/henri-samuel-designer/.

Relevant excerpt: History of the mansion acquired by Jerry Perenchio and designed by Henri Samuel.

Dávila, Arlene. *Latinos, Inc.: The Marketing and Making of a People.* University of California Press, 2001.

Relevant excerpt: Examines how Univision helped shape the Hispanic market's identity in the United States.

CHAPTER 10
The Telenovela Business

Erlick, June Carolyn. *Telenovelas in Pan-Latino Context.* Instituto de Estudios Latinoamericanos/Routledge, 2017.

Relevant excerpt: A comprehensive study on the importance of telenovelas in Latin American societies and their global expansion.

Gutiérrez, Félix F., and Jorge Reina Schement. *Spanish-Language Radio in the Southwestern United States.* University of Texas Press, 1979.

Relevant excerpt: Analyzes how Univision and Televisa shaped the Spanish-language television industry in the United States.

Sosa Plata, Gabriel. *The Television Duopoly.* Al Consumidor, 2010.

Relevant excerpt: Provides historical context on how Televisa monopolized television production, including control over telenovelas.

Young, James. "Mexico: Televisa Juggernaut Flexes Its Muscles." *Variety*, October 3, 2008.

Relevant excerpt: Analyzes how Mexican telenovelas gained international popularity.

Villamil, Jenaro. "Television for the Screwed." *Proceso*, March 19, 2013.

Relevant excerpt: Details the controversial statements made by Emilio Azcárraga Milmo about Mexican society.

Martínez, Andrés. "'La Vida' Loca: The Modern Mexican Telenovela Is an Oversexed Stew of Giddy Promiscuity, Weird Couplings, Substance

Abuse and Repressed Homosexuality. Let's Watch!" *Salon*, February 28, 2000. https://www.salon.com/2000/02/28/telenovelas/.

Relevant excerpt: Analyzes Telemundo's early attempts to produce telenovelas in the United States.

"Te Odio, Te Amo: Why Telenovelas Rule Latin Entertainment." Interview with Carolina Acosta-Alzuru. Alt.Latino, NPR, August 2, 2013.

Relevant excerpt: Academic insight on the role of Cuban writers with regard to developing telenovelas.

CHAPTER 11
El Tigre Returns

Stevenson, Richard W. "Hallmark to Sell Its Univision TV Group." *New York Times*, April 9, 1992.

Relevant excerpt: Describes Hallmark's decision to sell Univision and the financial impact, as well as how Perenchio, along with Azcárraga and Cisneros, bought and reorganized the company.

"Carlos Barba has been appointed president and… ," *Los Angeles Times* Archive, May 11, 1991.

Relevant excerpt: Covers Barba's resignation and the economic crisis that led to Telemundo's bankruptcy.

CHAPTER 12
Soccer Fever Hits the United States

Galeano, Eduardo. *El fútbol a sol y sombra.* Siglo XXI Editores, 1995.

Relevant excerpt: Soccer as a spectacle, passion, and cultural phenomenon. Discusses the business side and surrounding power structures.

Goldblatt, David. *The Ball Is Round: A Global History of Soccer*. Riverhead Books, 2008.

Relevant excerpt: Analyzes the influence of João Havelange and Guillermo Cañedo within FIFA.

Ostermann, Ruy Carlos. *Itinerário da derrota: Crônica de cinco Copas do Mundo sem Pelé.* Artes e Ofícios, 1992.

Relevant excerpt: Examines how television became a key factor in broadcasting soccer across the continent.

"Emilio Azcárraga: Presidente de Televisa, es uno de los hombres con más poder en México." *El País*, January 6, 1986.

Relevant excerpt: Details the power relationship between Emilio Azcárraga Milmo and FIFA.

"Futbol México '86: Así se hizo el mundial." *Proceso*, 1986.

Relevant excerpt: About Guillermo Cañedo and Mexico's strategic approach to hosting the World Cup.

"Throwback Thursday: The USA's Captivating 1994 World Cup Group." *Sports Illustrated*, July 4, 1994.

Relevant excerpt: Explores the lack of soccer culture in the United States prior to the arrival of Univision and Televisa in the market.

CHAPTER 13
Latina USA and Latin Music

Saralegui, Cristina. *Cristina!: My Life as a Blonde.* Warner Books, 1998.

Relevant excerpt: Autobiography of Cristina Saralegui, narrating her experience at Univision and her impact on Latinas in the United States.

Erlick, June Carolyn. *Telenovelas in the Latin World.* Instituto de Estudios Latinoamericanos/Routledge, 2017.

Relevant excerpt: Explains the impact of telenovelas and their connection to Latin music in Hispanic television.

Pacini Hernandez, Deborah. *Oye Como Va!: Hybridity and Identity in Latino Popular Music.* Temple University Press, 2010.

Relevant excerpt: Details the evolution of Latin music in the United States.

Estefan, Emilio. *The Rhythm of Success: How an Immigrant Produced His Own American Dream.* Celebra, 2010. (Also published in Spanish as *Ritmo al éxito: Cómo un inmigrante hizo su propio sueño americano.* Celebra, 2010.)

Relevant excerpt: Describes the trajectory of the Miami Sound Machine and the consolidation of the Latin crossover in the United States.

Jalil, Oscar (text), and David Sisso (photography). "Rolling Stone Interview: Corazón delator." *Rolling Stone* (Argentina), March 2003, 30–37.

Relevant excerpt: Analyzes the internationalization of Latin pop-rock music.

"*People en Español* Magazine Honors: Cristina Saralegui." *People en Español,* April 16, 1998.

Relevant excerpt: Explores the impact of Cristina Saralegui and her show on Latin culture in the United States.

Ogunnaike, Lola. "Crossover Star Tries Crossing Back; Ricky Martin Returns to His Latin Roots." *New York Times,* May 20, 2003.

Relevant excerpt: Mentions how Univision and Televisa contributed to the globalization of Latin pop music.

CHAPTER 14
Jerry Perenchio, Univision's Man with the Midas Touch

Feldman, Leslie Dale. *Rustics and Politics: The Political Theory of* The Beverly Hillbillies. Lexington Books, 2013.

Relevant excerpt: History of the TV series *The Beverly Hillbillies,* that inspired the name of Jerry Perenchio's mansion, Chartwell.

Hoffer, Richard. *Bouts of Mania: Ali, Frazier, and Foreman and an America on the Ropes.* Da Capo Press, 2014.

Relevant excerpt: Analysis of the boxing match organized by Jerry Perenchio and its impact on the boxing industry.

Bachelet, Pablo. *Gustavo Cisneros: Un empresario global.* Planeta, 2004.

Relevant excerpt: Biography of Gustavo Cisneros and his relationship with Jerry Perenchio and Univision.

Fernández, Claudia, and Andrew Paxman. *El Tigre: Emilio Azcárraga y su imperio Televisa*. Raya en el Agua/Grijalbo, 2000.

Relevant excerpt: Explains Televisa's role in Univision and the relationship between Jerry Perenchio and El Tigre Azcárraga.

Stevenson, Richard W. "Hallmark to Sell Its Univision TV Group." *New York Times*, April 9, 1992.

Relevant excerpt: Report on the sale of Univision and its impact on the television industry.

Barnes, Mike. "Jerry Perenchio, Consummate Hollywood Dealmaker and Former Univision Head, Dies at 86." *Hollywood Reporter*, May 24, 2017.

Relevant excerpt: Obituary recounting Perenchio's venture into television and his success with Univision.

James, Meg. "A Hollywood Player Who Owns the Game." *Los Angeles Times*, June 20, 2006.

Relevant excerpt: Explains Jerry Perenchio's history and strategy for dominating the Spanish-speaking market in the United States.

Sutter, Mary. "Televisa Ready to Cross the Border: Company Pacts with Univision on Programming, Pay TV, Music." *Variety*, December 20, 2001.

Relevant excerpt: Analyzes how Televisa and Venevisión became the exclusive content providers for Univision under the program license agreement.

Puig, Claudia. "Univision President Bolts to Rival Telemundo; Communications: Joaquín Blaya Was Concerned About the New Owner Using Fewer U.S.-Produced Shows." *Los Angeles Times*, May 27, 1992.

Relevant excerpt: Report on Blaya's resignation following Univision's acquisition by Perenchio and his partners.

CHAPTER 15
Opulence, Extravagance, and Power

Gross, Michael. *Unreal Estate: Money, Ambition, and the Lust for Land in Los Angeles*. Broadway Books, 2011.

Relevant excerpt: History of Chartwell and the mansions owned by media moguls in the United States.

Ratcliffe, Justin. "The Enduring *Enigma*." *Superyacht Report* 175 (January 2017): 171–79.

Relevant excerpt: History of El Tigre Azcárraga's yacht *ECO* and its influence on the superyacht industry.

Chernow, Ron. *The House of Morgan: An American Banking Dynasty and the Rise of Modern Finance*. Atlantic Monthly Press, 1990.

Relevant excerpt: To understand El Tigre's admiration for J. P. Morgan.

Montes, Geoffrey. "The Unlikely Backstory of the Most Expensive House in America." *Galerie* magazine, November 1, 2018.

Relevant excerpt: Design of Cartwell by Henri Samuel and its influence on luxury architecture in the United States.

"Inside a $195M Bel Air Estate with Secret Tunnels." Video, *On the Market* series, season 1, episode 19. *Architectural Digest*, October 4, 2019.

Relevant excerpt: Provides, through images, detailed features of the Chartwell mansion.

Meltzer, Peter D. "Rare Wine Auctions Set New Records in the First Half of 2018." *Wine Spectator*, July 18, 2018.

Relevant excerpt: Mentions the auction of Jerry Perenchio's wine collection after his passing.

Bailey, Joanna. "What Happened to the Playboy Private DC-9 Jet?" *Simple Flying*, January 5, 2021.

Relevant excerpt: About the *Big Bunny*: background material to help understand Jerry Perenchio's obsession with the *Playboy* airplane.

"Tales from a Failed Coup." *Economist* (via Reuters), April 25, 2002.

Relevant excerpt: Helps explain Gustavo Cisneros's personality and role in global politics and economics.

CHAPTER 16
The Never-Ending Sale

Fernández, Claudia, and Andrew Paxman. *El Tigre: Emilio Azcárraga y su imperio Televisa*. Raya en el Agua/Grijalbo, 2000.

Relevant excerpt: Explanation of Televisa's role in Univision and the relationship between Emilio Azcárraga Milmo and Jerry Perenchio.

Bachelet, Pablo. *Gustavo Cisneros: Un empresario global*. Planeta, 2004.

Relevant excerpt: History of Gustavo Cisneros and his role in the purchase and eventual sale of Univision.

Stevenson, Richard W. "Hallmark to Sell Its Univision TV Group." *New York Times*, April 9, 1992.

Relevant excerpt: Analysis of Univision's sale and the role of the three partners involved.

"NBC Agrees to Acquire Telemundo for $1.98 Billion in Cash and Stock." *Wall Street Journal*, October 11, 2001.

Relevant excerpt: Description of Telemundo's sale to NBC and its effect on Univision's market value.

Authers, John. "Televisa Executives Quit Univision Board." *Financial Times*, May 10, 2005.

Relevant excerpt: Mentions Emilio Azcárraga Jean's effort to renegotiate Televisa's programming agreement with Univision.

"Spanish-Language TV: Univision Goes Public." *BusinessWeek*, September 26, 1996.

Relevant excerpt: Describes the successful initial public offering of Univision led by Jerry Perenchio in 1996.

Chapter 17
The Story Comes to an End

Ball, Matthew. *Streaming Wars: The Future of Television.* March 2023. Available at https://www.thestreamingbook.com/.

Relevant excerpt: The impact of YouTube, Netflix, and Amazon on the Univision and Televisa business models.

Harrup, Anthony. "Mexico's Televisa to Merge Content Business with Univision." *Wall Street Journal*, updated April 13, 2021. https://www.wsj.com/business/media/mexico-s-televisa-to-merge-content-business-with-univision-11618353691.

Relevant excerpt: Explains the merger between Televisa and Univision and its impact on the media market.

Robles, Frances, Ken Bensinger, and Jeremy W. Peters. "Conundrum of Covering Trump Lands at Univision's Doorstep." *New York Times*, December 8, 2023.

Relevant excerpt: Discusses Enrique Acevedo's interview with Donald Trump and the impact it had on Univision.

Farrell, Mike. "Falco Nears Univision Exit." *Broadcasting & Cable*, March 7, 2018.

Relevant excerpt: Explains why Univision failed to go public.

Murphy, Aislinn. "More Details Emerge in Billionaire Thomas Lee's Suicide." Fox Business, February 24, 2023.

Relevant excerpt: Describes the details surrounding the death of Thomas Lee.

Ridley, Rob. "Azteca, Club América Make Landmark Debut on Mexican Stock Exchange." *The Stadium Business*, February 21, 2024.

Relevant excerpt: Launch of Club América shares on the Mexican stock exchange.

ABOUT THE AUTHOR

Javier Marín has owned Spanish-language media outlets in the United States since emigrating from Venezuela with his wife and two children in 2000. He is the founder of Tiempo Company, based in Washington, DC, which manages a number of brands including *Tiempo News*, *El Tiempo Latino*, and *El Planeta*. From 2016 to 2024, he was an investor in Univision's official soccer store. Marín is a graduate of the OPM program at Harvard Business School and currently lives with his wife, Carolina, in Maine.

www.ingramcontent.com/pod-product-compliance
Lightning Source LLC
Jackson TN
JSHW032052280925
91561JS00003BA/3
* 9 7 8 6 0 7 3 9 3 1 6 2 5 *